Understanding Psychological Disorders in Males

Understanding Psychological Disorders in Males

Margeret Tremblay

Clanrye International
www.clanryeinternational.com

Clanrye International,
750 Third Avenue, 9th Floor,
New York, NY 10017, USA

ISBN: 978-1-64726-639-4

Cataloging-in-Publication Data

Understanding psychological disorders in males / Margeret Tremblay.
p. cm.
Includes bibliographical references and index.
ISBN 978-1-64726-639-4
1. Men--Psychology. 2. Distress (Psychology). 3. Mental illness.
4. Psychology, Pathological. I. Tremblay, Margeret.

BF692.5 .U53 2023
155.332--dc23

For information on all Clanrye International publications visit our website at www.clanryeinternational.com

Contents

Preface

A psychological disorder refers to a condition that is typically identified by symptoms such as abnormal thoughts, behaviors and feelings. These disorders may be linked to different conditions including psychosis, depression, stress, sleep and anxiety. The prevalence of mental disorders such as somatic problems, depression and anxiety are influenced by gender. Some of the mental health issues faced by men include depression, generalized anxiety disorder, social anxiety disorder, obsessive-compulsive disorder, bipolar disorder and schizophrenia. Men are more prone to withdraw socially under stress and might not take actions to handle their stress. They are also more likely than women to be diagnosed with antisocial personality disorder and substance abuse. Mental stress in males is connected with a number of health issues that might influence their health including high blood pressure and consequent cardiovascular morbidity and mortality, erectile dysfunction, cardiovascular disease, and decreased fertility. This book provides significant information to help develop a good understanding of psychological disorders in males. It presents researches and studies performed by experts across the globe. Those in search of information to further their knowledge will be greatly assisted by this book.

This book has been the outcome of endless efforts put in by authors and researchers on various issues and topics within the field. The book is a comprehensive collection of significant researches that are addressed in a variety of chapters. It will surely enhance the knowledge of the field among readers across the globe.

It gives us an immense pleasure to thank our researchers and authors for their efforts to submit their piece of writing before the deadlines. Finally in the end, I would like to thank my family and colleagues who have been a great source of inspiration and support.

Margeret Tremblay

An Overview of Male Psychological Disorders

In a scene from an early episode of the popular American drama series *Mad Men*, the character Paul Kinsey warns: 'A modern executive is a busy man. He leads a complicated life. He has family and leisure – and he's supposed to keep *all* that straight.'[1] The show follows the lives of a group of men and women working in the ruthless Madison Avenue advertising world during the 1960s (hence the name *Mad Men*) and is now well-known for its depiction of the merciless and aggressive competitiveness of the industry and its portrayal of heavy drinking and adultery – features which are said to have characterised 1960s corporate culture. Perhaps not so typical of the lives of ordinary men in Britain, the show nonetheless communicates a sense of some of the pressures facing men in a rapidly changing post-war world. The degree to which men actually succeeded in 'keeping *all* that straight' in Britain and the United States (US) during the period has recently become a topic for debate among social commentators, and academic historians.[2] However, the ways in which men coped with professional and personal pressures are less well understood, and we know very little about the degree to which men suffered from emotional and psychological difficulties and how they dealt with them when they did.

Why this history is so poorly recorded is a matter for considerable debate. Many would argue that men are simply much less likely than women to be affected by mood disorders and that women are more naturally predisposed to such conditions.[3] There is a well-versed ancient link between femininity and 'madness', the origins of which are now well known, as are the concerns put forward by feminist commentators from the 1980s who argued that higher cases of psychological illness in women were directly related to the disadvantageous aspects of the female role.[4] Statistically, women do appear to suffer more frequently from depressive and anxiety disorders, featuring more regularly in primary care figures for consultations, diagnoses and prescriptions for psychotropic medication. This has remained consistent throughout the post-war period with current figures suggesting that women are approximately twice more likely to suffer from affective disorders than men.[5] However, this book will argue that the statistical landscape reveals only part of the story. For a start, 75 per cent of suicides are currently among men, and we can trace this trend historically to data that suggests this has been the case since the beginning of the twentieth century.[6] Alcohol abuse, a factor often related to suicide, is also significantly more common in men who are more than twice as likely to become alcohol-dependent than women.[7] This trend is well-established and is a consistent theme throughout the studies of general practice morbidity that emerged during the late 1950s.[8] Additionally, it has long been acknowledged that men often present with somatic, or 'physical' symptoms which might have an emotional cause. It is therefore highly likely that male cases of depression and anxiety disorders are underdiagnosed.[9] Indeed, family doctors practising in the 1950s noted that women tended to present with symptoms of low-mood, anxiety, lack of motivation and sadness (which, for the most part were easy to recognise); however, men were more likely to present with somatic symptoms, including a range of ill-defined disorders affecting the stomach, digestion, sleep and general wellbeing.[10]

Male psychological illness has not been entirely absent from history. In recent years, scholars have written extensively about male presentations of distress in the distant past. Mark Micale has demonstrated how, during the Georgian period, 'nervousness' in males from the upper social strata was commonly accepted and viewed as a sign of 'good breeding'. Advances in scientific and anatomical knowledge from the practice of dissection suggested that the central nervous system was fundamental to understandings of the body. Within Georgian society, the individuals thought to be most seriously affected by nervous distempers were those from the cultured classes who were considered to have more refined nervous systems that were more prone to collapse. The display of emotion in this period was not associated with sexual practice or effeminacy – being 'manly' in Georgian Britain primarily meant being virtuous and wise. Male emotionality, therefore, crossed no inappropriate boundaries, nor brought undue negative attention. Men were therefore quite comfortable looking inwardly and being reflective about their own physical and psychological experiences.[11] The Victorian period that followed ushered in a host of social and cultural changes associated with industrial and imperial pursuit. Bolstered by the evolutionary theories of Charles Darwin and Herbert Spencer, this period witnessed the emergence of new constructions of male and female, in which women were viewed as biologically inferior to men, dominated by their reproductive systems and prone to irrationality. Men, in contrast, were considered to be rational, 'restrained' beings.[12]

Despite the fact that, during the late nineteenth and early twentieth centuries, Charcot and Freud both included accounts of male 'hysteria', and notwithstanding narratives of 'neurasthenia' among intellectual men, it has been accounts of female insanity that have largely dominated the literature from this period onwards.[13] There is, of course, one important exception: the psychological and somatoform symptoms of trauma in combat. Unexplained and troubling symptoms of trauma have featured in all major combat zones, dating from early accounts of cerebro-spinal shock during the Napoleonic Wars; cardiac exhaustion during the Boer War; shell shock during the First World War, through to more recent experiences of gastric disorders during the Second World War and post traumatic stress disorder in modern times.[14] Male trauma in war has rightly attracted much interest among scholars and culminated in extensive literature on the topic; however, much less attention has focused on the experiences of ordinary men outside the extraordinary sphere of military combat. The aim of this book, therefore, is to gain a more precise understanding of the aetiology and presentation of psychological illness in ordinary men since the mid-twentieth century. I ask a number of questions about the ways in which men presented with symptoms to their doctors and I also consider whether or not we can gauge with any clarity how many cases remained undiagnosed in the community. In particular, the book aims to reveal more about *why* we know so little about male psychological illness, and why such an uncomfortable relationship existed between medicine, culture, masculinity and emotion. It looks in detail at the broad cultural forces that influenced the ways in which men understood their symptoms and coped with their problems. It also examines the gendered cultures that were embedded in medicine and the workplace because, as Judith Butler has argued, gendered behaviour is to some extent 'performative', in that it produces a series of effects that consolidate the impression of being a man or a woman – institutional and structural forces then operate to reinforce such behaviour.[15] However, the book is not only concerned with the cultural; it also examines the 'material' – the limits of medical knowledge and the range of organisational and professional factors that also influenced the understanding and treatment of psychological symptoms. I will argue ultimately that, once these factors are considered, a very different pattern of gendered psychological illness emerges. These insights have important implications, not only for the ways in which we understand gender and mental illness in the past, but also for service providers and policy-makers currently grappling with a somewhat incongruous situation in which 'men are currently half as likely as women to be diagnosed with depression, yet three times more likely to kill themselves because of it'.[16]

The post-war context

The critical social and cultural developments of the post-war decades have provided historians with rich material for analysis. The broad trends are now well known; however, it is important to remember that many of the developments affected men and women in unique ways. Britain's industrial and manufacturing base went into steep decline and mechanisation resulted in a drastic reduction of workers employed in primary and secondary sectors. Women entered the workforce in increasing numbers, energised by an expanding service sector that was well-suited to female employment. Patterns of consumption and leisure shifted markedly after the immediate austerity of the post-war period. By the late twentieth century, almost 12 per cent of consumer expenditure went towards furniture, electrical and other consumer goods; the figure in 1950 was just 4.7 per cent.[17] This trend was undoubtedly stimulated by the growth of popular press and commercial television advertising.[18] The age at which most men and women married began to decline from the 1930s and the demobilisation of men at the end of the war resulted in the post-war baby boom that has, of recent years, become the subject of much demographic debate. Gradually, through the 1960s and 1970s, women gained more control over their fertility following the introduction of the contraceptive pill; however, changes in social 'mores' were of course much slower and less dramatic than the well-versed adage 'the sexual revolution' would suggest. Class and status became a topic for analysis as rising incomes resulted in a blurring of class distinctions and the middle classes lost some of the economic and political advantages they had enjoyed before the war.[19] Inextricably linked to class and social change were the problems of youth and education. The expansion of secondary school education from 1944, the shift from a tripartite system to comprehensive schooling during the 1960s and the gradual expansion of university education resulted in higher numbers of working class children and young adults benefiting from an education previously denied to them.[20] Anxieties about class were duly exacerbated by concerns about race relations and housing shortages due to increasing numbers of immigrants from the West Indies and South Asia who were eager to find work in Britain. While immigrant people brought cultural and religious diversity, Christian Britain simultaneously witnessed a decline in religious practices from the late 1950s – a change that has been described as 'one of the most significant trends of our time'.[21]

The changes to the social, economic and cultural landscape of post-war Britain were ultimately complex and marked by currents and counter-currents that are not easy to explain by grand theories of social change.[22] Contemporary anxieties were nonetheless evident in the proliferation of social studies undertaken from 1945, which, as Chris Harris has remarked, were 'part of a post war mentalité which perceived there to be a sea-change taking place in social life which involved loss as well as gain'.[23] Willmott and Young's influential study of community in Bethnal Green in London's east end, and Elizabeth Bott's examination of marriage and social networks, attempted to investigate kinship relationships and support systems as families adapted to new economic and environmental circumstances.[24] The anthropologist Raymond Firth, meanwhile, focused his attention on middle-class families, as did Willmott and Young in their later publication on family and class in a London suburb.[25] The overriding message from such work was that fears about kinship networks being under threat were unfounded as familial relationships remained strong despite the on-going social and cultural changes. Preoccupations about class were explored in a number of studies, including Richard Hoggart's *Uses of Literacy* (1957) which examined the unintended consequences of 'mass education' of the working class. The sociologist John Goldthorpe and his colleagues published a series of texts during the 1960s examining the impact of increasing affluence on working class identity in which they argued that workers' class identity remained important to them, despite their increasing prosperity.[26] Concerns about new suburban housing estates and their effects on the mental health of housewives were also evident in research undertaken by clinicians during the 1960s. However, the conclusions were once again somewhat reassuring as findings suggested that psychiatric morbidity was no worse on new estates than it had been found to be in older urban developments.[27] Broadly, the surveys of the period articulated fears about new ways of living, but often unearthed a surprising degree of continuity and cohesion. By the mid-1970s, the sociological study of class identity had become less of a priority as the focus shifted to structural aspects of inequality.[28] Two other major concerns related to the subordination of women put forward by the women's movement, and the problems of youth delinquency – first identified as a problem during the 1950s but increasingly seen as a growing one during the 1960s and 1970s.[29] As numerous authors have chronicled, the 1960s and 1970s were marked by a cluster of liberal reforms on sexuality, abortion and obscenity, although, as Addison rightly points out, the permissive legislation of the period revised rather than abandoned previous boundaries.[30]

The social changes of the period undoubtedly affected the way in which men and women experienced their lives at work, at home and within families; however, contemporary studies focused largely upon 'structures' such as class and labour, and 'institutions' such as marriage and the family. Where they focused on gender, the pressures that were unique to women as wives, mothers and increasingly as workers attracted scrutiny.[31] Men were discussed tangentially as workers within class structures or as youths, but less frequently as husbands, fathers or male individuals. However, in popular culture, literature and film, representations of masculinity emerged more freely – for example in the epic war movies of the 1950s, such as *Bridge on the River Kwai* (1957) and *The Dam Busters* (1955). In romantic literature, the type of ideal man being 'hunted' by young women in Mills and Boon bestsellers was unsurprisingly square-jawed, professional, strong, silent and dominant. Most notably, he was 'inscrutable'.[32] 'Social problem' literature and film became a distinct genre during the 1950s and anxieties about youth and disaffection were reflected in a range of novels, plays and movies depicting the so-called 'angry young men'. As Sutherland notes, the salient features of these young individuals were 'anger, youth and bubbling testosterone'.[33] John Osborne's play *Look Back in Anger* (1956), adapted later for the screen, is among the best known for portraying the class tension and anti-establishment sentiment of the post-war years. Other books and films tackled the themes of ambition and social mobility. John Braine's *Room at the Top* (1957), for example, articulated many of the tensions facing working-class men who sought to achieve higher status and success. Ian Fleming's creation of the character James Bond in 1953 did much over the coming decades to reinforce the stereotypical image of masculinity through the themes of action and sexual prowess.[34]

Reflecting the darker undercurrents of the Cold War and political instability, the 1960s and 1970s were marked by an increase in the popularity of thriller and disaster novels where men, once again, were commonly depicted as valiant and dauntless, able to triumph over adversity.[35] Other works reflected the reform of obscenity laws in 1959 which not only affected the accessibility of literature that had been previously censored, but also ushered in a new wave of 'liberating' sex manuals, such as Alex Comfort's *The Joy of Sex* (1972). The concerns of the women's movement also heavily dominated popular culture during the late 1960s and 1970s and a new generation of writers began to explore 'what it was to be a woman' in fiction and film.[36] The plight of men in this new society did not escape the attention of novelists completely. Joseph Heller's darkly humorous novel *Something Happened* (1974), for example, built upon the concerns put forward earlier by authors such as George Orwell, William H. Whyte, David Riesman and Herbert Marcuse describing the conformity and emptiness faced by men in post-war Britain and the US.[37] The protagonist, Slocum, is restless and dissatisfied; he despises his job and does not care for his family, entering into regular equally unsatisfying adulterous affairs. As will become evident in the following chapters, although these themes emerged with regularity in the popular culture of the time, they were notable by their absence in organised debates about men and psychological illness.

Although the sociological studies in Britain failed to focus directly on men as individuals, in the US during the late 1950s, the sociologist Helen Mayer Hacker raised concerns about the traditional masculine role which 'proscribe[d] admission and expression of psychological problems feelings and general overt introspection, as summed up in the stereotype of the strong, silent man'.[38] Hacker drew attention to the fact that men, increasingly, were expected to show attributes of sensitivity, patience and understanding, yet they had not been relieved of the necessity of achieving economic success – nor were they permitted such catharsis as weeping or obvious displays of emotion. She highlighted a new range of contradictions in the male role at home and work, emphasising the importance of continued research in this area. Although such work would have been considered *avant garde* at this time, Hacker was not entirely alone in highlighting the disadvantages of the male role. In 1959, Ruth Hartley, for example, also criticised the socialisation of young boys into the male sex role, which was ultimately seen as unhealthy and the cause of unhappiness.[39]

In the US, by the 1970s, concerns about the negative aspects of living up to the demands of the male role led to a 'men's liberation' movement. Writers such as Warren Farrell, Herb Goldberg, Joseph Pleck and Jack Sawyer began to explore the 'problems of masculinity'. The Canadian psychologist, Sidney Jourard, writing in an edited collection of essays about masculinity in 1974, noted that although male emotionality was clearly manifest in autobiography, art and literature, in practice, men were still expected to appear tough, objective, unsentimental and emotionally inexpressive. Men who showed 'weakness', he argued, risked being viewed as 'unmanly by others'.[40] The men's movement was undoubtedly more influential in the US; however, during the 1970s a small collective of men in London began producing a magazine named *Achilles Heel*. This publication aimed to challenge traditional forms of masculinity and male power and to support the creation of alternative social structures and personal ways of being. The social theorist Victor Seidler, one of the original founders, noted that men were uncomfortable expressing emotional needs. To register weakness, he argued, brought into question 'the very sense of male identity'.[41] Men, it appeared, had struggled 'to escape an essentialism that for generations had been used to legitimate the oppression of women . . . Masculinity could not be "deconstructed", it could only be disowned'.[42] The *Achilles Heel* magazine published articles on a range of topics that included the family, fathering and work, and it continued until the late 1990s.[43] However, the degree to which their message influenced the lives of ordinary men remains unclear. In the three decades following the Second World War, although a range of intellectuals and social commentators were beginning to question the essential nature of 'maleness', and indeed the desirability of the male role, most men continued to experience their lives within the narrow framework of socially acceptable norms. As Jourard noted perceptively during the 1970s, 'manliness' appeared to carry a chronic burden of stress that was a key factor in health and wellness.[44] The notion that mental illness is rooted in life experience was advanced in much of the sociological literature from the 1970s; however, as will be demonstrated in Chapter 1 of this book, the emphasis on both sides of the Atlantic was routinely placed on the female role and the particular types of stress experienced by women.[45]

Any study of health and sickness must take into account not only the cultural and social landscape of the period, but also the contemporary framework of medical approaches that were formulated and ultimately adopted. The post-war decades were marked by increasing confidence in curative medicine as significant achievements were made in the fields of surgery, pharmacology and bacteriology. The treatment of mental illness was also largely dominated by biological psychiatry and the development of new drugs to treat severe psychological disorders and mild-to-moderate anxiety and depression. One of aims of this book is to explore the ways in which medical approaches that became dominant at that time influenced the kinds of conditions that gained most attention and the likelihood that they would be detected. Most importantly, it will argue that the prevailing medical approach influenced the training of doctors at medical school and consequently the ways in which conditions were understood and treated by general practitioners (GPs). Considered alongside contemporary cultural expectations of male behaviour, these factors are also central to our appreciation of why so many cases of male emotional disorder remained undetected, misinterpreted or diagnosed as somatic disorders.

During the mid-twentieth century, the biomedical model was, of course, not without its critics. Proponents of the social medicine movement such as John Ryle and Thomas McKeown, professors of social medicine at Oxford and Birmingham respectively, argued strongly that constitutional and social factors should be more closely considered and that 'observation' and 'historical analysis' of the patient were important techniques that had been increasingly underplayed.[46] In raising these concerns, the social medicine movement drew upon the views of earlier critics of 'new ways of living': rising consumerism, the breakdown of traditional values and kinship ties, and their possible effects on health.[47] Differing somewhat in their emphasis, other competing movements also emphasised the importance of factors outside the biological sciences. From the late nineteenth century interest in psychosomatic medicine, for example, led to research on the troublesome relationship between psychological, social and biological factors in disease.[48] Building on the work of such theorists, in his book *Psychosocial Medicine* (1948), Scottish physician James Halliday highlighted the role of social and emotional factors in physical disorders such as peptic ulcers, gastritis, rheumatism and cardiac disease.[49] Additionally, as Mark Jackson has recently shown, the post-war decades marked a period in which increasing concern developed about the negative health consequences of 'stress'.[50] Research developed in a number of broad areas within general medicine, psychiatric epidemiology, psychology, psychosomatic medicine and occupational health and the term 'stress' increasingly began to dominate debates about the negative health consequences of the pressures of modern living.[51]

Nevertheless, as the following chapters will demonstrate, despite the important contributions made by the social medicine movement to aspects of social and psychological causation of sickness, it never fully bridged the divide between prevention and cure, as those such as Ryle had once hoped.[52] As Dorothy Porter has shown, although numerous social medicine departments were established in British universities throughout the 1950s, none of them were ever incorporated into the training of clinicians. Instead, they remained peripheral to the main activities of medical schools.[53] The consequences were manifest in the concerns of H. J. Walton, a psychiatrist from the University of Edinburgh, who, by the late 1960s observed that GPs might be missing psychosomatic symptoms in their patients because of their training at medical school which placed 'great emphasis on basic scientific investigation . . . physical factors or theoretical matters'.[54] Among many medical students, Walton detected a lack of concern about the psychological component to illness, and he argued that some 'physically orientated' graduates actively disliked patients who presented with psychogenic aspects to their illness.[55]

Echoing the aims of the social medicine movement, the aspirations of psychosomatic theorists and stress researchers were aimed at reducing the burden of sickness by pressing for social improvements. However, as other authors have noted, the irony was that the debates increasingly emphasised *personal* rather than collective responsibility for managing stress and coping with life's pressures.[56] Similarly, in the field of occupational health, despite the fact that some studies drew attention to the ways in which conditions at work induced physical and psychological illness, discussions were broadly motivated by concerns about productivity. As such, most researchers employed a 'disease-centred' approach, which underplayed social and emotional factors that might influence sickness patterns.[57] It was ultimately not until the 1980s that studies began to concentrate on the emotional and psychological health of workers and, more broadly, a 'new' public health movement emerged proposing that disease could be prevented by wide-scale changes in personal habits.[58] As is now well known, the criticisms of curative medicine put forward by influential individuals such as Thomas McKeown and Ivan Illich during the late 1970s prompted renewed debates between the proponents of sophisticated medical intervention and those dedicated to the prevention of sickness by social improvements. The irony again was that the work undertaken by social theorists appeared to harmonise neatly with a new political discourse that emphasised the role of the individual in health. McKeown's work was subsequently cited selectively by those looking to 'roll back the state' and buttress claims that government-supported medical services should have a limited role in health.[59] Much of McKeown's thesis was ultimately discredited, but, nonetheless, the notion that social conditions and standards of living ultimately impact on health remains a relevant one. The remit of this book is not to evaluate the relative merits of either approach; indeed, most would now view targeted intervention and social change as complementary to each other.[60] However, the following chapters serve to illustrate how a post-war medical model that emphasised a curative, interventionist approach did much to impede the detection of male psychological and psychosomatic illness. Had the medical model focused additionally upon health issues in political, social and economic terms, it might contrastingly have provided the ideological motivation for explanations of the social causation of disease and consideration of the cultural construction of gendered behaviour that is so intimately connected with mental disorders. A more holistic approach might further have inspired changes in medical education towards the organised study of social pathology which, as Ryle proposed in 1947, might 'give a broader and more humanistic outlook to emerging doctors and fit them better for their important role in a changing society'.[61] As this book will suggest, the longstanding cultural association with women and mental illness further exacerbated clinicians' propensity to diagnose psychological disorders more readily in women than in men.

One of the central arguments presented in this book is that, for a variety of reasons, many of which are not completely understood, men have tended to present with distress in ways that fit less well with the traditional medical models of mental illness. Instead of presenting with classically dysthymic symptoms of low mood, for example, men have been more likely to report physical symptoms affecting the body and musculoskeletal system. I build on this argument throughout the following chapters and contend that it is one of the most fundamental reasons why men do not appear in data for psychological illness as regularly as women. Any discussion of psychosomatic symptoms must necessarily engage with the growing literature on somatisation – a topic that has been widely debated between psychiatrists and anthropologists since the mid-1950s.[62] In 1977, the American psychiatrist Arthur Kleinman wrote a seminal article criticising psychiatry's 'breathless search' for a universal form of depression across cultures.[63] While acknowledging that there may well be a basic depressive syndrome characterised by depressive affect, insomnia, weight loss and other mood changes, Kleinman argued that this syndrome 'represents a small fraction of the entire field of depressive phenomena' and that it was a 'cultural category constructed by psychiatrists in the west'. By definition, he argued, 'it excludes most depressive phenomena, even in the west'.[64] Kleinman developed these ideas over a long career as a psychiatrist and anthropologist, expounding the notion that 'cultural values and social relations shape how we perceive and monitor our bodies, label and categorise bodily symptoms', and that we therefore 'express our distress through bodily idioms that are both peculiar to distinctive cultural worlds and constrained by our shared human condition'.[65]

Kleinman's ideas were soon well-established and later expanded by a group of other anthropologists and psychiatrists interested in cross-cultural psychiatry. Laurence Kirmayer, whose interest in the subject was rooted in his own family's experience of immigration to Canada, became another key researcher in the field.[66] Kirmayer pointed out the conceptual confusion in the use of the term somatisation, setting out three distinct meanings that could be found in contemporary literature. In western biomedicine, for example, patients were expected to recognise that the roots of their distress lay in psychological or social conflict and articulate them as such to a physician. However, if somatic symptoms presented without organic cause, patients were assumed to be somatising. A second interpretation, and the one promoted by Kleinman, was that somatic symptoms present in place of an emotional problem where the body is a metaphor for social and emotional experience. Finally, psychoanalytically inflected theories of somatisation inferred that emotions could give rise to somatic signs and symptoms.[67] Kirmayer pointed out that, despite the differences in these interpretations, they nonetheless all shared a common core: that 'somatisation always involves a discrepancy between where an observer believes a problem, concern or event is located, or how he expects it to be expressed, and the subject's experience and expression of it in the body'.[68]

There has been criticism of the broad notion of somatisation on a number of levels. Biological psychiatry claims that the concept is relativistic: if our perception and presentation of symptoms is entirely culturally determined, there can be no 'true' psychiatric disorders, proving problematic for clinical practice and treatment. Some also argue that the notion of somatisation somehow buttresses a dualistic concept of medicine, which presumes the physical body is isolated from the mind, proposing instead that emotion is 'embodied' in bodily processes.[69] These matters are still widely debated and are difficult to untangle. Two psychologists from the University of California, Berkeley,

John F. Kihlstrom and Lucy Canter Kihlstrom, in an attempt to reconcile opposing camps, have pointed out that the concept of somatisation might be the wrong place to look for a resolution to the mind-body problem, because for many patients, 'problems do not lie anywhere in their bodies. Rather, they are using their bodies, the language and culture of medicine, and the institutions and processes of the health-care system to express and manage their personal and interpersonal difficulties in a way that would be otherwise difficult or impossible'.[70] Thus, understanding somatisation perhaps requires 'not [just] that we look into the patient's body, but rather into the patient's life and the world in which he or she lives'.[71] I situate the accounts that follow from this perspective.

At some basic level, the ideas promoted by the social medicine movement and the concepts put forward by cross-cultural psychiatrists, ascribed to a broadly 'biopsychosocial' model of medicine in which the biological, the psychological and the social are seen as playing an important role in health and illness. The 'biopsychosocial model', as formally articulated by the American psychiatrist George Engel in 1977, criticised the contemporary scientific medical model for its exclusive focus on biological processes, which excluded behavioural and psychological influences. Engel argued that the medical model should take into account the social context in which a person lives. He claimed that:

> By evaluating all the factors contributing to both illness and patienthood, rather than giving primacy to biological factors alone, a biopsychosocial model would make it possible to explain why some individuals experience as 'illness', conditions which others regard merely as 'problems of living'.[72]

The biopsychosocial model was also not without its critics. Although Engel claimed that his model was non-dualistic, some have suggested that by 'reifying the psychosocial components as different from the biological' his ideas were in fact dualistic.[73] It has also been criticised for its eclecticism, broadness and vagueness, because 'if everything causes everything, one cannot fail to be right, while at the same time nothing informative is really being said'.[74] Others have cautioned that his perspective did not really fit the criteria for a 'model' and could never be more than an idea or a theory.[75] In analysing the material for this project, I accept that many of these criticisms may be valid; however, I contend that a model of medicine in which patients' subjective experiences are considered important, and which accepts that the interactions between the bio-psycho-social domains are complex, offers us (and in particularly me as a historian) the best opportunity to expand our knowledge of psychological and psychosomatic ill-health. The renowned psychiatrist and academic Suman Fernando has observed that symptoms are often experienced as internal and external at the same time; however, western medicine largely considers that illness is experienced as *either* external *or* internal, with one impacting on the other.[76] As the following chapters will demonstrate, when it came to understanding the ways in which men expressed pain and distress, the reductionist model of disease that viewed subjective and objective experiences as 'distinct and separate from each other',[77] provided a barrier between doctor and patient that was in most cases very difficult to overcome.

Structure and design

Writing in the 1950s, Hacker noted that interest and research into the male social role had been 'eclipsed by the voluminous concentration on the more spectacular developments and contradictions in feminine roles'.[78] Part of the problem, she argued perceptively, was that a 'concept' had not emerged for male behaviour, since 'men have stood for mankind, and their problems have been identified with the general human condition'.[79] Hacker's use of the word masculinity was a precursor to the way in which the term has been used in modern times. As Tosh has shown, this is of relatively recent coinage, dating back in common parlance no further back than the 1970s.[80] During the nineteenth century, the term 'manliness' most usually described the gendered lives of men. Manliness implied a single standard of manhood, expressed in certain physical attributes and moral dispositions. Masculinity (often used in the plural 'masculinities') in contrast, fits more comfortably with the post-modern view of the world, with its proliferation of identities and contradictory discourses.[81] Since the work of Joan Scott in the mid-1980s, and following on from the emergence of women's studies, scholars have become increasingly interested in the concept of gender.[82] Key to this concept has been the ways in which male and female identities are socially constructed. Scott argued that 'the story is no longer about the things that have happened to women and men, and how they have reacted to them; instead, it is about how the subjective and collective meanings of women and men, as categories of identity have been constructed'.[83] However, it was not until the 1990s that scholars began to look explicitly at the history of masculinity – a controversial undertaking from the outset because of the risk that it might be colonised by researchers who were concerned with promoting anti-feminist scholarship.[84] Despite obvious tensions, a burgeoning scholarship ensued, with contributions to the debate not only from historians but also from sociologists, and those working in social policy and the health sciences. In line with broader debates about gender, opinion tends to be divided into two camps: one proposes an essentialist notion of manhood and suggests that misguided attempts by women to change the natural order of gender balance have resulted in a 'crisis in masculinity'; the other contends that gender is socially constructed, historically contingent – not 'natural', necessary or ideal, thus exciting the potential for change.[85]

Central to studies of masculinity has been the concept of hegemonic masculinity put forward by the Australian sociologist, R. W. Connell. This is the notion that at any one time there is a normative ideal of masculinity to which men aspire because it is the most honoured way of being a man. It requires all other men to position themselves in relation to it and, ideologically, it has legitimised the global subordination of women to men.[86] It is argued that this model of masculinity has gained ascendancy through culture, institutions and persuasion – although, as Connell points out, it was never assumed to be 'normal' in the statistical sense because only a minority of men might enact it. Most importantly, the concept offered the potential for older forms of masculinity to be displaced by new ones and for less oppressive ways of 'being a man' to become hegemonic.[87] Although the concept is now used widely in scholarship about men and masculinity, it is not without its critics. Margaret Wetherell and Nigel Edley, for example, argue that the term is 'not sufficient for understanding the nitty gritty of negotiating masculine identities and men's identity strategies'.[88] Employing a social psychology perspective, they suggest that a definition of dominant masculinity 'which no man may actually ever embody' might not be appropriate.[89] For a range of reasons, the concept of masculinity itself has also been criticised. It is, for example, often widely used without being precisely defined; it appears to 'essentialise' the character of men and further assumes a false binary or 'dualism' of gender relations.[90] Although it is not the remit of this book to repeat such debates in detail, any scholarship that deals with the lived experience of men must necessarily engage with the discussion. The approach that I take in the following chapters is that the terms masculinity and masculinities remain useful when examining male health and behaviour.

As Robertson and Williams recently pointed out, 'masculinities' should not be seen as character types and attributes held by individuals; they can alternatively be recognised as 'processes of arranging and "doing" social practice that operate in individual and social settings'.[91] Using this approach, I have been able to understand better the possible links between male behaviour and practice, and men's mental health in a range of settings both within and outside medicine from the 1950s. I thus avoid the notion that there are a range of essential male traits that engender stoic, unemotional and independent behaviour, instead arguing that male customs were (and still are) often constrained by social structures and institutional gendered practices. As a historian, I would also contend that there are still advantages in employing the concept of hegemonic masculinity. The version of masculinity that was most 'honoured' during the post-war period required the projection of strength and control – qualities that did not fit well with a notion of male nervous instability. As Mark Micale has shown in his work on male nervous illness in earlier times, these values were a hangover from the Victorian era when 'the spectrum of emotions deemed appropriate for adult men in Britain greatly diminished' – a point that will be developed more fully throughout this book. [92] This is of course not to say that all men 'achieved' or complied with this version of masculinity. Indeed, as the testimonies from clinicians in this book will illustrate, much of the male psychological and psychosomatic illness that presented in primary care could be correlated with unsuccessful attempts to live up to this ideal.

Of recent years, historians have highlighted a tension that has developed between earlier social histories, which focused primarily upon experience and agency, and more recent cultural histories, which focus upon discourse and representation.[93] As Michael Roper has rightly noted what is often missing from linguistic analyses is an adequate sense of the material: the practices of everyday life and the human experience of emotional relationships.[94] Historians of masculinity have therefore suggested that future studies would benefit from a focus, not only on broad cultural codes, but also upon how men related to these codes.[95] In the words of Roper and Tosh, new histories need to 'explore how cultural representations become part of subjective identity'.[96] This is a challenging task, for we cannot know with any real certainty the subjective processes that operate to mediate between individual men and cultural formations of masculinity. We can only ever hope to 'correlate' certain aspects of male behaviour with the set of cultural codes that predominate at any one time. Roper cautions that earlier social histories which focused on the material practices of daily life tended to make 'untheorised' assumptions about the motivation for certain behaviours, sometimes resulting in accounts that amounted to 'little more than the historian's own unexamined projections onto the past'.[97] To overcome this in his own work, Roper uses a psychoanalytical framework to analyse the unconscious elements of soldiers' behaviour during the First World War, emphasising the importance of 'mothers' and 'maternal support' in the subjective experience of the troops. However, I would question the extent to which it would be possible, or even advantageous to apply any specific theory to explain the associations between discourse, representation and patterns of emotional behaviour among the men under study in this book. A psychoanalytical perspective, for example, would underplay the importance of the historical, medical and social context of the post-war period, resulting in a reductive account of male emotional illness.[98] The approach I take, therefore, is that 'good' history need not necessarily offer certainties, but can nonetheless provide possibilities and insight into the complexities of human experience. As Robertson and Williams recently pointed out, although we need to acknowledge that the 'meaning and language' we attach to bodily experiences changes with culture and through time, this should not lead us to abandon attempts to obtain an 'adequate' understanding of the material.[99] As such, I hope to develop a more nuanced understanding of post-war society, gender and psychological distress, taking into account not only cultural codes, but also the evolution of medical practice and the broader social and economic factors that had such impact on the daily lives of men and women in Britain from the 1950s. I offer convincing suggestions about the connections between discourse and behaviour, but do not claim unproblematically to couple them together.

The chapters that follow by no means provide an exhaustive account of male experience. It has been outside the scope of this project, for example, to consider in any great depth the specific problems faced by black and minority communities or the complexities related to issues of class and geography. I do, however, touch upon these wherever the material allows. The book does not focus directly on the history of psychiatric services, for this subject has been covered fully elsewhere, and, as will become evident, men rarely engaged with services for moderate to minor mental disorders.[100] The history of male psychological illness is somewhat unchartered water and it is hoped that this project will inspire further research to unravel the different mental health challenges that were faced, for example, by ethnic minorities as they moved to Britain following the Second World War.[101] I am also aware that this history has not been written primarily from the perspective of ordinary men themselves. Although some individual narratives are included, it is broadly an account of how medicine and society sought to understand male psychological illness. However, by the end of this book it will become evident that seeking the views of a large group of men about their emotions during the post-war period might prove to be unproductive. As Mark Micale has argued so perceptively in his study of male emotional illness in earlier times, the 'true male malady' has, since the Victorian era, been men's chronic inability to reflect on themselves non-heroically without evasion and self-deception.[102] To be self-aware has been seen as 'unmasculine' and health has been 'regarded rhetorically as a feminised concern'.[103] Additionally, men's problems have been less visible because historically it has been the male 'gaze' that has undertaken observation and examination, and, as Hacker pointed out over fifty years ago, a male norm by which others have been measured.[104]

I build my arguments about psychological illness in men from the analysis of a wide range of archival material, including the personal papers of clinicians who had a specific interest in mental health. I also examine medical debates about mental illness and the education of doctors at medical school and in general practice. The insights from this material are supported by the oral testimonies of fifteen retired GPs who had experience in practice during the 1950s, 1960s and 1970s and whom I interviewed at length.[105] The study also includes analysis of material from pharmaceutical companies and GP prescribing patterns for anxiety, depression and psychosomatic illness. It draws additionally on debates from industry that can be found in published primary material on the workplace and health – a topic that gained considerable attention in the decades following the war as the nation strived to expand its economic growth and productivity.

Chapter 1 is situated in primary care and explores the ways in which male psychological disorder presented to GPs. It examines the ways in which cultural and social forces influenced medical ideas about gender and mental illness, and illustrates how the biological, interventionist model of medicine in Britain impeded the efforts of those who sought to engage more constructively with debates about the social and emotional dimensions of disease.

The mental health of workers is addressed in Chapter 2, where I argue that debates about sickness absence, absenteeism and stress were dominated by concerns about productivity, resulting in a failure to investigate male psychological illness in the workplace, despite clear evidence of its existence.

The use of alcohol as a coping mechanism among men is the central theme of Chapter 3. I show how inertia within the medical community and the eventual dominance of the disease theory of alcoholism hindered the detection of alcohol abuse among men. I also suggest that the culture of heavy drinking among British men at work and during leisure time did much to obscure damaging levels of alcohol consumption that were very often regarded as normal.

Chapter 4 examines trends in psycho-pharmaceutical prescribing among GPs. The aim of this chapter is to question statistics that suggest unproblematically that women were at least twice as likely to receive a diagnosis and prescription for a psychological disorder. By including categories of drugs that contained 'hidden' tranquillising compounds, often directed at men for gastric disorders, and by examining some of the vagaries of the data, I argue that men in fact feature more obviously in this story.

Chapter 5 addresses what I have termed 'special cases': the mental health of doctors themselves and debates about the psychological health of immigrants who had come to Britain in the decades following the Second World War. By the 1980s, research had begun to uncover a significant problem with alcohol, drugs and mental illness within the medical profession. At the same time anxieties were emerging about the ways in which those with non-British backgrounds were coping with the strains of joining new communities. The two are explored simultaneously, not because their experiences were comparable in any direct way, but because they are together illustrative of many of the broad themes already explored in this book, and serve to advance the core arguments put forward in earlier chapters.

I conclude by suggesting that this history has begun to expose and uncover male psychological distress where it seemed previously hidden, but was in fact prevalent – either existing undiagnosed in the community, or presenting in complex psychological and psychosomatic forms in primary care. I argue that because women have 'reported' psychological symptoms with more regularity, this does not necessarily mean that they are more likely to be predisposed to them. This is especially important when, as the book will demonstrate, men have historically been much less likely to identify symptoms in themselves – and far less likely to seek help when they do. Rebalancing our view of the gendered landscape could have far-reaching consequences, not only for historians of mental illness and psychiatry, but for those working currently in the field of mental health where some persist resolutely, and perhaps mistakenly, to focus on the apparent disparity in psychological health between the sexes. If we are to understand more about why so many men commit suicide, we must expend more energy looking at changing cultural practices that have for so long influenced men's ability to recognise, report and manage emotional distress.

1

Mental Disorders and General Practice

Introduction

At a meeting of the Royal Society of Medicine in November 1958, the psychiatrist Michael Shepherd and a group of colleagues observed that most of the previous work on the epidemiological aspects of mental disorder had been focused on institutionalised patients where the population had been 'conveniently circumscribed for the purposes of investigation'. Research, therefore, had been concerned predominantly with major psychiatric disorder. In order to obtain further knowledge about mental illness, Shepherd argued that there was a need for systematic study of the minor psychiatric disorders and their prevalence in the community.[1] Shepherd, a well-respected Professor of Psychiatry, established the General Practice Research Unit at the Institute of Psychiatry in London during the late 1950s. The aim of this unit was to study, by epidemiological methods, 'the causes, nature, extent and distribution of extra-mural mental disorder in the setting of general practice, where, under the conditions of the British National Health Service, information is obtainable about the health of the bulk of the population'.[2] In stating this aim, Shepherd and his colleagues were articulating a view widely expressed by those working in general practice during the post-war period: that family doctors fulfilled a unique role in medicine and should be more widely involved in epidemiological research. The proposal offered general practice the opportunity to gain professional status within medicine, for, as David Hannay has pointed out, at mid-twentieth century, it was viewed as less prestigious than other specialisms and those who opted for it were 'considered to be less able or to have fallen off the specialist ladder'.[3] On the one hand, therefore, moves to promote research in general practice could be seen as one of a number of measures put in place to establish the field as a discipline in its own right – measures that also included the founding of the College of General Practitioners in 1952, the development of vocational training and the evolution of departments of general practice.[4] On the other hand, the work undertaken and records held by family doctors did indeed provide unique insights into patient populations and offer opportunities for research into the incidence of a wide range of diseases, prescribing patterns and clinical decision-making processes.

In an attempt to further my understanding of male psychological illness, I focus on general practice in this first chapter, in part because of the proliferation of research studies that emerged from primary care on mental illness during the period. Combined with the personal recollections of doctors working in practice from the 1950s to the 1980s, these studies provided me with rich material. Although it is the case that much male mental illness remained undetected in the community, as we shall see, a significant amount of male psychological and psychosomatic illness presented in primary care. The local doctor's surgery also provided a space within which much 'family illness' emerged that was often connected to sick men who were reluctant to seek help for psychological problems or addiction. A good deal of nervous illness in women and children, for example, was related to broader psychosocial problems and difficult interpersonal relationships at home. As this chapter will illustrate, this might go some way towards explaining why women appear to predominate in statistics for mental illness. As Elianne Riska has noted: 'The history of medicine can be perceived as the tale of the rise and fall of medical discourses that have provided a lens through which the physician has constructed disease and its "cause".'[5] Certainly, the story of male psychological illness and its place in general practice, suggests that physicians, as a product of their time and place, played a key role in both reflecting and reinforcing not only the prevailing medical model of psychiatric disorder, but also the dominant model of masculinity that promoted strong, tough providers. Indeed, most physicians at this time were men themselves, and therefore bound by the same nexus of constraints and expectations as their male patients.

Shifting concepts of mental disorder

Recent academic interest in the history of psychiatric disorders suggests there was a notable shift from an age of 'anxiety', post-Second

World War, to a period from the 1970s in which depression emerged as the dominant concept. Allan Horwitz, writing about the American experience, argues that this in part reflected the criticism directed at psychiatry's diagnostic system by critics such as Thomas Szasz and D. L. Rosenhan during the post-war period.[6] Biological psychiatry required 'specificity' – distinct diagnoses and treatments directed at specific symptoms. The concept of major depressive disorder, as it emerged during the late 1970s, was able to fit this bill more suitably than the large range of ill-defined anxiety disorders, often caused by life's difficulties, which 'lacked the diagnostic specificity needed to give disease entities medical legitimacy'.[7] The increasing emphasis on depression also reflected developments in psychopharmacology and, later, the emergence of the new selective serotonin reuptake inhibitors (SSRIs). These proved a 'promising market' in light of concerns about dependency problems with many of the older anxiolytic drugs, in particular the benzodiazepines. The SSRIs claimed to raise levels of serotonin in the brain and harmonised both with the notion of biological specificity and the concept of chemical imbalance – concepts that were to become deeply embedded in both clinical and popular accounts of depression. A point made, not only by Horwitz but also by others such as David Healy, is that the development of new drugs 'shaped the nature of the illness that it was supposedly meant to treat'.[8] These developments were crystallised with the release of DSM III in 1980, in which the condition 'major depressive disorder' encompassed amorphous and short-lived psychosocial problems as well as serious and chronic depression. Anxiety disorders, in contrast, focused specifically on distinct disorders and individual phobias such as agoraphobia, obsessive-compulsive disorder and post-traumatic stress disorder.[9] In Britain, the situation differed somewhat as the standard diagnostic tool for mental illness has been the *International Classification of Diseases* (ICD). Although revision nine, published in 1979, included the condition 'major depressive disorder', 'generalised anxiety states' still featured, in addition to 'distinct phobic disorders'.[10]

Mark Jackson has also drawn attention to the fact that, during the immediate post-Second World War period, society struggled to come to terms with economic depression, the rise in totalitarianism and the fear of atomic warfare, resulting, he argues, in 'an upsurge of anxiety'.[11] Jackson argues, however, that alongside the shift away from the age of anxiety and the move towards a focus on depression in the late 1970s, many commentators turned to the concept of 'stress' to explain a host of clinical conditions and physio-psychological processes. According to Jackson, the concept of stress 'resonated with attempts to come to terms with a rapidly changing world' and stress reactions were more easily quantifiable than anxiety.[12] Motivated by the work undertaken by late nineteenth- and early twentieth-century stress researchers, such as Walter Cannon (1871–1945), Harold Wolff (1898–1962) and Hans Selye (1907–82), and psychosomatic theorists such as Franz Alexander and Helen Flanders Dunbar, increasingly epidemiologists, clinicians and social commentators implicated stressful life events in a range of physical and psychological disorders.[13]

Undoubtedly, these broad intellectual histories do indicate a clear move, metaphorically and clinically, away from anxiety towards a period during the late twentieth and early twenty-first centuries in which depression appeared to emerge as the modern epidemic. However, the remainder of this chapter will illustrate that during the 1950s, 1960s and 1970s, in practice, debates about the diagnosis, classification and cause of mood disorders (and associated somatoform conditions) remained a highly contested area where much variation existed among practitioners.

Studies on psychiatric morbidity

Surveys of health and sickness have a long history that begins much earlier than the period that is covered by this book. Early studies were motivated by a desire to produce statistical information about the population, amid concerns about the effects of poverty, poor living conditions and social disorder. The first of note is often awarded to Charles Booth for his study of late nineteenth century working class life, *Life and Labour of the People* (1889 and 1891).[14] However, much earlier, Edwin Chadwick's *The Sanitary Condition of the Labouring Population* (1842) and the *Health of Towns Commission* (1843) drew upon interviews and data from Boards of Guardians and general practitioners (GPs). Seebohm Rowntree, in his study of York, *Poverty, A Study of Town Life* (1901), attempted to move the discipline of sociology from its literary and journalistic affiliates towards a 'social science'.[15] His study involved the 'intensive' method of interviewing 11,560 families (a total of 46,754 people) in an attempt to discover a true measure of poverty.[16] Increasingly through the twentieth century, the developing method of sampling enabled surveys to be undertaken more economically.

The hardships and traumas experienced during the Second World War prompted explicit unease about the nation's health. Concerns were particularly focused upon the effects of long hours of work, rationing, blackouts and the general stress of war.[17] A report undertaken by the Ministry of Health, *On the State of the Public Health During Six Years of War* (1946) suggested that many outpatient departments and doctors' surgeries were reporting large numbers of people complaining of tiredness and feeling 'rundown'. The summary report for the Ministry of Health in 1944 observed that a range of minor ailments had increased, prompting the General Register Office to put forward plans for an index of morbidity to measure major and minor illness. The result was *The Survey of Sickness 1943–1952* (published in 1957), in which a sample of 4,000 people were interviewed about all aspects of their health.[18] The insights drawn from this research revealed much about broad trends in morbidity. However, when it came to psychological illness, the survey also exposed a range of methodological problems that continued to hamper the pursuits of those working on the epidemiological aspects of mental illness for the next thirty years or more. The authors noted that the fieldwork entailed a range of problems related to the classification of illness. For example, where two symptoms were obviously connected, they would be put together; where this was not conclusive, they were noted separately.[19] This presented particular problems where a physical symptom might have a psychological cause. It was acknowledged that many people might be reticent disclosing the 'exact nature of their illness', and that some respondents retained more objective memories of their condition than others.[20] As this chapter will suggest, factors like these were to frustrate researchers over the coming years and led the authors to acknowledge that it was debatable whether the study would in fact bring them any 'nearer to a true picture of the state of the health of the community'.[21]

The Survey of Sickness revealed that psychoneuroses and all categories of mental disorder were significantly more common in women. However, with what was to become a defining feature of much of the research to follow, the survey also found that 'ill-defined illness' – sickness that did not fit into clear categories – accounted for a significant amount of morbidity. Men featured in large numbers for ill-defined illness and also for consultations for indigestion and gastrointestinal disturbances.[22] As will become evident in this book, there is good reason to suggest that many vague diagnoses were related to psychosomatic and psychological illness in men. Motivated by such high levels of neurotic illness, and the concomitant anxieties about the economic cost of sickness absence, from the late 1950s, much research took place in general practice with the aim of understanding more about the causes and prevalence of mental illness. Following the foundation of the College of General Practitioners in 1953, increasingly GPs were prompted to undertake such research themselves.[23] In 1958, the first national morbidity survey was published, authored by W. P. D. Logan and A. A. Cushion. This was a study of the clinical records from 106 general practices (171 doctors) across England and Wales. Echoing the findings from *The Survey of Sickness*, the research indicated that psychoneurotic disorders were much more common in females, but that ulcers of the stomach, particularly duodenal ulcers, were more frequently diagnosed in men.[24] Women also featured with regularity in an interesting category entitled 'Consultations for reasons other than sickness or injury'.[25] Unfortunately, the study did not elaborate on what precisely these consultations covered; however, the oral histories of general practitioners suggest that women often visited the doctor to disclose personal problems, many of which related to male members of the family.

Through the 1950s and 1960s, many studies appeared in the medical press on the extent of psychological illness in general practice populations. By 1974, nonetheless, commentators conceded that rates of recorded mental illness differed greatly between doctors and between practices.[26] Anthony Ryle, a GP from London (and son of John Ryle, the renowned Professor of Social Medicine at Oxford University) highlighted the disparities between studies in an article published in the *Journal of the College of General Practitioners* in 1960. Ryle suggested an approximation could probably be made that 'between 5 and 10 per cent of the population were likely to consult their doctor at least once with symptoms of neurosis', yet some studies estimated that, during a five year period, as many as 40 per cent of patients were at risk.[27] Ryle put forward a host of explanations that might account for such a wide variation in recorded diagnoses between different investigators. First and foremost of these was 'the absence of any satisfactory criteria of diagnosis'.[28]

Measuring and classifying mental illness

As community psychiatry increasingly began to replace asylum-based care of individuals with mental illness, psychiatry began to focus on the less severe categories of psychiatric disorder.[29] As Michael Shepherd pointed out, during the mid-1960s, 'the influx into treatment situations of earlier, milder and more transient cases has helped to bring about a radical alteration of perspective . . . In consequence, the epidemiologist . . . has been forced to extend his observations from institutional populations to include the community at large'.[30] Nevertheless, despite increasing research into the nature and causes of moderate to mild psychiatric disorders, no uniform method of diagnosis and classification emerged.

At the heart of controversies on this topic were two fundamental difficulties. The first was the relationship between 'psychotic' and 'neurotic' conditions. R. E. Kendell, Professor of Psychiatry at the University of Edinburgh, remarked in 1976 that the concept of depressive illness 'embraces a wide range of different clinical phenomena and spans the historical distinction between psychosis and neurosis, yet at the same time, the prevailing mood of sadness, helplessness and hopelessness gives it a common core, a unifying theme'.[31] The confusion, he argued, reflected in part a broader philosophical clash between the Meyerian bio-psychosocial approach espoused by Adolf Meyer (1866–1950), which framed mental illness as 'reaction types' that could be understood within the context of life-situations, and the Kraepelin school, as advanced by Emil Kraepelin (1856–1926) who viewed psychological symptoms as biological, discreet disease entities. Some clinicians were of the view that only one category of organic, depressive illness existed and that symptom severity could be located somewhere along a continuum, while others promoted the idea that there were two or more discreet versions that variously included a range of neurotic and anxiety-related symptoms. Nevertheless, a majority of research articles accepted broadly that 'endogenous' or 'psychotic' depression (what we might now diagnose as major depressive disorder) was more likely to embody the 'classical' aspects of melancholic depression: feelings of hopelessness, sleep disturbance, appetite and weight change; whereas, 'exogenous' or 'reactive' depressive states were often typified by feelings of anxiety neurosis and were more likely to be triggered by environmental stress. However, there were many semantic differences between descriptions, with authors variously invoking a host of alternative terms, including: organic depression, cyclic depression, affective disorder, periodic depression and neurotic-depressive reaction. As Kendell pointed out, these semantic differences had produced many misunderstandings in the past and sustained many disputes. The confusion was so widespread and deeply ingrained that, he argued, the profession might be well advised to abandon all terms 'and start afresh'.[32] If any agreement existed at all, it was that the reactive or neurotic class of depression was more difficult to conceptualise.

The second limitation faced by researchers of psychiatric morbidity in general practice was that by restricting psychiatric disorders to the psychotic/neurotic framework, psychosomatic presentations were often excluded from consideration. As Shepherd noted, this often resulted in misleadingly low estimates because many emotionally disturbed patients presented with somatic complaints.[33] A study by John Fry, an early pioneer of research in general practice, for example, found that during the late 1960s, prevalence rates (per thousand) for neurosis among his patients were 238 for men and 528 for women. His conclusion was that the pattern of distribution showed 'a marked preponderance of female patients' and that this conformed broadly with earlier reported figures from the same practice.[34] Notable in the method and design of his study, however, was the fact that the diagnostic category of neurosis 'did not cover psychosomatic conditions or physical illnesses with a neurotic complaint'.[35] In contrast, research undertaken at another 'average' suburban practice by R. E. Perth found that 39.4 per cent of patients had suffered at least once during five years from some kind of psychosomatic complaint and that 'half the work done during surgery hours was taken up by [these] conditions'.[36] Women, of course, appeared regularly in numbers diagnosed with a wide range of psychosomatic disorders, including headaches, skin disorders and chest pains; however, men predominated in diagnoses of peptic ulcer and epigastric pain – conditions that, according to Perth, were often of psychogenic origin because symptoms disappeared or improved with psychological treatment.[37]

The lack of clarity surrounding the epidemiology and nosology of psychological illness was further compounded by the lack of a reliable screening tool to aid practitioners in making assessments about the mental health of their patients. Until the mid-1970s, the screening tool most often used in research was the Cornell Medical Index (CMI). Originating from Cornell University College, New York in 1949, its purpose was to provide 'an instrument suitable for collecting a large body of pertinent medical and psychiatric data at a minimum of the physician's time'.[38] The index contained a total of 195 questions relating to bodily symptoms, past illnesses, family history, behaviour, mood and feeling. Although the index was widely used in general practice research, by the 1970s practitioners had begun to suggest that the questionary scores and practitioners' assessments did not correlate with sufficient accuracy. Indeed, Shepherd noted in 1966 that much of the variation between general practice studies could be accounted for by 'observer factors'.[39] A study of psychiatric outpatients also showed that, when rated with the CMI, many patients would have been 'missed' because their scores fell within the normal range.[40] A number of other methods existed to aid with diagnosis, including the Hamilton Rating Scale, the Beck Depression Inventory and the Wakefield Self Assessment Depression Inventory.[41] However, as commentators pointed out, there were significant problems with early measuring scales which were often hampered by a lack of clarity about what was being 'measured': distress or disorder; psychological, emotional or mental wellbeing.[42] The psychologist and epidemiologist, Barbara Dohrenwend, observed later that these early tools gave general indications of stress, analogous to the measurement of body temperature: elevated scores tell you that something is wrong, but not what is wrong.[43] High scores might indicate a normal reaction to stressful circumstances, or alternatively, a firm case of neurotic disorder. A further problem was refining the balance between consideration of affective and somatic symptoms, which, as we have seen, often proved an insurmountable obstacle.[44]

Michael Shepherd reputedly felt that designing a screening questionnaire that could apply to everyone was impossible.[45] However, David Goldberg, a psychologist and psychiatrist who worked closely with Shepherd as a trainee at the Maudsley, developed the General Health Questionnaire (GHQ), which was eventually published as a Maudsley Monograph in 1972. Goldberg's screening instrument was designed to detect the less severe psychiatric disorders – the so-named 'dysthymic states' – and to identify the inability to carry out normal functions. It therefore detected personality disorders and patterns of adjustment associated with 'distress', but not schizophrenia or severe psychotic depression. The main version contained sixty questions, but abbreviated versions were developed for speed of use and consisted of thirty, twenty or twelve items. Although the questionnaire was designed to be completed by patients, Goldberg was confident that a high percentage of respondents were 'remarkably frank in admitting symptoms'.[46] The GHQ has been rated consistently as a leading example of how health measurement methods should be developed, and, in initial studies, scores correlated well with psychological assessments undertaken by a psychiatrist.[47] However, the questions about symptoms that reflected physical illness relate to pressure or pain in the head, hot or cold spells and 'feeling run down'. Somatic symptoms that were more common in men, such as gastric disorders, might not have been detected by GHQ questions. Furthermore, the physical items were excluded completely from abbreviated formats because they produced a number of 'false-positive' responses.[48]

Somatoform presentations in men

In his much-cited book, *Psychiatric Illness in General Practice* (1966), Shepherd cautioned that there were many difficulties involved in supplying general practitioners with a formal definition of a psychiatric case. He suggested that there were a host of psychosomatic symptoms where no organic cause could be found. It was in this area, he argued, that most disagreement on diagnosis could be found.[49] In his study of psychiatric morbidity in general practice undertaken across Greater London, Shepherd formulated a classification system divided into two classes: 'formal psychiatric illness', which included psychosis, neurosis, dementia and personality disorder; and 'psychiatric-associated conditions', which included physical illnesses and symptoms where 'psychological mechanisms' might have played a part in the condition.[50] It is surprising, nonetheless, how many doctors failed to include psychosomatic symptoms in their history-taking, leading Shepherd to suggest that GPs may be under-reporting neurotic illness.[51]

The most common symptoms seen in men who presented in primary care related to the digestive system: dyspepsia, 'epigastric pain' and constipation. Lower back pain and impotence were also viewed as likely to have a psychological aspect. Other symptoms included chest pains and skin rashes – and some physicians felt that there was a psychogenic aspect to asthma.[52] Gastric symptoms and backache appeared repeatedly in all studies of morbidity in general practice and researchers often noted that men were unlikely to recognise the associations between their symptoms and emotional disorder. W. A. H. ['Arthur'] Watts, a GP from a large surgery in Ibstock, Leicestershire who had developed a keen interest in depressive disorders, noted that these diagnoses were often very difficult.[53] In a study on depression undertaken among his own patients, he cited numerous case histories. One case provided was a typical example of a man in his early fifties with symptoms related to gastric disorder. When X-ray results returned with negative results, the man eventually admitted that he had been feeling 'morose' and had difficulty sleeping. Asked whether he had ever had thoughts about suicide, he replied that he had, but added: 'I never would have told you had you not asked me.'[54] Watts published widely on depression and anxiety and included a chapter on the clinical pictures of depression in his much-cited book, *Depressive Disorders in the Community*, published in 1966. In this publication, he provided numerous case histories of male and female patients who presented with unusual physical symptoms related to psychological disorders. One man, a regular attender at an out-patient dermatology clinic, developed symptoms of chronic urticaria. Simultaneously, he appeared to have lost interest in his hobbies and his sex life. The patient was diagnosed with mild depression, and treated with a potent mix of antidepressant and antipsychotic drugs. Watts noted that the man soon improved and that, like many of the mild cases, he was 'relieved' because he had 'felt he was getting neurotic and felt guilty because he was so feeble about things'.[55]

Evidence of male psychological illness presenting as somatic illness was not only visible in published material, but also conspicuous in the notes kept by doctors about their patients and in the oral history testimonies of retired practitioners. There was broad agreement that gastric symptoms provided a 'respectable' reason for visiting the doctor and that men found any underlying psychological symptoms very difficult to talk about. Glen Haden, a retired family doctor from Somerset, recalled that he would try and 'probe' further if he had a suspicion that there was 'something they weren't telling you about', but that 'men were very reluctant to do so. And of course . . . they very often presented with gastric or gastro-intestinal symptoms'.[56] Other doctors were less comfortable pursuing a search for emotional causes, reflected perfectly in the testimony of Giles Walden, who recalled: 'I must admit, whether it was just me, but I didn't probe the sort of psychological aspects of it at all . . . I think there was resistance [from patients] to any kind of that. You know, you mustn't admit to defeat or inadequacy in any way.'[57] Another GP pointed out that if he began talking to men about psychosomatic symptoms, he had to be 'very careful, because the reaction would be "So you think I'm a hypochondriac!"'.[58] This doctor felt that it was all bound up with 'the macho thing for men . . . women will talk about their feelings . . . men rarely do that. Even when they're really good friends, they rarely do that'.[59] Robert Manley, who spent his entire career in general practice in the West Midlands, also confirmed that male anxiety often presented as gastric symptoms. Speaking about patients with digestive disorders, his testimony was typical of those interviewed on the subject:

> I have no doubt that amongst all these people there were a lot who were also worriers . . . So, in other words, it was anxiety presenting as gastric symptoms. Similarly, what is now called, well in those days it was called spastic colon, and now irritable bowel, we prescribed

> DSNT [double-strength nerve tonic], a mild sedative, because we thought people might be worrying. But, I don't think we really . . . speaking for myself, I don't think we penetrated very far into their psychological disorders. Nor do I think they would be very willing to admit them themselves, because, you know, men don't complain, do they?[60]

During the 1950s and 1960s, John Fry published extensively on the epidemiology and natural history of gastric disorders and many other common medical conditions found in primary care. Fry, a founder member of the College of General Practitioners and a prominent figure in his field, served as a GP in Beckenham, Kent, from 1947 until his retirement in 1991. Fry favoured the use of 'observation' and 'facts and figures' in his research, which he undertook among the patients on his list. In his published research articles on neurosis, Fry was inclined to exclude psychosomatic symptoms from his criteria for diagnosis and hence found that female cases predominated.[61] In one study on psychoneurosis, he found that females outnumbered males by a rate of 5:1.[62] Although Fry acknowledged that somatic symptoms might be associated with psychological illness, he did not appear explicitly to address the possible connection between high levels of *male* gastric disorder, other ill-defined illnesses and psychological distress. By observing symptoms in great detail, Fry focused particularly on 'the natural history' of an illness and warned that physicians should always 'think in terms of organic diseases when making the initial diagnosis'.[63] He kept meticulous notes from his consultations which were recorded in alphabetical order and included the name and sex of each patient as well as the first and last date of symptoms. He also noted any other extraneous factors that he felt might be relevant to the diagnosis. These entries indicate he saw many male patients with symptoms of psychological distress, often masked by alcohol abuse and somatic symptoms. Gastric disorders were particularly common. A male patient, born in 1916, for example, presented to the surgery regularly with gastric dyspepsia between 1960 and 1966. Fry's notes indicate that the individual was suffering from 'overwork and tension', for which he recommended 'less work' and 'rest'. Another male, born in 1900, presented to the surgery in 1959 with dyspepsia, from which he had apparently suffered 'for years'. The notes suggest that, as a child this patient had endured a 'very disturbed home life' and that he also complained of 'chest pains and anxiety'. The patient was prescribed sodium amytal – a sedative barbiturate, which Fry prescribed with regularity. Similar diagnoses included 'epigastric pain', often concurrent with descriptions of patients as 'unhappy' or 'stressed at work'. Others were noted to be experiencing 'marital discord'.[64] Constipation and other bowel disorders also featured regularly in accounts from family doctors. Graham Hadley, a GP from Birmingham recalled that his 'local proctologist reckoned he had a fair share of uptight, tight-arsed patients who may well have had psychiatric problems as well'.[65]

The quintessential gastric disorder that was thought, at least in part, to be associated with stress or 'distress' was peptic ulcer – a condition that was also significantly more common in men. John Fry developed a keen interest in ulcers and published widely on the topic. From his own patient population, with methods he described as 'simple' and 'based essentially on adequate records over a long period of time', he observed that the condition was much more common in men than women, and was particularly prevalent in males between the ages of thirty and sixty.[66] Fry suggested that there was no obvious comorbidity in ulcer patients, with the exception of psychoneurosis, which was associated with a number of cases. In circumstances where patients were 'tense', he recommended the use of sedatives, which were useful in helping the sufferer 'cope with their symptoms'.[67] The role of anxiety in ulcers was also acknowledged by other physicians. The internationally renowned gastroenterologist, Francis Avery Jones (1910–98), for example, specifically remarked that 'worrying inwardly' and 'bottl[ing] up' were factors that might aggravate the condition or influence its chronicity, emphasising that: 'It is sometimes difficult to appreciate the degree of frustration or resentment that may be hidden.'[68]

The medical and social history of peptic ulcers has been well documented and the remit of this chapter is not to repeat existing accounts. However, it is worth briefly revisiting contemporary debates about the causes of peptic ulcer because they reveal much about medical approaches towards organic disease and psychosomatic disorders. The broad trends are well known. Acute gastric ulcers (found in the stomach) were first documented at the beginning of the nineteenth century. Reaching a peak late century, they were more common in young women. This trend changed significantly during the early decades of the twentieth century when female cases declined sharply, to be replaced by rising male mortality from peptic ulcer.[69] The increase in male numbers could be accounted for largely by cases of duodenal ulcer, which were found in the top section of the intestine as opposed to the stomach. Numbers peaked during the 1950s and began to decline by the 1960s. Complications were a common cause of death and included severe haemorrhage and perforation, the latter requiring urgent surgery.[70] Early treatments dispensed by the GP were limited to antacid medication and patients were usually advised to follow a bland diet and take plenty of bed rest. Serious cases were treated with surgery: gastroenterostomy and later, vagotomy, which was a procedure to limit acid secretion.[71] During the 1970s, the Scottish pharmacologist, Sir James Black, introduced cimetidine, a H2 receptor antagonist, which inhibited stomach acid production, allowing ulcers to heal without surgery. This became the mainstay of treatment until the 1980s when the Australian physician, Barry Marshall, discovered that Helicobacter pylori (H pylori) bacteria were the cause of most ulcers.

The discovery of H pylori revolutionised views on the aetiology and treatment of peptic ulcers, causing what some have described as a 'surge of biological reductionism'.[72] As Susan Levenstein argued recently, this new biomedical model offered the opportunity to move peptic ulcer from a stigmatised 'psychosomatic' cubbyhole into a more dignified 'infectious one'.[73] However, there is still heated debate about the role of psychological factors, and some still maintain that psychological stress probably functions as a cofactor with H pylori, stimulating the production of gastric acid or promoting behaviour that causes a risk to health.[74] In formulating a holistic model for peptic ulcers, commentators such as Levenstein have re-energised a biopsychosocial framework endorsed much earlier by physicians, psychosomatic theorists and social researchers who viewed ulcers as one in a long line of 'diseases of civilisation', caused by social change, the rapid pace of industrialisation and the pressures of modern life.[75] One of the most prominent figures to promote such theories was James Lorimer Halliday (1898–1983) who worked as a Regional Medical Officer with the Scottish Department of Health. Halliday supported a holistic view of medicine and emphasised the role of social and emotional factors in physical disorders.[76] He argued that psychosomatic illness was a response to 'noxious psychological factors of environment' and suggested that curative medicine could no longer be contented with the academic question 'what has the patient got?' Instead, he proposed, physicians should ask the more valid question 'why did he take ill when he did?'[77] As Rhodri Hayward has recently shown, for Halliday, the morbidity statistics provided by the Scottish Department of Health disclosed not only patterns in the pathologies of claimants, but also revealed 'a complex archaeology of social, cultural and political influences'.[78]

Halliday provided psychoanalytically inflected criticism of a variety of changes in the 'world of the child' and the 'world of the adult' to explain the rise in psychosomatic illness in the mid-twentieth century. He was critical, for example, of the increasing popularity of bottle-feeding and the growing emphasis on child rearing in accordance with medical 'experts', arguing that these moves had resulted in a loss of body contact with the mother. He was also disparaging of the 'preoccupation with bowel training', where, as he put it, 'when the clock struck certain hours, little pots were punctually applied to little botts'.[79] Most critically of all, Halliday noted that, 'with the introduction of a relatively abundant supply of household furnishings . . . the masses had become possession-conscious'.[80] Families were becoming smaller, and houses were increasingly set apart from one another so that playmates were neither so numerous nor available. Then, at the age of four or five, every child was dispatched from the home to the communal nursery or day school, to sit tests and examinations that were anxiety- and panic-causing.[81] The changes 'in the world of the adult', argued Halliday, had resulted in the drives and impulses of emotional life becoming 'increasingly disturbed, diverted, frustrated or distorted in response to the progressively accelerating changes of the psychosocial environment'.[82] He noted in particular that man had become increasingly separated from 'mother earth', as urbanisation had resulted in more people being cut off from the 'times and tides of nature'. The growing indifference to cosmic rhythms; the rise of the machine and the spread of unnatural shift-work patterns; and job insecurity had resulted in what Halliday described as 'a progressive increase of inner insecurity'.[83]

Halliday was clearly articulating a range of cultural anxieties. His concern was that the rapidly changing world had resulted in the increase of anxiety, insecurity and helplessness, which were duly implicated in rising numbers of psychosomatic conditions. Evidence of this growing insecurity, he argued, could be found in the expanding popularity of patent medicines and the spread of magazines devoted to such subjects as vigour and personal health.[84] This association between the civilising process and disease was not new;[85] however, Halliday's observations on the sex-incidence of disease are particularly revealing in what they say about men and masculinity during the period. He argued that the changes in the milieu of adulthood affected the two sexes differently, and, as a consequence, the incidence of most psychosomatic illness was greater in men. He noted that the process of emancipation had resulted in women gaining access to 'many new interests and satisfactions'; yet, it was still socially acceptable for them to express emotion freely. Men, in contrast, were beginning to experience a greater range of anxieties; yet emotional expression for them was largely still viewed as inappropriate.[86]

The notion that gastric disorders were in some way related to the psyche was also not new, but founded upon the work late nineteenth and early twentieth century stress researchers such as Cannon, Selye and Wolff, who all variously examined the troublesome relationship between psychological, biological and social factors in disease. As Herbert Weiner has shown, psychosomatic theorists mid-twentieth century espoused a range of different approaches. Helen Flanders Dunbar, the first editor of the American journal *Psychosomatic Medicine*, proposed that individual personality characteristics tended to be associated with certain conditions. Hypertensive patients, for example, tended to be 'shy and perfectionist', but with 'volcanic eruptions of feeling'.[87] Franz Alexander, another key figure in the development of the psychosomatic movement, fostered a psychoanalytic model whereby different diseases were thought to be caused by specific unconscious conflicts. Hypertension, in Alexander's view, was thus understood to be the result of the patient's fear of their own 'repressed' aggression.[88]

Peptic ulcer attracted much attention from physicians and commentators who were sympathetic to a holistic approach because it appeared to strike individuals with specific characteristics and often after stressful life events. John Ryle observed in 1932 that duodenal ulcer patients tended to be 'lean and nervous men – often tense and muscular, with brisk mental and physical reactions . . . Psychologically, these folk [were] energetic, restless, conscientious, intent on their projects'. The 'male type', noted Ryle, 'spends his energies freely, often bolts his meals, often smokes excessively and generally lacks the aptitude or opportunity for quiet in his life, which falls more frequently to the lot of womankind'.[89] According to Ryle, nervous influences played their part because anxiety and mental conflict seemed to aggravate symptoms. Hence, 'a restless stomach accompanies a restless mind'.[90] Ryle and others argued that the life and occupations of the city were more productive of the disease and that symptoms often followed financial difficulties, family illness or some other distressing event.[91] In a study of peptic ulcers in the decade leading up to the Second World War, the leading social researcher, Richard Titmuss, concurred with Ryle that urban metropolitan areas were implicated in the incidence of peptic ulcers, with numbers in London 'considerably in excess' of the rest of England and Wales. Titmuss drew a correlation with rising mortality from ulcers and the depression of the 1930s, noting that the subsequent economic recovery after the War coincided with a decline in peptic ulcer.[92]

The Second World War caused considerable concern when it was found, almost immediately, that it produced a rise in mortality among military personnel from both gastric and duodenal ulcers, and a more general rise in other gastric disorders.[93] In recent years, these increases have become the focus of historians, who note the shift from 'functional somatic disorders' (such as war neuroses and 'disordered action of the heart' which were commonly seen during the First World War) to a rise in numbers of peptic ulcers during the Second World War. As Edgar Jones has argued, dyspepsia and peptic ulcer dominated the medical agenda of 1940, creating a crisis that threatened to undermine the fighting capability of the British Army.[94] A nervous disposition and an 'ulcer constitution' were identified as predisposing factors but the military diet and smoking were also thought to play a part.[95] However, studies soon showed that the incidence of ulcer in the civilian population had also grown rapidly, giving rise to the idea that wartime stress more generally could induce gastric illness.[96] Ian Miller has argued that theories about the psyche and its role in gastric disorders produced profound changes in treatment and that in the army, the interaction between mind and abdomen began to intrude therapeutic action. Thus, according to Miller, psychological approaches were increasingly given priority over physiological therapy. However, Edgar Jones and Simon Wessely have cautioned against the idea that 'psychiatric models for unexplained symptoms gained ascendancy over more intellectually suspect organic claims', proposing instead that functional somatic disorders do not in fact 'disappear', 'rather, they change their form in response to powerful medical and cultural forces'.[97] Certainly, considerable mystery still surrounds the natural history of peptic ulcer, and no convincing explanation has been found for the rise and fall in cases during the mid-twentieth century.[98] As Levenstein points out, there has been an ingrained resistance in modern medicine to examining disease in an integrated manner that incorporates both psychological and biomedical elements.[99]

In the decades following the Second World War, family doctors who were sympathetic to a psychosomatic approach did draw an association between psychological distress and physical symptoms, but these doctors were in the minority. The views of those who fostered a holistic approach were sought during a debate that took place during the late 1950s about the place of psychiatry in general practice. A working party of the Council of the College of General Practitioners was appointed in

1956 to study the importance of psychological medicine in primary care, the final version of which was published in the *British Medical Journal* in 1958.[100] During this investigation, written evidence was obtained from twenty-seven members of the College who had expressed an interest in psychological medicine. Additionally, details were sought about the subjects taught at medical school in Britain. The correspondence from this investigation suggests that GPs were struggling to deal with a wide range of psychosomatic and neurotic presentations in both sexes. One contributor, a Dr S. I. Abrahams, provided a list of symptoms that were 'difficult to fit in' and which had 'taxed [his] therapeutic resources'. Among the examples provided were the details of a forty-year-old fishmonger who complained of 'pain in his nose, fear of heart disease and cancer etc.' This particular individual also suffered from 'guilt feelings over cowardice in action and an act of infidelity'. Abrahams added that the man was of 'obsessional makeup' and that he compensated for his symptoms by over-exercising. Another male patient, aged forty-five, presented with a 'fear of cancer of the throat, with spasm of pharyngeal muscles'. After an in-depth consultation, it appeared that the basic problem was 'a feeling of inadequacy' which emerged whenever decisions had to be made. According to Abrahams, this 'originated in domination by his mother, who was still alive'.[101] Philip Hopkins, a general practitioner from Hampstead in London, cautioned that 'what might be called gastritis by one doctor becomes acute anxiety state with dyspepsia in the records of another'. Drawing specifically on Logan and Cushion's study, Hopkins specifically highlighted the 'large number of conditions which are in themselves, vague and indefinite'. Had these symptoms, Hopkins argued, 'been found to be due to some physical disease, they would have been put under the appropriate headings'.[102] Reflecting on his own experiences in practice, Hopkins expounded the importance of psychosomatic symptoms:

> A patient might come with a headache, a backache or abdominal pain . . . it mattered little which symptom. If encouraged, the patient would do more than recite a list of symptoms; he would relate them to times, incidents and other factors which were important . . . often enough, the presenting symptom acted as a mask, an excuse with which to come to the doctor . . . If the opportunity were given, the mask could be dropped. If, on the other hand, the doctor gave the impression that he was not prepared to listen . . . but was content to prescribe a tonic or a sedative, then the real trouble remained concealed.[103]

Hopkins was a founder member of the College of General Practitioners, but, most notably, he was the founder and President of the Balint Society and also a founder member of the Psychosomatic Research Society. The Balint Society was named after the influential Hunagarian psychoanalyst, Michael Balint (1896–1970). As the remainder of this chapter will illustrate, physicians who were receptive to and trained in Balint's methods were more likely to be sympathetic to a holistic approach towards their patients. However, as we shall see, despite Balint's significant influence among some GPs, it seems likely that a majority of family doctors formulated their understanding about complex somatoform complaints from within the prevailing reductionist medical model. Doctors' training and attitudes, combined with the harsh day-to-day realities of practice life, resulted very often in what Shepherd described as, at best, a 'tolerant indifference' to the role of psychological factors in disease.[104]

Training and approaches in post-war general practice

In part reflecting the low status of general practice, doctors entering the field in the years immediately following the introduction of the NHS could expect little or no formal training for the role as a family doctor.[105] During the 1950s, some medical undergraduate courses made arrangements for 'attachments' to GP surgeries; however, in only three British medical schools was this made compulsory. By the time the first Chair of General Practice was established in Edinburgh in 1963, there were still only eight medical schools offering all students some experience of general practice.[106] In 1967, the General Medical Council (GMC) recommended that this provision should be expanded, a motion supported by the Undergraduate Education Committee of the Royal College of General Practitioners. However, it was not until 1986 that all British medical schools had departments of general practice.[107] From 1952, following undergraduate qualification, all doctors were required to serve a 'pre-registration' year, during which time they work under provisional registration with the GMC. After this year, fully registered doctors could then undertake specialist postgraduate training in their chosen field. In the early years of the NHS, general practice was not seen as a 'discipline' for postgraduate study: it had no journal, no chair in any university and no academic organisation.[108] The need for formal postgraduate training had been highlighted in the two influential Cohen Reports of 1948 and 1950. Lord Cohen, who chaired the investigations, stated that, post-registration, new recruits should undertake a further three years of specialised training for general practice.[109] However, there were no real developments until the formation of the

College of General Practitioners in 1952.[110] The College began publishing ideas about vocational training in their reports between 1965 and 1967, and, in April 1968, the Royal Commission on Medical Education endorsed the College's findings. Five years of postgraduate training, synonymous with training for other specialties, was recommended – comprising three years of general professional training, followed by two years of vocational training for general practice.[111] Between 1965 and 1985, vocational training schemes of many different kinds were developed across Britain, and, although the Royal Commission's recommendations were not fully implemented, modified schemes, usually of two years in hospital posts, followed by a year in general practice, were organised.[112] It was nonetheless not until 1976 that parliament passed the National Health Service Vocational Training Act, requiring three years of mandatory postgraduate training for general practice.[113]

Given the lack of training for general practice in the broad sense, doctors entering the field during the 1950s and 1960s were unprepared to deal with the kinds of psychological illness that presented in surgery. A working party of the Council of the College was appointed in 1956 to investigate psychological medicine in general practice. Reporting in 1958, it established that there were wide variations between medical schools in the provision of training at undergraduate level, with some providing regular lectures on psychology and others providing nothing at all.[114] Compulsory attendances at clinical out-patient and in-patient units were similarly variable. The report concluded that the subject should be taught more thoroughly to all undergraduate medical students and that opportunities for postgraduate training in psychological medicine should be available for those with a special interest in the subject. It further noted that 'a grounding in the humanities [was] of value in acquiring maturity and wisdom'.[115]

The lack of preparation for general practice and for dealing with the psychological conditions that presented in primary care, was widely evident in the testimonies of doctors who had experience of practice during the period. As Robert Manley recalled: 'Like everybody else going into general practice in 1961, I was completely untrained for the peculiar skills required . . . although fascinated by the idea of it.' Speaking about the attachment training schemes that existed in some areas at that time, he maintained that 'a lot of these were unsatisfactory . . . they were really exploited as helping hands, and there was virtually no group training or meetings of anything of that sort.'[116] One Professor of General Practice, who developed a well-respected regional postgraduate vocational scheme, roundly summed up the situation:

> My generation of doctors . . . were appallingly trained in mental and emotional illness, I mean 'destructively' trained, in my humble opinion. We were given some former psychiatric teaching by professors whose patients were all in mental hospitals, who all had florid psychoses, and we'd got absolutely no awareness of the scale of the problem, and we'd got absolutely no training in how to manage it in everyday life. So we came out of our . . . top universities . . . completely naked to deal with this mass of problems that confronted [us]. It was a complete shattering shock.[117]

The prevailing biomedical model within which students were taught at medical school did much to obscure psychological and emotional aspects of disease – a point made regularly by GPs interviewed for this research. For the most part, those who were trained at the top universities noted that the education they received was what they described as 'traditional'. This was particularly so for those who had trained briefly under the renowned psychiatrist, William Sargant (1907–88), at St Thomas' Hospital in London.[118] An anecdote from one doctor about his early days in clinical training reflected the sentiments of many retired GPs and is worth repeating in its entirety:

> [I remember] being told that anatomy dissection started on the second of October, and to report to Anatomy in Room A. And I remember standing outside with a load of other medical students, not knowing what to do. Nobody was there welcoming us. Eventually I think one of us decided, well, we'd better go in, and we went in, and there were the, you know [cadavers], I won't go into the details. And I've always looked back at that as a sort of, kind of, maybe subconscious deliberate desensitisation training . . . to make you tough, make you able to withstand unpleasantness and to, to distance yourself from the patient. And there's nothing more 'distancing' from you than a dead patient that you've spent eighteen months cutting up . . . And so, in the mid-1970s, a lot of us felt that we were too distant from our patients.[119]

Another doctor, speaking candidly about his training, maintained that:

> [It] wasn't about anything to do with behaviour. It was: people have an illness, you give them a drug, they get better, or you give them a drug and they don't – so you give them another one, or you send them for an operation . . . There wasn't an awareness of the other aspects.[120]

The prevailing reductionist approach to medical training did not go unchallenged. Balint was the most influential figure in this respect. He emigrated to England in 1939, and is said to be one of the first in the world to study the possibility of using psychotherapeutic tools in general practice.[121] After a number of hospital and child-guidance posts, Balint moved to the Tavistock Clinic, London, in 1947.[122] In 1950, with his wife, Enid, he set up a series of seminars for GPs for the discussion of psychological problems in general practice.[123] The central focus of these seminars was the doctor-patient relationship. Balint believed that the doctor's response to a patient's complaint was as important as any drug or treatment administered. He put forward the concept of the 'apostolic function', which, in his words meant that:

> Every doctor has a set of fairly firm beliefs as to which illnesses are acceptable and which are not; how much pain, suffering, fears and deprivations a patient should tolerate, and when he has the right to ask for help or relief; how much nuisance the patient is allowed to make of himself etc., . . . These beliefs are hardly ever stated explicitly but are nevertheless very strong. They compel the doctor to do his best to convert all his patients to accept his own standards and to be ill and to get well according to them.[124]

Balint stated that the effects of the apostolic function were far-reaching because they restricted a doctor's freedom: 'certain ways and forms simply do not exist for him' or are 'habitually avoided'. Such limitations, he noted, were determined chiefly by the doctor's personality, training and 'ways of thinking'. The resolution, according to Balint was 'a compromise between the patient's proposition and the doctor's responses'.[125] Specifically, Balint maintained that doctors had been conditioned by the biomedical model of training: 'The present state of medicine, with its emphasis on organic diagnosis and the corresponding neglect of psychological factors, prompts the doctor to organise illnesses around anatomical, or at least physiological – that is, around some concrete – pathology'.[126] Consequently, the doctor 'helps' the patient organise their 'illness' around certain symptoms.

Balint's ideas were published in an article in *The Lancet* in 1955, and developed further in his book, *The Doctor, His Patient and the Illness*, published in 1957. Some senior figures in the field describe the publication of this book as 'a watershed in the development of general practice', because it provided a theoretical justification for general practice; rejected the 'inferiority' of the generalist; and emphasised the importance of whole-person medicine and holistic care.[127] However, opinion is divided on the broader influence of Balint's work. In reality, his seminars at the Tavistock Clinic were attended by a very small number of GPs. One of the original group, John Horder, who was instrumental in the development of general practice and President of the College between 1979 and 1982, remarked that 'it was only a small minority of GPs who recognised the potential of Balint's work' and that many regarded those involved with the movement 'with suspicion'.[128] It nevertheless, had a profound influence on his own personal approach, because he had never before been taught 'to listen'. He also felt that Balint 'challenged some of the well-established beliefs and practices handed down in teaching hospitals, particularly the bias in favour of physical suffering'.[129] Others who were involved with the Balint movement maintain that the small number of doctors who worked with him went on to achieve much wider influence 'as his disciples', through vocational schemes that developed in some areas of the country.[130] Certainly, many of his ideas are evident in the book, *The Future General Practitioner* (1972), which is widely extolled as the most important text to be published in the field.[131] The divide in opinion about Balint's methods and influence is certainly palpable in interviews with retired GPs. Whereas some were sensitive, if not to Balint's original ideas, at least to the notion that practitioners should examine their own attitudes, others were highly critical and completely dismissed his approach. Younger doctors who were more open to alternative ideas often found it impossible to convince older colleagues who were more traditional in their style. Dr Robert Manley, for example, who had read Balint's book and was quite keen to join seminar groups in the early 1970s, recalled: 'I found it difficult to persuade my partners that there should be any change whatsoever in the practice. They were very, very conservative.'[132] Another stated that, although he was aware of the Balint movement, he was 'a bit confused by it all', adding that his practice colleague, 'who was a bit of a hippy', would have been 'more interested in that side of it'.[133]

What is clear from the interviews is that doctors who were sympathetic to a holistic approach were more successful in detecting hidden psychological disorders in patients of both sexes. However, the reverse was true for those whose style of practice was more traditional. As Balint pointed out, for many doctors, psychological symptoms remained 'beyond the professional pale'.[134] This was particularly significant when it came to diagnosing cases of male psychological or psychosomatic illness because, most doctors, at least until the late 1970s, were also male, and thus both the doctor and the patient found themselves bound by a complex set of medical, cultural and social beliefs which made any discussion of mental illness very difficult. A broader focus on communication and language in doctor-patient consultations did not come until the late 1970s, by which time the general consensus was that most family doctors were not well equipped to deal with psychosomatic disorders and many of the social problems that presented in practice. A study of tape-recorded consultations between patients and doctors during the mid-1970s revealed what was described as 'professionally dreadful' skills (or lack of skills), leading to recommendations for new teaching techniques.[135] In its conclusion, the report reiterated that doctors' performance should not be measured simply in terms of their diagnostic and prescriptive skills, but also by their ability to create and maintain long-term human relationships. Further, it was noted that all doctors were 'both a product and a prisoner of the training system which has produced them'. The prevailing scientific approach had thus resulted in a situation where doctors often accepted the initial offer of symptoms and 'failed to detect a not so obvious psychological and/or psychosomatic disorder'.[136]

Widely contrasting attitudes are evident in the accounts of doctors who had experience of practice during the period. Nowhere was this more apparent than in views about nervous illness and the status of psychiatry and allied professions. While some physicians took psychological symptoms very seriously, and, despite busy schedules, found time at the end of surgery to re-book patients who needed longer to talk about their problems, others had little time for 'neurotic' presentations and considered them to be a drain on resources. This was undoubtedly in large part due to their training, but in some measure due to the personality of the doctor. H. J. Walton, a psychiatrist at the University of Edinburgh, noted that, among doctors, 'suspicion and scepticism about psychiatry begins early'. Confirming the long-held belief that psychiatry did not carry prestige among medical school departments, he argued that 'many medical students view psychiatrists as emotionally unstable and as confused thinkers'.[137] Walton, in a study of attitudes among medical students, made some interesting observations about their views on psychiatry and mental illness. Evidence from a final-year class suggested that approximately half the class were what he described as 'organically-orientated' and not interested or responsive to psychological illness. A quarter of these did not wish to treat patients with minor psychiatric disorders, while another quarter were uncertain whether they would be prepared to accept cases of psychoneurosis at all.[138] One student stated explicitly that he '[did] not want to treat psychoneurotic patients in his practice'; another described himself as 'reacting very unfavourably to a large range of patients with psychological components in the illness [and] disturbed that functional illness will form a large part of later practice'.[139]

Although Shepherd, in his study of general practice, found that family doctors were in general tolerant and enlightened, there was nonetheless a significant amount of antipathy towards mental illness. One participating doctor, for example, stated that neurosis was caused by self-indulgence.[140] Several others refused to participate in the study at all. One maintained that psychiatrists encouraged neurotic patients to avoid their responsibilities; another was of the opinion that all neurotic patients were ungrateful and that nothing could be done for them.[141] Shepherd found that the degree to which doctors were aware of the social and domestic background of their patients' illnesses varied considerably, and that the majority seemed to accept the phrase 'once a neurotic, always a neurotic'.[142] Looking back with hindsight over their careers, a number of the doctors who were interviewed for this project were critical of their own attitudes during the early years of practice. Christian Edwards, who was a family doctor in Hampshire, admitted that 'in his youth' he thought that patients with psychiatric symptoms were inadequate: 'Lack of moral fibre, pull yourself together and you'll be alright. But of course you learn that depressives have no way of helping themselves really'.[143] Indeed, the term 'lack of moral fibre' (abbreviated in patients' notes to LMF) emerged more than once in the interviews – a hangover from associations of weakness assigned to soldiers with war neuroses during the Second World War. Richard Stanton, who was very sympathetic himself to the Balint approach, remembered being very critical of a colleague who used to write disparaging comments in his patients' notes:

> On one occasion he just wrote, the whole – all his entry was 'witter witter'. And another one he wrote was 'TTHLOAD' . . . and I asked [the receptionist] 'What's this one?' 'Talks the hind leg off a donkey'. [laughter].[144]

Another recalled that, just before he retired, a colleague of his pointed out some bad habits he had developed over the years:

> I was completely unaware of what I was doing [laughs]. They said, 'Do you realise, you told me [your] technique of getting rid of a

> patient in the surgery?' If I felt they'd had enough time, apparently I used to move to the edge of my chair, and then sort of get a bit closer, and then I would stand up. And then, you know, usher them out. I was completely unaware that was something I did.[145]

In contrast, some highly sympathetic attitudes were evident. Dr Adams, a GP from the West Country who had trained originally as an anaesthetist in the Forces, described himself as 'very interested in people'. He developed an interest in Gestalt therapy and viewed psychiatric symptoms as having a 'purpose' in that they were often an indication that something was not working well in the patient's life. Adams saw his role as helping raise the patient's awareness of this. His view was that pharmacological treatment was usually unnecessary and just 'papered over the cracks'. Adams was not an ardent follower of Balint and saw him as a kind of 'guru', arguing that a 'map of anything is only ever the map of the person creating it'. His approach instead was 'person-centred' and he maintained firmly that 'the only person who really understands you is yourself'.[146]

When it came to views about the gendered distribution of psychiatric disorders, many of the general practitioners who practised with a traditional approach were of the opinion that women were biologically predisposed to mental illness. Some of them were willing to admit that this inevitably influenced their own patterns of diagnosis. Robert Manley recalled:

> I think there was a gender split. Whether it was in the presentations or whether it was in my mind, I don't know. I mean, the idea of hysteria as a woman's condition was still very much a popular concept in medicine. And menopausal and menstrual changes of mood and so on. Those were current ideas attributed more to psychological than to physiological disorders. And it was very easy to be patronising.[147]

Such views were widely espoused, and evident in the testimony of one very senior and well-respected GP who was emphatic that, 'The female is genetically or biologically more prone to emotional and depressive illnesses.' Urging me to 'read it up', he maintained: 'I don't think it's cultural, and I don't think it's environmental . . . I think women get it more, for reasons that I think are not, not yet known.'[148] The same doctor felt that Balint was revolutionary because he demonstrated that symptoms might be a metaphor for 'feelings' – feelings that most often presented in women – 'because *they* were the problem patients, those GPs had brought to him [Balint] . . . a huge skew towards difficult, middle-aged women who hadn't "been sorted"'.[149] Indeed, the stereotypical figure of the hysterical or hypochondriac woman widely permeated popular gendered perceptions, with frequent references among doctors to 'bored housewives' and 'fat notes'. One doctor explained, signalling with hand signs that, 'If you took a pile of women's notes "that high" the men's notes would be "down there"'.[150]

Such views must be seen within the context of their time and were formulated upon the longstanding notion that women were dominated by their reproductive systems and prone to irrationality. These ideas remained dominant through the 1950s and 1960s and were still influential into the 1970s. Their influence can be seen in much of the published material on mental illness in the years following the war. Stephen Taylor's report on standards in primary care, *Good General Practice*, which was submitted to the Cohen Committee, for example, was interspersed with value-laden remarks about 'hysterical' women; 'feckless', 'overwhelmed' and 'sluttish' mothers; and 'suburban housing estates [where] whining anxiety hysterics predominate'.[151] Even Arthur Watts, whose approach to depressive disorders was generally sympathetic, observed that women's irritability around the time of menstruation left them liable to 'fly off the handle at the least thing'.[152]

Those who were generally open to Balint's ideas, or at least to psychodynamic approaches, often observed that the person who presented at the surgery was not necessarily the patient with a problem. The notion of 'family illness' became an important concept during the 1960s and 1970s and became the focus of a number of publications. F. J. A. Huygen's book, *Family Medicine: The Medical Life History of Families*, published in 1978, was probably the most well-known of these and was described as influential by several general practitioners in interviews. Huygen was a GP from Holland who used his practice population to observe the long-term physical and psychological health of families. From these observations, he formulated a theory of family dynamics. Using the comprehensive data he had collected from patients alongside his own personal knowledge of them, Huygen connected the medical with the social to reveal hidden illness and better understand unexplained symptoms. His case histories are interspersed with examples of female patients attending with symptoms that were due to problems with male relatives at home: male relatives who were most likely experiencing psychological pressures of their own. Huygen cited one case, for example, where 'the symptoms of the mother – nervousness, sleep disturbances – could, in every instance be related to family problems'. The woman's husband had begun shift work and had experienced difficulties adapting to it, becoming 'irritable and tense at home'. Huygen noted that the wife developed symptoms, 'which mirrored family interactions'. Similarly, in later years when tensions developed with teenage children, 'the mother translated this into somatic symptoms presented to the doctor'.[153] Roger Lea and John Souton, two doctors practising in the West Country, both mentioned that Huygen's work had been influential. Dr Lea maintained that:

> The family is a unit, and any dysfunction in that family would present with the one who found it most easy to get to the doctor, that is the – usually the wife . . . and she would bring the children. And therefore, the consulting patterns of men were much lower.

Lea described Huygen's book as 'inspirational' and that it was, for him 'quite helpful to realise that actually, patients were part of a unit'.[154] Unsurprisingly, Philip Hopkins, with his openness to psychosomatic presentations, also observed that women might present with illness in response to difficult domestic circumstances. In a chapter on 'stress disorders', he gave the example of one woman who had visited him with 'hot flushes, headaches and bouts of depression'. All treatment had failed. Eventually the woman divulged that 'her husband had been coming home drunk at night for some months'. It took Hopkins a little while to persuade her that the symptoms might be related to her husband's behaviour; however, with time there was some improvement and she was better able to cope with her affairs.[155] However, as Marshall Marinker noted in his contribution to Irvine Loudon's history of general practice, the family-therapy approach did not achieve centrality in Britain where the concept was of greater importance to some general-practice theorists and family-oriented doctors than to most practitioners and their patients.[156]

The realities of practice daily life

For those entering practice in the late 1950s and the 1960s, the medical and cultural problems of dealing with patients with psychiatric illness were further frustrated by long working hours and the meagre conditions of general practice. A survey of general practice undertaken between 1951 and 1952 by Stephen Hadfield, then Secretary to the

British Medical Association (BMA), had identified large variations in practice, but poor facilities and long hours were undoubtedly common themes throughout. Hadfield found that doctors undertook consultations with approximately twenty-five patients in ninety minutes of morning surgery and long rounds of home visits where they would invariably visit five homes in one hour. In many of these homes, he would be expected to see two, three or even four patients when he was expecting to see one – a development for which, according to Hadfield, the NHS was responsible.[157] Evening home visits were common, even when a rota system with colleagues existed. During times of epidemics, high pressure continued for weeks at a time.[158] Added to these challenges were administrative duties of paperwork, mail and dealing with large volumes of advertising matter distributed by pharmaceutical companies.[159] These findings were reflected most articulately in Richard Moore's memoirs of his family's medical heritage, *Leeches to Lasers: Sketches of a Medical Family* (2002). Speaking of his own early years as a locum in the 1960s, Moore recalled surgeries with little equipment, no heating and hard benches for patients to wait for consultations. One surgery he attended was a converted stable where 'the straw and hay had been removed, but no further adaptations for its new role seemed to have been made'.[160] After an education at a teaching hospital with specialist resources, Moore found himself 'wandering in a world of tonics and placebos more reminiscent of the nineteenth than the twentieth centuries'.[161] Eventually settling permanently in Shrewsbury, Moore's surgery was positioned on the first floor of a 500-year-old building, and he ran the practice initially with two partners and the help of only one part-time receptionist. Moore soon realised he would be required quickly to develop working relationships with colleagues, plus the knowledge and skills of management, accounting, budgeting and planning. 'No attention,' he recalled, 'had been paid to such mundane but fundamental matters in preparation for [his] life's work.'[162] Consultations were 'rushed' and 'communication with patients was not good'. The situation was even worse at the branch surgery where there were no records or facilities 'other than what [they] carried in [their bags]'.[163] Moore recalled that during the early years, he and his two partners covered all the demands of the practice, 365 days a year. This entailed domiciliary obstetrics (twenty-five to thirty births a year), night and weekend calls, with only one half day off a week. The working day consisted of three surgeries and ten or twelve home visits on most days, plus a surgery on most Saturday mornings. 'This did not seem arduous in the 1960s,' he recalled, 'because such commitments were usual'.[164] Moore's experiences were consistent with the recollections of GPs who participated in this project and widely evident in contemporary published material. Shepherd, in his study of general practice found that many practitioners in poor, overcrowded urban areas had so much physical sickness to contend with that they were consequently 'less tolerant of neurotic disorders'.[165] It is hard to imagine quite how challenging were the circumstances faced by GPs during the period, but they are summed up powerfully by David Morrell, who was the first doctor from an academic department of general practice to become President of the BMA:

> My vocational training lasted three days . . . the early weeks and months in the consulting room were confused and I was filled with feelings of guilt. The knowledge and skills acquired in hospital just did not seem relevant to many of the problems presented, and when a proper 'hospital-type' patient presented, there was never time to carry out the type of examination which I had learnt . . . I was . . . simply conscious of my own inadequacies and the constant demand for care.[166]

Reflections

Looking back over epidemiological studies on mental illness undertaken during the post-war period, the trends seem straightforward: women were at much greater risk of psychological illness and were diagnosed with it at least twice as often as men. However, the material in this chapter has suggested a more complex picture. The Introduction to this book opened with the sobering statistic that 75 per cent of suicides are currently among men, suggesting that there is much we do not yet know about male distress. It is important to note that suicide is sometimes a misleading proxy for mental health: the act is not always 'irrational' and there are circumstances in which an individual's wish to die might be entirely understandable – in older people with multiple physical illnesses, for example.[167] However, it is widely acknowledged that people with mental health problems are at greater risk of suicide. Although overall rates have declined during recent years, and the ratio of male-to-female suicide rates changed over time, male suicide rates have been consistently higher throughout the nineteenth, twentieth and twenty-first centuries.[168] Research into suicide during the 1950s acknowledged that men outnumbered women, but rarely shed any light on why this might be.

Broad discussions about suicide were framed by the relative values and disadvantages of the two most common research approaches: the study of epidemiological trends and in-depth studies of suicidal rumination and attempted suicide.[169] Epidemiological studies often focused on comparative data between different regions or in specific areas. Peter Sainsbury's study, *Suicide in London* (1955), for example, noted higher numbers in the West End and North West areas and lower rates in Southern boroughs and many of the large working class districts.[170] His research clearly documented higher rates among men, but 'did not extract any particular environmental factor that appeared to determine this differential sex incidence'.[171] Other studies tested hypotheses relating to a range of variables such as class, age, the loss of a spouse, divorce and isolation. American research indicated that suicide was more common in the lower classes; however, in Britain, there were no specific investigations on class and suicide during the period.[172] In research published much later during the 1990s, the psychiatrist Norman Kreitman, who wrote widely on suicide and depression, argued that suicide was significantly more common among classes IV and V, echoing findings across the Atlantic.[173] Kreitman and his colleagues suggested that suicide was associated with social deprivation, chronic mental illness and alcohol abuse. Downward social drift and unemployment were also noted to be key factors in suicide – both factors that were more common in the lower social classes.[174]

In contrast, F. A. Whitlock found that suicide was generally more common in the more affluent classes. With specific relation to sex differences, he noted that male suicides were particularly connected with loneliness and isolation, especially in old age, and that males who were vulnerable to suicide appeared also to express themselves in other violent ways.[175] These key factors were to be developed in more recent debates about the different ways in which men and women express distress. However, Whitlock acknowledged that, at that time, existing research could say very little about the mental health of communities or about the prevalence of mental illness and alcoholism – which, as will be demonstrated in Chapter 3, were closely correlated. Summing up, he concluded that 'any attempt to bracket together the epidemiological findings in male and female suicide will scarcely do justice to the complexity of circumstances that vary according to the age and sex of the patient'.[176] Psychiatrists and physicians were keen to find ways of preventing suicide by investigating whether those who had succeeded had made earlier attempts and by examining whether or not individuals had been under medical care at the time of their death. Once again, views differed between studies. R. W. Parnell, a research physician, and Ian Skottowe, a psychiatrist, found in 1957 that among 100 suicides from inquest registers between 1949 and 1956, 53 per cent were not under any medical care. Warning signs nonetheless were apparent in the majority and were evident in extracts from witness statements. The fact that individuals seemed to behave 'normally', even though they may have appeared to be in low spirits, often prevented family, friends and doctors from attempting to 'certify as insane' or refer for psychiatric treatment.[177]

In contrast to Parnell and Skottowe's findings, Alan Capstick, a senior medical officer from Cardiff, found that 78 per cent of 881 suicides considered by him had been treated by their doctor for symptoms that were 'probably' related to psychiatric illness. Because so few of these cases (18 per cent) had been referred for psychiatric support, Capstick called for doctors to raise their awareness of symptoms that might indicate suicidal ideation. Unfortunately, Capstick's data was not divided by sex, so it is not possible to gain insight about the gendered presentation of patients' symptoms prior to suicide. C. A. H. Watts included an entire chapter on suicide in his book on depression in the community and discussed many of the same trends as Sainsbury and other researchers. Watts noted the large numbers of men in statistics, but showed that women were more likely to 'attempt' suicide as a gesture – a cry for help. Detecting men who were vulnerable to suicide seemed particularly difficult and Watts urged that GPs had a special responsibility in detecting depression in its early stages: 'By being better diagnosticians, doctors in general medicine and general practice can probably do more to lower the suicide rate than the psychiatrists themselves'.[178] Indeed, other GPs often remarked that it was difficult to pre-empt suicides, illustrated in the poignant recollections of Jeremy Barrington who remembered a male patient he had treated for depression following a bereavement. After some time, he appeared to improve and presented at the surgery one day in good spirits. The patient told the doctor that he planned to visit his sister to help with her garden: 'He said he was better . . . felt better'; however, 'he went to stay with his sister, dug her potatoes, bagged them up and hanged himself in the shed.' Barrington felt that the brief psychological improvement had been because 'he had decided he knew what he wanted to do'.[179]

By the late 1960s social psychologists, sociologists and epidemiologists were beginning to draw attention to the different ways in which men and women might express anguish and distress. These concerns should be seen as one dimension of broader concerns about the health consequences of life stress, social inequality and modern working life. As other authors have pointed out, such anxieties should be seen as a product of a specific historical moment, driven in part by a desire to challenge political structures, and to address contemporary concerns about poverty, crime and warfare.[180] Debates were politicised between those who viewed the causes of psychological and psychosomatic disorders as related to environmental factors such as social and economic inequality, and those who promoted the theory of individual constitutional vulnerability. Ultimately, western countries, working within an increasingly biological medical model of mental illness and armed with the availability of new psychotropic drugs, tended to move towards a strategy that encouraged physicians and politicians to treat individuals rather than dealing with deep-seated social problems.[181]

The feminist movement motivated some of the psychological and sociological research undertaken during the 1970s.[182] Many investigations that took place during this period suggested that women were more vulnerable to depression due to the role they fulfilled in society. An influential figure in this respect was the sociologist, George W. Brown, who published widely on depression and gender. As the title suggests, his study, *Social Origins of Depression: A Study of Psychiatric Disorder in Women,* co-written with Tirril Harris in 1978, proposed unequivocally that social circumstances and life-difficulties unique to the female role, caused depression in women, and in particular for working-class women.[183] In his later work, he argued that serious or traumatic life events were experienced differently by men and women, and that women were especially vulnerable to depression in reaction to stressful events that had greater 'role salience' for them. By role salience, Brown was referring to the idea that women would identify most acutely with events that involved their children and home, and were likely to hold themselves as responsible for crises in these spheres.[184] Other scholars put forward valid criticisms of Brown's work, criticising the methodology employed in his earlier work and the conceptual definition of the social variables involved in their analysis.[185] Brown's earlier work could certainly not claim to be entirely representative since it excluded men altogether. The authors designed their 1979 study upon the somewhat sweeping assumption that 'women probably suffer from depression more than men', and that 'they were more likely to be at home and thus available for interview during the day'.[186] His later work was based on self-reported depression, thereby relying upon men being honest about their emotional states. As this book has suggested, this methodological problem has proved difficult to overcome. Additionally, Brown and his colleagues excluded the presentation of somatic symptoms from their analysis.[187]

Walter Gove's authoritative contribution to debates on gender and mental illness suggested that the difficulties associated with the domestic role caused married women in particular to be vulnerable to psychiatric symptoms and that this explained why women were diagnosed with mental illness more often than men.[188] The American psychiatrist, Bruce Dohrenwend and his wife Barbara, challenged Gove's theories by arguing that psychological disorders were greater in the lowest social classes and thus related to the stress of their particular environment.[189] In their work on sex differences in psychological disorders, the Dohrenwends proposed instead that new research methodologies introduced since the Second World War accounted for larger numbers of women in statistics. Their thesis was that pre-war studies were more likely to rely on criminal records, recorded cases of antisocial behaviour and data on alcohol and drug abuse – all categories that were less likely to expose female cases. Post-war, they maintained, investigations focused on interviews with respondents and screening tools such as the Cornell Medical Index. These methods, they argued, concentrated on symptoms of depression and anxiety, indicative of neurosis, and therefore it was 'not surprising that scores on such measures [were] generally higher for women than men'.[190] The Dohrenwends concluded that the impression that women were more likely to experience psychological symptoms was 'a function of changes in concepts and methods for what constitutes a psychiatric case'.[191]

In Britain, Monica Brisco, a psychiatrist from the Institute of Psychiatry, also contended that Gove's research did not stand up to careful examination, arguing that, among researchers, there was no consensus about which sex actually experienced greater strain.[192] Brisco extended her analysis over a ten-year period from the late 1970s to include a number of important factors associated with gender and psychological disorders. Firstly, her research suggested that women were able to identify 'feeling states' more effectively than men. Secondly, she maintained that women were able to 'show rather more feelings, particularly those of an unpleasant nature than men'; they were thus more likely to seek the advice of a doctor for emotional support.[193] Thirdly, Brisco's research suggested that men avoided admitting negative feelings and found facing up to symptoms of anxiety as 'stigmatising'.[194] Finally, she suggested that GPs were aware that women felt more comfortable discussing psychological problems and that this might, in turn, affect their response.[195] Unable to resolve the polarised debates about nature and nurture, Brisco argued that the relationship between them was far from simple. She nonetheless concluded from her own research that girls were socialised to express feelings more openly than boys, which resulted in a greater awareness of feeling states and, hence, a greater need for emotional support. As one of the potential sources of support was the general practitioner, it was therefore, according to Brisco, not surprising that more women were diagnosed more frequently with psychological problems.[196] Other authors noted more broadly that the 'ethic of health is masculine' and that therefore men looked upon illness 'as a feminine characteristic to be shunned'.[197] Echoing the findings from general practice in this chapter, by the 1980s, observers began to identify that men 'kept depression to themselves' by concealing or camouflaging it.[198] Because the socialisation into manhood accentuated achievement, competence and success; toughness, confidence and self-reliance, for many men, psychological illness became 'a private experience, unshared with others'.[199]

Whereas femininity had long been associated with emotionality and irrationality, normative masculinity was constructed as 'a man who was in control, both of his inner self and his external environment'.[200] However, 'masculinity' did not entirely circumvent the medical gaze, for it instead became the focus of medical and psychological studies into coronary heart disease during the late 1950s. Two American cardiologists, Meyer Friedman and Ray Rosenman put forward the concept of the 'Type A personality' during the late 1950s. Type A personalities were defined as being ambitious and highly driven individuals who were often impatient, excessively organised and anxious, leading, according to Friedman and Rosenman, to raised serum cholesterol and an increased vulnerability to coronary heart disease. Type B behaviour personalities exhibited converse behaviour patterns. Type A became a powerful concept through the 1970s and 1980s and was developed in a book for a lay audience *Type A Behaviour and your Heart,* published in 1974. As Barbara Ehrenreich has pointed out, with the discovery of the Type A personality, cardiologists had not found the elusive molecular 'cause' of coronary heart disease, but instead a unique category of personality that existed without reference to any known categories of psychological disorder.[201] Thus, the characteristics that prevented men from expressing emotion and seeking help for psychological symptoms were medicalised and recast as a health hazard for men. As Riska observes, the concept of Type A personality led to a realisation that the conformity to a narrow definition of masculinity could be lethal for men. When middle-class breadwinners conformed to the moral values of traditional masculinity, they got a medical label for their pursuit. Unlike women, however, for whom the medicalisation of femininity was usually psychological – for men the cost was entirely physical.

2

Workplace Mental Health: Myths and Missed Opportunities

Introduction

In 1942, the Medical Research Council's Industrial Health Research Board initiated an investigation, led by Dr Russell Fraser and Dr Elizabeth Bunbury, into neurotic illness as a cause of absence from work. Prompted by concerns about industrial efficiency during wartime, the research focused on light and medium engineering industries from Birmingham and Greater London and attempted to gauge the 'true incidence' of the condition and 'its effects on production'.[1] Their study of 3,000 workers found that 9.1 per cent of male workers and 13 per cent of female workers had suffered from what was described as 'definite' neurosis.[2] The number of male cases uncovered in this study was significantly higher than those that were to emerge later in studies during the 1950s and 1960s from general practice, which broadly suggested a female to male ratio of 2:1. Once again, a familiar feature of this study was that greater numbers of men were diagnosed with what Fraser described as 'disabling psychosomatic symptoms' (3.5 per cent of men and 2.1 per cent of women). When the figures are taken together, it would appear that psychological and psychosomatic illness was a significant problem for men as well as women.

Fraser's research methodology was progressive for its time. Unlike other studies that used sickness certificates alone as the basis for investigation, Fraser's study of workers included two clinical examinations: physical and psychological. Workers' home life and environment were also examined by a social worker so that information about domestic arrangements and leisure activities could be included. Employment sickness records were also consulted. Although the author acknowledged that the wartime context of the study meant that the findings might not reflect those in peacetime, he concluded that neurotic illness was an important cause of industrial disability among the workers studied.[3] However, the research undertaken into health and work during the decades following the Second World War was shaped by broader cultural, political and economic factors and focused primarily on unemployment, physical and chemical hazards and absenteeism, underestimating the prevalence and impact of mental illness.[4] The remainder of this chapter explores the various agendas that underpinned these debates and also examines the broader construction of masculinity that endorsed a machismo culture at work, preventing open discussion about male mental illness.

Developments in occupational health

As is well known, legislation governing workplace health and safety evolved over the nineteenth and twentieth centuries, largely in response to concerns about the risks posed to workers by hazardous materials and dangerous practices. As Vicky Long has noted, from the mid-nineteenth century, developments in industrial and occupational health were implemented in response to public concerns, but also shaped by the broader political and economic context.[5] The series of Factory Acts passed by the British parliament from 1819 initially sought to mitigate the poor conditions endured by women and children. By 1855, a rudimentary industrial medical service was introduced by law and, in 1895, notification of important industrial diseases, such as lead, phosphorous and anthrax poisoning, was introduced.[6] A cornerstone of the developing legislation was the 1833 Factory Act, which established a range of provisos limiting the working hours of young persons of less than eighteen years of age and the appointment of factory inspectors with power to enforce regulations.[7] Legislation towards the end of the nineteenth century required that workers in dangerous trades be examined by certifying surgeons who notified cases of occupational disease. Following the introduction of the Workmen's Compensation Act of 1897, many employers voluntarily appointed physicians as a means of protecting themselves against compensation claims.[8] At the turn of the twentieth century, the state had built a statutory medical service for factory workers, provided by approximately 1800 part-time certifying factory surgeons (later known as factory doctors).[9] Their remit was threefold: to examine young persons under eighteen years of age for fitness for work; to undertake examinations of persons employed in dangerous trades; and to investigate cases of notifiable industrial disease. Throughout the first half of the new century, workplace legislation continued to develop, adding to regulations about specific trades to cover entire production processes. However, by the late 1960s, as industrial technology advanced, the shortcomings of such a prescriptive approach to factory health and safety were becoming clear. Following the recommendations of the Robens Report in 1972, the Health and Safety at Work Act, 1974, fundamentally changed the principles of workplace health and safety. Based on the concepts of self-regulation, goal-setting and voluntary codes of practice, this new legislation placed the responsibility for workplace welfare on employers and employees. Such a brief overview of occupational health in Britain should however not be read as an uncomplicated development of state intervention. As Long argues in her account of the rise and fall of the healthy factory, industrial health 'evolved from the contested negotiations between trade unions, employers, the medical profession and the state, as each sought to achieve their objectives through an array of strategies'.[10] Periodically, approaches to the health and safety of the workforce were also influenced by the requirements of, and responses to, the broader global context: the growth and decline of the British Empire and the two World Wars.

From the early twentieth century, concurrent to developments in occupational health were modifications to working practices as the principles of 'scientific management' were applied increasingly to production processes. At the turn of the century, influential figures such as Frederick Taylor, Henry Ford and Frank and Lillian Gillbreth introduced the new concepts of piece-rates, time and motion studies, and automation. Originating in the United States (US) but later introduced in Britain by British industrial psychologists, the underlying principles of scientific management were that the correct selection of employees and appropriate methods of work were central to maximising production and improving the welfare of workers. In 1921, Charles Myers co-founded the National Institute of Industrial Psychology with Henry Welch to promote scientific management and ostensibly improve standards for workers. Myers stated in his influential text, *Industrial Psychology* (1929), that the aim of the field was to 'discover the best possible human conditions in occupational work'.[11] In Britain, automated operation processes were introduced increasingly to a range of manufacturing industries that required very large outputs.[12] Although one of the principles of scientific management was to improve standards of work and welfare for workers, from the 1940s, the impact of scientific management on employees in fact became a source of concern and debate.[13] Whereas, during the inter-war period, debates had been dominated by concerns about physical and mental 'fatigue', the decades following the Second World War saw a shift in approaches to industrial medicine towards a focus on the psychological pressures of new working practices.[14]

Sarah Hayes has shown recently that the debate about automated processes was exceptionally polarised. Some industrialists argued that the new methods would lead to reduced demands on physical health and result in a less hazardous environment, while others feared the 'dehumanisation' of the workplace.[15] Indeed, in 1959, concerns prompted the World Health Organization (WHO) to convene a study group on the problems of automation. Seen within the context of wider social change and technological development, the group noted that it was difficult to separate the effects of automation from other influences, such as management style.[16] The tone of the report was tentatively positive and the group cautioned against the propensity towards pessimistic appraisals that 'warn humanity against the industrial hell towards which it is inexorably moving'.[17] They argued, for example, that any risk of automated work being rendered 'meaningless' would be offset by less monotony and repetition. The report called for 'less hysteria', and concluded that more emphasis should be placed on preparation, education and 'responsible' media coverage.[18] However, commentators would later protest that modern manufacturing processes did indeed lead to workers experiencing monotony, isolation and a lack of control, causing physical and psychological ill effects – ill effects that were ultimately treated surgically or pharmacologically and compensated financially.[19] Ultimately, the polarised and conflicting debates presented employers with the opportunity to ignore the health implications of automated processes, despite evidence that the new practices impacted on the physical and mental health of workers.[20] As I have argued in Chapter 1, the technical and medical model of intervention in health that prevailed, not only underplayed the importance of the psychosocial environment at work, but resulted in missed opportunities more broadly when it came to detecting the prevalence and causes of psychological illness in male workers.

Absenteeism and sickness absence in post-war Britain

From the 1960s, the topic of absenteeism had generated considerable debate among industrialists and psychologists. The term was used to refer to short-term employee absence that occurred without suitable notification and without official sanction by medical personnel, and it differed from sickness-absence, which was a formally certified period of time off work due to illness. Absenteeism implied 'voluntary' absence for one or two days and was interpreted as a way in which employees might take time off to avoid pressure, or in retaliation against the employer as an expression of job dissatisfaction. Despite widespread concern about the effects of absenteeism on production and efficiency, by the early 1980s, no satisfactory explanatory framework for the phenomenon had been found.[21] Part of the problem stemmed from a lack of accurate records and difficulties identifying which absences were in fact 'voluntary'.[22] In attempting to explore the issue, most commentators focused upon the individual employee's motives for taking unsanctioned time off work and examined factors such as age, sex, rank, wage and length of service. Some concluded that some workers were simply 'absence prone', implying that taking time off work was a habit. However, Professor John Chadwick-Jones, formerly Director of the Occupational Psychology Research Unit at Cardiff University, was critical of explanations that focused upon the individual employee's motives for taking short-term leave. Instead, he formulated a 'theory of absenteeism' as a social phenomenon, 'as part of a social exchange between employees and management'.[23]

Certainly, a number of clear and distinct patterns emerged from the literature.[24] For example, short-term absenteeism was negatively associated with age (older workers were less prone to absenteeism than younger employees).[25] Workers in lower ranks were more likely to be absent than those at managerial level, the assumption being that senior managers were either more assiduous or that the flexibility inherent in senior roles allowed personnel to attend to personal matters in their own time more easily.[26] The most striking pattern was the observation that women had consistently higher rates of absence than men. In a well-cited article published in 1962 in the *International Labour Review*, Viviane Isambert-Jamati explored factors that might contribute to high numbers of female absenteeism. The author noted that the problem was related to the responsibility for dependent children and that this was manifest in figures that suggested married women took more time off work than widows and spinsters.[27] The highest rates of absence indeed occurred in women between the ages of twenty-five and twenty-nine 'reflecting the fact that there were young children to be tended'.[28] Supporting this explanation, other researchers noted that a great deal of female absence occurred during the morning,[29] the theory being that women were required to undertake household chores and childcare responsibilities at this time of day. Isambert-Jamati's research indeed suggested that some women felt that employment contradicted what they saw as their 'proper social function'. When asked about their feelings towards their job, those who felt 'that their proper place would be, and should always have been, at home, [were] far more numerous in the group of frequent absentees than in the group of regular workers'.[30] Female labour turnover was also consistently higher than male, again accounted for by personal factors that affected women's ability to work, such as childbirth, sickness in the family and care of children or relatives.[31] This high labour turnover often coincided with absenteeism and was particularly high during winter months, where families fell sick more often, and during the summer school holiday period.[32] The study of daily variations of absence also exposed interesting patterns whereby workers were more likely to be absent on a Monday than on other days of the week. This trend was not new and had prompted commentators much earlier to formulate expressions such as 'Blue Monday', 'Colliers' Monday', 'Drunken Tuesday' and, for the fortnightly paid, 'Lazy Wednesday'.[33]

Debates on absenteeism thus focused on broad trends from scanty data and upon what might be done by the employer to minimise loss of productivity. Hilde Berhend noted in 1959, that by themselves, patterns and trends did not tell the researcher much about the *causes* of absenteeism.[34] Although there was broad consensus that high rates of absenteeism might be associated in some way with expressions of low job satisfaction, she cautioned that no clear-cut frontier existed between sickness and psychological malaise, pointing out that 'psychosomatic diseases and voluntary absences may both represent escapes from an unbearable situation'.[35] In a review of literature in 1973, Chadwick-Jones noted that a very small number of authors had considered disorders of personality and neurotic and psychosomatic illnesses as causes of absenteeism. Fraser's study of neurosis in factory workers and Helen Flanders Dunbar's *Psychosomatic Diagnosis* (1943) were cited as notable examples; however, Chadwick-Jones expressed surprise that 'this field should be so neglected'.[36] Undoubtedly, the focus of literature upon individual motivations and attendance behaviour resulted in missed opportunities to uncover and expose psychological and psychosomatic disorders in men. As this chapter will argue, symptoms of 'distress' in men commonly presented as ill-defined disorders that might prompt a short spell of time off work. As authors writing about alcoholism in industry had also observed, much Monday morning absence was caused by heavy drinking over the weekend – a connection seemingly lost to those undertaking research into short-term absence. The situation was duly exacerbated by the focus on female workers and the fact that employees were often untruthful about why they had been absent.[37]

By the late 1960s, absence due to medically certified sickness also presented considerable problems in industry, costing, in economic terms, around £400 million a year.[38] As with absenteeism, patterns of sickness absence followed some broad, recognisable trends, once again suggesting that women experienced more sickness absence than men. In 1968, statistics from the Office of Health Economics suggested that men insured under the national insurance scheme experienced 479 spells of certified sickness absence for every 1,000 men at risk. For women, the rate was higher at 520 per 1,000.[39] The authors noted that the number of episodes of absence had increased at a moderately steady rate between the mid-1950s and the late 1960s, but that the trend was towards more frequent, but shorter spells of absence.[40] Again, concerns were raised that uncertified absences of less than four days most likely made up a significant total of absence among the working population; however, no national statistics for these absences were available.[41] Younger male employees appeared to have more short spells of sickness than older workers, while older male workers had longer spells that were less frequent. These patterns were confirmed in a range of employment arenas.[42] Shift workers tended to have fewer episodes of sickness, but were more likely to be off work long-term.[43] A number of researchers focused on the types of unique stresses experienced by workers in specific jobs, concluding that, despite higher stakes and high pressure, job satisfaction was more common in managerial positions.[44] Sickness rates were greater among miners and quarry workers, whereas agricultural workers appeared to take less time off work.[45] Among rural communities, the consensus was that farmers rarely sought medical advice, often ignoring sickness and disease until crisis prompted emergency care. A number of GPs who were interviewed for this project remarked that agriculture was very tough and that farming families during the 1950s and 1960s lived in primitive conditions. Remembering emergency home visits, one GP recalled that homes were desperately cold and that life was very hard: 'I mean sometimes I couldn't take my jacket off it was so cold . . . but lovely people. And very non-complaining. And things you never see nowadays – people with locked hips from osteoarthritis shuffling along, men in their fifties.'[46] Another doctor who spent his life practising in rural Devon concurred, recalling that farmers 'rarely complained of minor disorders' and because they were 'working on their own account, they would put up with a lot of – considerable physical symptoms, before they complain'.[47] The tough circumstances faced by farmers were reflected in the fact that suicide was more common among them than in other occupations. Roger Lea, who practised in a rural community, felt that farmers communicated very poorly and that they 'were lonely' sort of people: 'And if they got depressed, they just worked and they carried on.'[48] Suicide, according to another GP who lived in a farming community, was more common among farmers because, in terms of access to licenced firearms, they 'had the means to do so'.[49] Indeed, more recent research has suggested that, historically, farmers, veterinarians, doctors and those serving in the police force have been more likely to take their own lives – all occupations where the access to firearms or toxic substances might facilitate suicide.[50]

Drawing on data from the General Household Survey (1972), the sociologist Peter Townsend noted that unskilled men were three times more likely to suffer from 'limiting, longstanding illness, disability or infirmity' than professional men. From the survey, he observed that, in comparison with professional men, unskilled workers lost an average of four-and-a-half times as many days from work in the year, demonstrating 'the disadvantage of the partly skilled and unskilled professional classes'.[51] As UK unemployment began to rise during the 1970s, commentators suggested that an inverse correlation relation existed between morbidity and socioeconomic status. M. Harvey Brenner, who published extensively on the links between mortality, morbidity and the economy, argued that 'economic instability and insecurity increase the likelihood of immoderate and unstable life habits, disruption of basic social networks and major life stresses – in other words, the relative lack of financial and employment security of lower socioeconomic groups is a major source of their higher mortality rates'.[52]

Patterns of illness shifted throughout the period from the 1950s to the 1980s, in part reflecting improved diagnosis and treatment, preventive measures and changes in the incidence of diseases.[53] Days of work lost through respiratory tuberculosis, for example, decreased significantly between the mid-1950s and the mid-1960s, as did the incidence of pleurisy, anaemia and skin diseases.[54] Peptic ulcers (diagnosed more frequently in men), although still a significant problem throughout the 1950s and 1960s, were decreasing in number.[55] Agar and Raffle's study of London transport workers, published in 1975, suggested that diseases of the stomach and duodenum were decreasing among older workers, but increasing in younger men.[56] The most noticeable trend, discernible in all studies of sickness absence, was the large rise in coronary heart disease, psychiatric diagnoses, musculoskeletal disorders and gastric disorders (other than peptic ulcer).[57] Although authors formulated somewhat different methods of categorising these conditions, it is clear from research undertaken throughout the period that they became an increasingly important factor in sickness absence. Testimonies from GPs who were practising during the 1960s and 1970s suggest that gastric disorders and backache featured as the most common psychosomatic conditions. One GP who was interviewed for this book noted perceptibly that, although heavy lifting was indeed a genuine cause for musculoskeletal conditions, 'you also did get the feeling that some of this back pain was a metaphor for having a heavy load somewhere in their lives'.[58] Another recalled: 'The commonest way of presenting was of course the backache . . . so you either took that at face value, and gave them a week's rest or something – or probed a bit further to find out what was going on.'[59] The study, *Off Sick*, published by the Office of Health Economics in 1971, utilised data from the mid-1950s and noted a large increase in numbers of workers absent through 'sprains and strains', 'nervousness debility and headache' and 'psychoneuroses and psychoses'.[60] Most research suggested that women were more likely to experience psychoneurosis – usually by a significant margin. Logan and Brooke's survey of sickness, for example, examined the number of illnesses, days of incapacity and consultations for selected diagnoses and found from their sample of 4,000 interviewees that the mean monthly prevalence rates in 1950 for psychoneurotic disorders and personality disorders in all ages over 16 were 106 for men and 155 for women.[61] However, reflecting studies undertaken in general practice, a defining feature of all the research undertaken from the 1950s was the large number of men appearing in statistics for gastric disorders. Comparisons between studies are difficult because these symptoms were variously described in studies as gastro-intestinal disturbances, indigestion and epigastric pain. Nonetheless, there was clear evidence that men consulted their doctors, and frequently took time off work as a result of gastric symptoms.[62]

Taylor's study of oil refinery workers published in 1968, which won the Occupational Health Prize of the British Medical Association in 1967, was notable for its attempt at clarifying some of the complexities related to sickness absence.[63] The study (exclusively among men, due to its focus on refinery workers) examined patterns of sickness absence among workers who were divided into groups of never sick, frequently sick and long-term sick. Findings were matched to a control group. The methodology, in many ways similar to Fraser's earlier study on neurosis, included information not only collected from documents and records, but also from interviews, health examinations, investigations into family and personal past, social background and present home circumstances. The research suggested broadly that, although the men in the frequently sick group had nearly three times as many spells of sickness absence as their matched controls, there was very little difference in the types of illness experienced.[64] There were, however, three conditions that were significantly more common among both the frequently sick and long-term sick groups than the control, or never sick groups: nervous breakdown, peptic ulcer and incapacitating back-pain.[65] Taylor was perceptive in employing a range of investigative techniques, which allowed his researchers to draw more meaningful conclusions from the data. Unlike studies drawn from occupational sickness records alone, his approach allowed researchers to gather a large amount of medical, social and psychological information about each worker, which could be examined for associations with sickness absence. As a result, in comparison to other studies, a considerable amount of male neurosis was revealed.[66] Factors such as having had an 'unhappy childhood' and experience of parental divorce emerged as significant in the groups of men who were frequently off sick, as did the loss of a parent by death before the age of 60, which proved influential in 40 per cent of men who were frequently sick, in contrast to 20 per cent of the controls.[67]

The fact that Taylor's study revealed appreciable numbers of men who were explicitly defined as diagnosed with neurosis, is significant enough; however, when these cases are combined with the large numbers of musculoskeletal disorders, gastritis and dyspepsia – and an intriguing group of 'ill-defined' disorders – it would be reasonable to suggest that a number of these diagnoses were psychosomatic presentations of psychological disorder. When it came to neurosis, back-ache and peptic ulcer, Taylor had begun to make connections between a worker's social circumstances, his history, his medical diagnosis and absence patterns. However, his study lacked further analysis of gastric disorders other than ulcers, and made nothing whatsoever of conditions described as 'ill-defined'. This was somewhat surprising given that numbers in this category equalled those diagnosed with neurosis at 21.4 per cent of those frequently sick. A significant 30 per cent of frequently sick men appeared in the data for gastritis and dyspepsia, and for each of these conditions, cases in the control group were very small.[68] As Chapter 1 suggests, there was certainly a consensus among GPs that gastric disorders were a common psychosomatic presentation among men. One doctor remembered a male patient who presented annually with peptic ulcer symptoms, although no organic cause was ever found:

> It later transpired that his symptoms mainly occurred in the early part of the year. And it was eventually decided that, because of his job, he had a lot of critical things to produce by April the 1st, and it was probably anxiety leading up to that that produced his symptoms. And he tried all sorts of things – antacids were about the only thing available then . . . Then I think, after April the 1st, or from sort of May time onwards, it all abated. And all right for the next nine months.[69]

Authors interested in occupational health outside Britain were more forthcoming about drawing associations between repeated absence, neurosis and peptic ulcer. Some went further and drew a direct correlation between neurosis, heavy drinking and stomach disorders. One Australian study of repeated sickness absence in a range of occupations specifically noted: 'Neurosis, smoking and peptic ulcer, found to be linked with drinking, and the physical consequences of drinking to excess, no doubt contributed to the liability of the drinker to be absent repeatedly.'[70] The author of this research unequivocally stated that social factors, such as conjugal failure, drinking and other 'personal maladjustment', contributed to repeated sickness absence.[71] The same author, in a study of neurosis among male telegraph workers in Australia, found that one-third (33 per cent) of the 516 workers who were examined were considered to have, or to have had, disabling neurosis.[72] Most subjects mentioned more than one influence as being contributory to their symptoms. Among personal and domestic reasons, those most commonly cited were family ill health, money worries and marital discord. Occupational influences included inability to cope with the job, monotony and job dissatisfaction.[73] Similar concerns were raised by contributors to an international, interdisciplinary series of symposia on society, stress and disease that took place through the 1970s. In the fourth of a resulting series of publications edited by Lennart Levi, Sweden's first Professor of Psychosocial Medicine, two Swedish authors examined stress and strain among Scandinavian, white-collar workers.[74] They drew strong correlations between high levels of mental strain, the use of sedatives and tranquillisers, gastric disorders and nerves. The study did not include analysis of gendered patterns of illness, but nevertheless made the explicit observation that workers who reported psychological reactions to mental strain at work had 'a much higher frequency of medical complaints, above all in the form of gastric and nervous troubles'.[75] Their conclusions were that psychological and psychosomatic reactions were likely to occur simultaneously.[76]

All studies of mental illness in industry were hampered by the same methodological problems that affected epidemiological studies in general practice. As was demonstrated in Chapter 1, there was no clear definition of what 'mental illness' actually meant, and the classification of symptoms differed widely between studies. Writing later in 1980, a group of social psychologists from the University of Sheffield noted that there had been a complete lack of reliable empirical work on the subject because researchers had been unable to define or conceptualise adequately mental health or mental illness and that there had been a lack of valid measures for use with work populations.[77] Terms such as 'nervous breakdown' and 'neurosis' were often used interchangeably, with no clear account of the symptoms included.[78] Up until the late 1970s, in studies of occupational health, the term depression was rarely used, although some researchers referred to 'depressive neurosis', with no full explanation about what this inferred.[79] In many cases, depression and a whole host of other psychological symptoms were subsumed under the broad heading of neurosis. Some investigators included psychosomatic symptoms in their research, while others discarded them altogether.[80] Those who excluded them invariably revealed fewer numbers of men since they were more likely to present with somatic symptoms. Other research included psychosomatic symptoms only if they presented concurrently with psychological symptoms that conformed to the WHO's definition of a mental 'case'.[81] In 1957, making a case for the importance of epidemiological studies at work, R. S. F. Schilling argued that observing patterns of disease in groups might be the only way of detecting some occupational hazards and their influence on health.[82] However, he conceded that, particularly in relation to neurosis, there were numerous problems with the relatively simple association of cause and effect in much industrial disease, which had inevitably led to a narrow concept of industrial medicine.[83] Schilling raised concerns about studies undertaken at work, where treatment records were likely to be 'an unreliable mix of minor accidents and illness'. Furthermore, he noted that whether or not a worker reported for treatment depended on many things: 'Some make light of minor ailments; others make the most of them.'[84] The personality of medical staff and the prospect of loss of wages were seen as important factors that might influence a worker's decision to seek treatment. Calling for simpler and surer methods of assessing psychological illness, Shilling noted that many errors occurred in observing clinical signs and taking histories of symptoms so that 'much that is recorded may be unreliable'.[85]

Accurate sickness trends were also very difficult to trace through certificated medical absence since a great deal of controversy surrounded the question of medical certification, its value and effect.[86] In order to claim sickness benefits from the Department of Health and Social Security, workers usually needed to be certified as unfit for work by a medical doctor, usually a GP. However, it was generally accepted that GPs' training did not equip them with the ability to measure an employee's capacity for work.[87] As this chapter and the oral history testimonies throughout this book suggest, 'diagnoses suggestive of neurosis [were] often vague, and because in the eyes of some physicians and patients, a stigma attaches to mental disorder a more acceptable symptomatic diagnosis may be given on the certificate'.[88] One GP interviewed as part of this research recalled that it 'was a real . . . real problem, having a psychiatric illness on your note. So . . . we would call a psychiatric illness a physical one, because that was acceptable, and it was acceptable to their friends and their boss and everything else'.[89] Likewise, a senior professor of general practice concurred: 'Because the man didn't want to be labelled as psychological, the doctor would go along with it.'[90] The same GP remembered that one of his patients, a senior executive, drove over thirty miles outside the local vicinity to collect his prescription, for fear that someone might discover he was being prescribed psychotropic drugs.[91] The situation not only caused problems for patients, but also for GPs who were often placed in a difficult situation when deciding whether or not to issue a sickness certificate. One GP, contributing to a symposium on absence from work in 1969, noted that 'workmen do not usually want to bother a doctor' and that it was 'not part of the general practitioner's function to maintain industrial discipline or morale'. Indicating how unsatisfactory the whole process appeared to be, he added: 'There was a time in my career when I occasionally tried to refuse people certificates – but in the interest of my coronary arteries, I have given up arguing.'[92]

Certainly, evidence suggests that workers were often reluctant to discuss the causes of short-term absence with their employers and that some men refused to take part in workplace health investigations.[93] Those who did give consent to participate were often impervious to advice about health. An investigation during the 1960s, which explored the attitudes of senior staff in industry towards health investigations, noted that advice on smoking, drinking and eating habits was seldom received positively, possibly due to the employee's 'reluctance to remember advice which he found unpalatable'.[94] Moreover, studies that featured groups of men who, in statistical terms, appeared to be rarely ill often exposed interesting ambiguities. The 'never-sick' group in Taylor's oil refinery study, for example, 'almost without exception . . . denied that there was anything wrong with their health, their home or their work'.[95] This prompted Taylor to question whether such responses were untruthful or whether these individuals simply lacked insight into their own health and social circumstances.

As Chapter 1 illustrated, concerns about the rise of nervous disorders and 'stress-related' illness emerged in part from broader anxieties about a rapidly changing world and the impact of conflict and cultural upheaval on mental and physical health.[96] The eclectic range of physiological, psychological and psychosocial theories that emerged during the post-war period each claimed their own position within the debate about whether causes could be traced to the social environment or found within the individual. When it came to studies in industry, regardless of the perspective taken by investigators, productivity was primarily the motive for research. A study of long-term sickness among British civil servants undertaken during the late 1960s, for example, was borne from rising concerns about efficiency and occupational health.[97] The survey was interpreted by the service's medical advisor, the epidemiologist Daniel Thomson, who showed 'little sympathy for employees and limited awareness of contemporary research on the potential impact of work on health'.[98] Thomson was preoccupied with individual rather than corporate responsibility and described stress reactions in workers as 'largely of their own making' caused by personal shortcomings.[99] Stress-related ill-health, according to Thomson, was not necessarily the product of greater pressure at work, but instead, the product of 'lowered stress thresholds', offering employees 'a convenient means of avoiding seemingly unbearable pressures'.[100] Absenteeism was seen as a 'broader malaise affecting modern society'.[101] Unsurprisingly, the study of civil servants exposed a familiarly gendered pattern of sickness absence: women were more likely to be off sick than men, and, while male workers were more likely to experience heart disease, women were more prone to mental illness. As Jackson has argued, although these patterns might well have reflected the difficulties experienced by women in balancing work and domestic responsibilities, they also betrayed common assumptions about gender that were woven into debates about industrial health and sickness. This is particularly interesting, since physiological studies of stress undertaken by the pioneering stress researcher, Hans Selye, uncovered very little difference between the sexes. Indeed, he maintained that stress reactions were universal and non-specific.[102] It is clear from the civil servant study and from wider studies on occupational health, that a preoccupation with efficiency and the methodological problems associated with the collection and analysis of medical data, did much to hamper the potential to expose and explore male psychological and psychosomatic illness.

Masculine culture in the workplace

Although the framework of industrial and psychological investigations into workplace health was unhelpful in the sense that it often missed opportunities to uncover cases of male mental illness, additional factors exacerbated the problem. As Arthur McIvor has shown, during the post-war period 'the workplace was an important site for the incubation and forging of male identities'.[103] The 'essence' of masculinity, McIvor notes, with particular reference to the heavy industries, has been associated most often with physical prowess, toughness, homophobia, risk-taking and a lack of emotional display.[104] Masculinity at work has been the subject of much historical debate in recent years and scholars rightly point out that neither masculinity nor femininity were fixed constructs; instead, 'a range of masculinities and femininities coexisted around the traditional breadwinner and housewife paradigm'.[105] As Eileen Yeo has shown, masculinity is also 'fractured by class, race and ethnicity in settings where some versions of manhood are privileged and others subordinated'.[106] Nevertheless, in workplace culture the discourse of the 'hegemonic hard man' was the most influential.[107] As McIvor has illustrated so strikingly with his oral histories of the heavy trades, working-class masculinities were nurtured in the tough street culture of the neighbourhood and in dangerous, dirty and physically exhausting work.[108] This often 'brutal' world was mediated by the camaraderie of the workplace: black humour and repartee – and by heavy smoking and drinking outside work.[109]

Machismo behaviour had implications for both physical and mental health. McIvor suggests that there were two co-existing 'degenerative pressures upon health and workers' bodies': capitalist exploitation and masculine values.[110] Risk-taking at work was an important feature of male working-class culture, and it is not easy to determine precisely why workers took risks with their health – whether it was in order to impress their peers, or because they felt pressured by management.[111] David Walker has argued that machismo culture should not be seen as simply 'male strutting', but instead as 'emerging from and acted out as a consequence of the exploitation of the worker at the point of production'.[112] In Walker's opinion, the overriding need to earn a sustained income meant that workers did not necessarily 'seek out' danger, but were made to accept hazardous working conditions.[113] It is certainly the case, for example, that when safety equipment was first introduced in construction, steel works, mining and shipyards, many employees initially resisted wearing them.[114] Nick Hayes has shown, with particular reference to the construction industry, that improvements in welfare provision for workers 'debased the accepted currencies of physical endurance and self-provision'.[115] Unions noted that many operatives thought there was 'something cissy about safety and fanc[ied] themselves as tough guys'.[116] Ultimately, for construction workers, life on site might have been 'harsh, uncertain and dangerous', but it was also 'informal, manly and self-defining'.[117] Whatever complex motives lay behind risk-taking culture at work, it is clear that men were socialised into overcoming instinctual fears and apprehensions so that 'working in poor, dangerous conditions became the norm'.[118]

Central to workplace masculine culture was the importance of not appearing 'weak', which was manifest in oral testimonies and autobiographies of workers from the mid-twentieth century. Being 'at loggerheads' with management in the coal mining industry, for example, was a marker of the 'stoic struggle' against exploitative managers, employers and foremen.[119] Within Scottish mining communities, older miners encouraged youths to avoid any display of emotion, and this was viewed as training to be 'hard men'.[120] As Johnston and McIvor observed in their study of the Clydeside heavy industries: 'Any sign of weakness, emotion and vulnerability could lead to being pilloried: the butt of jokes, scathing banter, vicious nicknames and sometimes very public humiliation.'[121] Such attitudes were widely evident in the oral histories of doctors. Richard Stanton, a retired GP from Devon, recalled that he had to be very careful talking to men about psychosomatic symptoms 'because the reaction would be "So you think I'm a hypochondriac?". . . it's all to do with the macho thing for men, isn't it'.[122] Similarly, Sarah Hall, a GP with extensive medical experience in the East End of London, recalled that penetrating beneath the hard surface of market workers from Smithfield and Covent Garden was often very difficult:

> They make ridiculous jokes, really stupid jokes. They know they're being stupid. It's their way of maintaining their mood. So they've got this amazing front on them that's really hard to get through. And they'd be like, in the consulting room: 'Hi love, how are you?' You know. And, so they'd be loud and cheerful. And it was very, very difficult to get past that . . . it was that 'matey' thing.[123]

Indeed, this machismo culture meant that many men resolutely refused to visit the doctor. GPs practising in the West Country observed that farmers were particularly reluctant to seek help. One doctor recalled that 'the farming fraternity, the hunting, shooting, fishing fraternity, were far more stoical and prepared to self-treat, and, when they came our way, one was usually more impressed by their symptoms'.[124] Another noted specifically that farmers appeared to encounter problems with depression in their middle years, but that 'they sometimes never appeared with any symptoms – until they committed suicide'.[125]

During the 1950s and 1960s, a whole generation of men also brought the experiences of war to their working lives. Pat Ayres noted in her study of masculinities in post-war Liverpool: 'The manhood of those returning from serving abroad in the army of merchant service had been tested in the most overt way.'[126] Post-war, the demands of national service ensured that large numbers of young men continued to experience the discipline of the army. Michael Roper, in his study of management, observed that military service had a significant influence on the men he interviewed: 'The physical hardships and discipline . . . had educated them in the cult of toughness . . . masculinity was won through . . . having learnt what discipline meant [and] was sustained by ritual purgings of the "feminine" parts of themselves.'[127] Roper's study of managers also illustrates how the experiences of white-collar workers differed from 'hard men' working in heavy industry and manufacturing. Managers described 'a constant struggle to quell suspicions that they were unmanly or "soft"' and 'graded management hierarchies according to the level of aggression required to perform at each level'. Workers often felt they had 'failed to assert a sufficiently "hard" masculinity'.[128] The cult of toughness was manifest not only in the stories told by men, but also more literally 'embodied' in workers' postures, gestures and firm handshakes – and in their appearance, for example, with close-cropped hair.[129] On the shop floor, new Fordist practices, automation and conveyor-belt production were viewed as less 'manly' than traditional methods. However, as Ayers argues, the workplace remained an exclusively male milieu and, consequently, constructions of masculinity adapted and were remodelled 'in order to accommodate change without damaging men's sense of themselves as true men'. Ultimately, the experience of 'manliness persisted'.[130]

Occupational health

Historical reflections on occupational health and industry in Britain since the Second World War have exposed the complex political agendas at play between employers, employees, the government and trade unions. Central to the argument made in this chapter is the suggestion that the ability to identify and observe male psychological illness at work was obscured by these agendas and compounded by a construction of masculinity characterised by toughness and a lack of emotional display. In dealing with the topic of health at work, there has been hot debate among historians about the role of trade unions in occupational health. Critical interpretations suggest that union policies have tended to neglect the health of the worker in favour of a focus on wages, job security and financial compensation policies.[131] Johnston and McIvor argue, for example, with reference specifically to the risks of asbestos in Scotland, that 'the unions absorbed and reflected the macho attitudes of their dominant male workforce, rather than vigorously challenging this high-risk workplace health culture.'[132] However, alternative interpretations, including more recent analyses by Johnson and McIvor on workers' respiratory illness, suggest that the unions played a pivotal role in working to protect members.[133] Joseph Melling, while not exonerating the unions, argues that they acted 'within constraints imposed upon them by other actors as well as their own members'.[134] According to Melling, the trade unions were often working with limited information about health risks and were prompted to balance any risks against those associated with loss of earnings or reduction in employment that might accompany rigorous safety standards.[135] However, when it came to psychological illness, the trade unions were reluctant to intervene. Vicky Long has shown that during the 1930s, healthcare workers increasingly viewed the Trades Union Congress (TUC) as an organisation legitimately interested in the provision of healthcare and that a number of psychologists were keen to collaborate on investigations into workers' mental health. J. R. Rees, for example, Medical Director of the Institute of Medical Psychology at the Tavistock Clinic, was keen for the TUC to fund work at the institute, arguing that psychoneuroses were an important focus area for research since they caused one-third of all sickness from industry. However, these appeals were met with indifference, suggesting that trade unions may have been reluctant to accept that their workers' health problems may have had a psychological basis.[136] It is interesting that, despite a broad paradigm shift in discussion away from physical fatigue towards debates about the psychological health of workers, the TUC was reluctant to engage with debates about psychoneuroses, 'wary of the stigma still attached to mental illness'.[137]

During the immediate post-war period, opportunities to investigate the impact of mental illness among workers were also hampered by elemental questions about who should be responsible for occupational health in the first place. In her extensive exploration of political debates about industrial health, Long notes that the expansion of medical personnel in factories during the Second Wold War 'gave rise to the belief that a state industrial medical service would be inaugurated after the war in tandem with the new NHS'.[138] However, despite the TUC's efforts to secure such a service, the demands for this provision were resisted.[139] The Ministry of Health argued that 'industrial workers had no health needs that could not be met by the general health-care services', and suggested that industrial healthcare provision would simply duplicate that which would be available on the NHS.[140] The situation was duly exacerbated by the shortage of doctors with training and experience in industrial health – a fact that ultimately buttressed the arguments put forward by the Ministry of Health. The Industrial Hygiene Service that was eventually established employed 'technical experts' to ensure the health of the working environment. In so doing, focus shifted firmly away from the importance of preventative measures.[141] Thus, opportunities to investigate male health were almost certainly lost in the politics of occupational health. As McIvor notes, the state's over-reliance on scientific discourse, the lack of a preventative programme and the consequent narrow focus on specific occupational diseases did little to erode high-risk workplace health cultures.[142]

As the material in this chapter and the subsequent chapter on alcohol abuse suggests, debates about the health of workers in other countries often focused more openly on the problems of mental illness and alcoholism in industry. There are no straightforward explanations for this; however, it is clear that in the international arena, different cultural values and contrasting approaches to state intervention in matters of health resulted in alternative models of occupational health. Scandinavian researchers, for example, were prominent in studies undertaken on occupational health, and often cited in British journals.[143] The 'Nordic model' of welfare has been the topic of widespread debate and is held by some as an egalitarian and equitable example of state-regulated healthcare, funded by taxation.[144] Leaving the politics of this debate aside, if the origins of the Nordic welfare model are considered, it is possible to see why workers' health featured prominently in debates. As Mary Hilson has shown, the Scandinavian social democratic welfare state that developed was characterised by a number of guiding principles. Primarily, there was of course the expectation of state involvement via taxation. However, this was assisted by a strong work ethic where 'willingness to work' was a condition for receiving benefits. Social reform thus was seen to integrate the working classes and prevent social unrest, primarily through 'creating the means for individuals to support themselves'.[145] Scandinavian welfare was closely connected to the pursuit of economic efficiency and intended to be prophylactic, in that it provided the state with the means to create the 'good' society. Bolstered by deep-rooted Nordic values of individual responsibility for social welfare through sobriety, education and respectability, the prophylactic policy also extended to the realms of healthcare. Under the influence of a strong temperance movement, almost all Nordic countries, for example, experimented with some form of state control of alcohol during the early twentieth century.[146] This preventative approach was more likely to stimulate productive research into the health of workers and stood in marked contrast to the disease model that dominated in Britain. Hilson rightly warns against oversimplified histories that assume the same trajectory for all Nordic countries, and cautions against whig histories of the state welfare model. Nevertheless, the Nordic model has undoubtedly been characterised by collectivism and conformism, where welfare states have evolved peacefully without the open conflict that has been more typical in other countries such as the Britain and USA. Moreover, within the Nordic model, the trade unions have been more central to debates and held close links with the social democratic leadership.

On the international scene, state intervention in health was not necessarily the primary factor to influence the direction of debates about the psychological health of workers. For a set of completely different reasons, the concept of prevention also became embedded in psychiatric approaches in the USA. Here, psychiatric thought was shaped by the mental hygiene movement, which became influential from the first decade of the twentieth century. The National Committee for Mental Hygiene (NCMH) was founded in New York in 1909 by a number of leading psychiatrists and influenced in particular by Clifford Whittingham Beers (1876–1943) and Adolf Meyer (1866–1950). Beers, who had spent several years himself in psychiatric institutions following suicide attempts and mental breakdown, wrote a book entitled *A Mind that Found Itself*, which was published in 1908. Beers intended this publication to be 'a prelude to the formation of a national movement', which initially sought to improve institutional care. However, following Meyer's involvement, the objectives shifted significantly to encompass a broader move towards the promotion of health and the prevention of mental illness.[147] Surveys sponsored by the NCMH suggested that 'the bulk of individuals requiring psychiatric treatment were not in institutions' and the journal *Mental Hygiene*, which was first published in 1917, stressed the importance of preventative medicine, education and research into factors that affected the mental health of the population.[148]

Early interest in industrial psychology thus, in part, stemmed from the influence of the mental hygiene movement.[149] The importance of social and psychological factors in mental health at work was certainly reflected in the work of leading researchers such as the psychologist Elton Mayo (1880–1949), who emphasised the key role of the environment and human interaction in his authoritative text, *The Human Problems of an Industrial Civilization,* published in 1934. Increasingly, research that appeared in the *American Journal of Psychiatry* stressed the need for industrial physicians to 'concern themselves with the recognition of emotional factors underlying behaviour, which so frequently resulted in inferior output, high sickness rates, high labor turnover and absenteeism'.[150] Building on this approach, many large corporations developed psychiatric programmes for their workplaces, and feature articles in national newspapers attracted the attention of the general public.[151]

In addition to existing concerns about absenteeism and automation (that were commonplace in Britain), American literature regularly encompassed research on alcoholism, neurotic reactions and the more general application of psychiatry to business and industry.[152] Many of these publications included case studies of interviews and medical examinations with male workers who were affected by emotional distress and psychosomatic illness. Writing in 1959, for example, W. Donald Ross, in his book *Practical Psychiatry for Physicians,* described an exchange with a coal worker complaining about shortness of breath. Having made passing reference to the death of a fellow miner in a rock fall, the worker 'skirted around' the subject to focus again on his symptoms. When it was suggested that the death of his friend might have bothered him a good deal, the worker admitted that he 'hadn't liked to talk about it' but had 'worried considerably about it' and was then able to consider the impact of this trauma on his own feelings and anxieties about the hazards of mining.[153] This book included an entire chapter on 'psychophysiological problems' in which Ross explored a host of somatic presentations that might be caused by emotional distress, including: musculoskeletal disorders, asthma, chest pain, gastrointestinal disturbances, ulcerative colitis and spastic colon.[154] Another chapter examined job stresses that were specific to workers of different grades, and the author observed that executive workers were not only prone to anxiety and depression, but also to a host of psychosomatic illnesses which included indigestion, headaches and hypertension.[155] It is notable that Ross, despite what might seem like a progressive approach, still subscribed to the notion that women were biologically predisposed to emotionality, arguing that changes in attitude among women 'spring from the different motivations at different times in the ovarian cycle'.[156] Nevertheless, as Chapter 3 of this book will demonstrate, such texts did not shy away from sensitive issues such as alcoholism among workers – in marked contrast to formal discussion in Britain that was in almost complete denial that a problem existed at all.

A focus on preventative measures in the USA was almost certainly also connected to the system of employer-sponsored health insurance that developed from the 1930s. As David Blumenthal has noted, two historic events prepared the way for the emergence of employer-sponsored insurance. The first was President Franklin D. Roosevelt's decision not to pursue universal health coverage after his election in 1932, and the second was a series of federal rules enacted during the 1940s and 1950s on how employer-sponsored insurance should be treated with regard to federal taxes and in labour negotiations.[157] Roosevelt's decision created an opportunity for commercial insurers to step in and sell insurance to employers to provide protection for workers faced with the growing cost of illness. Simultaneously, the federal government's decision to limit employers' freedom to raise wages, resulted in employers expanding benefits to workers as a package to attract employees. Finally, in 1954, contributions made by employers to the purchase of health insurance for employees were ruled as non-taxable income to workers.[158] Consequently, private health insurance soon became an established feature of American life which appeared to diminish 'the need for government action but also had spawned a strong new insurance industry with a stake in the status quo'.[159] When compared to a system of universal coverage, opinions about the benefits and drawbacks of an industry-sponsored approach have been deeply polarised. However, leaving the politics aside once again, it is perhaps easy to see why, within a healthcare system that developed within the employment arena, employer-sponsored research and prevention programmes were more common in the USA. Contrastingly, in Britain, the NHS came to be seen as the most appropriate arena for the diagnosis and treatment of conditions that were not specifically related to health risks at work.

Reflections

Writing in the *British Journal of Industrial Medicine* in 1985, Rachel Jenkins, Professor of Epidemiology and Mental Health Policy, stated that:

> Industrial policy makers, scientists and the informed public have, until recently, concentrated their attention on three major work-related areas: unemployment, physical and chemical health hazards and absenteeism. Mental illness in the workforce has been of subsidiary interest and attention has focused on the separate issues of whether work is an aetiological factor in mental illness.[160]

Jenkins' article outlined many of the methodological anomalies and cultural biases that had hampered research into the mental health of workers since the Second World War. She noted, for example, that previous studies had tended to rely on the diagnoses given by GPs on sickness certificates and suggested that the estimates derived from these investigations were notoriously low. In her own research on psychiatric morbidity among executive officers in the Civil Service, Jenkins' respondents filled out the General Health Questionnaire (GHQ) and participated in a psychiatric interview. Results were then combined with analysis of employment sickness records and followed up twelve months later. The GHQ was intended specifically as a screening tool to detect those who either already had a psychiatric disorder or were at risk of developing one.[161] Early empirical studies using this tool suggested a good level of consistency and reliability, and investigators also sanctioned its use in employment settings.[162] Using this methodology, Jenkins found that psychiatric symptoms were common among her respondents and that there was 'no pronounced difference between the sexes'.[163] Jenkins underlined the fact that official statistics underestimated the extent of the problem, since they relied on the GPs ability to diagnose psychiatric illness. Citing work from Goldberg published in 1976, she argued that 'it is known that between a third and a half of psychiatric disorders presenting in general practitioners' surgeries remains undetected by the general practitioner.'[164] Additionally, she maintained that, 'since stigma and discrimination may accrue to receipt of a psychiatric diagnosis, the general practitioner may avoid writing such a diagnosis on the certificate of an employed person'.[165] The stigma associated with mental illness, she argued, prompted many individuals to present in primary care with a physical symptom since this was more socially acceptable than a psychiatric illness. Friends, relatives and GPs, she maintained, 'often share[d] this view'.[166]

By the 1980s, social scientists interested in occupational health were also drawing attention to the problems with previous studies. A group of psychologists at the Medical Research Council's Applied Psychology

Unit in Sheffield, for example, argued that the problem with empirical work thus far had been the inability to define or conceptualise the terms 'mental health' and 'mental illness' and the fact that there had been a lack of demonstrably valid measures for use with work populations.[167] Cary Cooper, who went on to become an internationally renowned professor of organisational psychology, argued that previous studies had been undertaken within single disciplines and that interdisciplinary work between psychology, sociology, medicine and management might expose more useful insights.[168] In a study of occupational sources of stress, co-authored with colleague Judi Marshall, Cooper articulated increasingly widespread concern that the field had been constrained by methodological problems related to the measurement of stress and psychological illness. They remarked that too few studies had explored psychosomatic presentations of psychological illness and added that finding adequate control groups for research had been problematic.[169] Drawing attention to the fact that a number of extra-organisational factors, such as family problems and financial difficulties, also contributed to stress and mental illness, Cooper and Marshall called for more research into the broader relationship between home and working life. In their 'model of stress at work', the authors concluded that there were multiple sources of stress at work, which, combined with the individual characteristics of the worker and personal pressures, could result in both physical and mental symptoms: hypertension, depressed mood and escapist drinking.[170]

In a continuation of her work on civil servants, Rachel Jenkins also published in 1985 a study of psychiatric morbidity and its association with labour turnover. Once again employing the GHQ and a system of interviews, the study incorporated not only investigation into aspects of job motivation and satisfaction, but also factors related to social support networks, relationships and financial circumstances of participants. Jenkins maintained that it was misguided to attempt to understand labour turnover by focusing primarily on workers' attitudes towards their employment. Instead, she concluded that minor psychiatric illness (including alcohol abuse) was an important cause of labour turnover for both men and women and that a range of social, psychological and economic factors should be included as possible causes.[171] Calling for further research, her concerns reflected the sentiments of a growing number of researchers working in fields allied to medicine and psychiatry that were keen to further their understanding of such a complex problem. Lennart Levi, writing in 1981, indeed suggested that official data on stress at work was 'only part of the story' because there were 'other indicators of a bad person-environment fit at work and elsewhere, such as alcoholism, suicide, mental and psychosomatic disorders'. These, he argued, were very common phenomena, yet no reliable data existed concerning the components of the total situation at work and outside it.[172] As numerous commentators were beginning to point out, interest in mental health was far greater in some other countries, in particular the USA, where industry had begun to develop a range of innovative programmes to investigate and manage psychiatric disorders among workers. However, in Britain, research remained 'scanty', and, as Jenkins noted, psychiatry as a whole appeared to show little interest in the field of mental health in the workplace.[173]

3

Alcohol as a Coping Mechanism

Introduction

Lord Stephen Taylor of Harlow, speaking in the House of Lords in 1965, recalled that he once knew a French GP who was 'much mystified by the English disease of the "nervous breakdown"'. The friend had observed: 'We do not have this in France. *En France c'est l'alcoholisme* (In France it is alcoholism)'.[1] By the mid 1960s, concerns about alcohol abuse among industrial workers emerged in a number of international studies about psychological illness, driven largely, as the previous chapter has illustrated, by concerns about sickness absence in industry. A study of Australian male telegraphists, for example, drew explicit attention to the inter-relationship between sickness absence, drinking, gastritis and peptic ulcer. Drawing a direct association between drinking and neurosis, the author argued that the subsequent 'physical consequences of drinking to excess no doubt contributed to the liability of the drinker to be absent repeatedly'.[2] As with much of the research on this topic, nonetheless, there was no clear consensus when it came to deciding whether the alcohol abuse was caused initially by the worker's constitution, or by the pressures of any personal or professional problems he might be experiencing. Research papers from the Netherlands articulated similar difficulties. A follow-up study of male alcoholics undertaken by clinicians at a treatment centre in Groningen proposed that troubles and conflicts in the marital and family sphere were usually present in patients; however, these conflicts were 'dependent on the pathological drinking – either being caused by it or, if present before, being intensified by it'.[3] In Britain, even less was known about the antecedents of drinking behaviours, and debates about alcohol took much longer to develop. Despite clear evidence that men were more likely to present (and take time off work sick) with somatic symptoms, such as gastritis and peptic ulcer, often exacerbated by the use of alcohol, few investigators sought to explore the extent to which men self-medicated with alcohol for the relief of depression and emotional release. This chapter examines the complex clinical, social and cultural forces that influenced debates about alcohol abuse in Britain from the 1950s and it suggests that historically, the failure to examine drinking as a 'coping mechanism' in men has had important implications for the broader interpretation of patterns of psychological illness.

Reflections on alcoholism

The disease concept of alcoholism that became dominant during the post-war period had its roots much earlier in the late eighteenth- and nineteenth-century theories put forward simultaneously by America's Benjamin Rush (1746–1813) and Britain's Thomas Trotter (1760–1832). Their theories are now well known and broadly describe the central characteristics of alcoholism that are still familiar to us today: namely, 'powerlessness' over the substance and the 'progressive' nature of the illness. By the turn of the twentieth century, the 'disease' of inebriety had begun to find its way into medical textbooks and academic psychiatry.[4] In Britain, the Society for the Study of Addiction to Alcohol and other Drugs (formed originally in 1884 as the Society for the Study and Cure of Inebriety), emphasised a medical, materialist conception of disease, despite its original aim to pursue a social medicine and public health approach. As Berridge notes, initial developments were a product of the particular state of the medical profession during a period in which physicians were, for the first time, treating 'specific' diseases with 'specific' treatments with some success. It seemed, therefore, 'only natural to extend this disease formulation to other conditions', such as homosexuality, insanity, alcoholism and drug addiction.[5] The central theme of the society was 'the crusading advocacy of a disease theory of inebriety to what was seen as an outmoded, moralistic approach' and its membership 'lay firmly in the medical sphere'.[6] In promoting alcoholism as a disease as opposed to a vice, the society lobbied to secure state legislation and a medical treatment structure.[7] A brief change of focus followed during the First World War, when concerns about efficiency during wartime prompted discussions about the control of alcohol more broadly. Pre-war discussions had been notable for not focussing on licensing laws and other 'non-medical legislative aspects of the drink question'.[8] During the inter-war period, nonetheless, these concerns receded and debates refocused on alcoholism as a racial and eugenic concern – although following the developments in psychiatry related to war neurosis in soldiers, there was limited and cautious acceptance in some circles of a psychological aspect to addiction.[9] For a number of reasons, a major shift took place in the mid-twentieth century towards a disease model of alcohol addiction, requiring medical treatment.[10] Berridge has shown that a strong biomedical emphasis developed and flourished in the post-Second World War period due to a new scientific optimism and faith in technology, which bolstered the belief in the power of clinical medicine. Simultaneously, the efficacy of psychological methods had been questioned as the process was increasingly viewed as 'tedious and long-drawn out'.[11] During the 1950s, those working within the field argued that the state should play a greater role in the provision of hospital-based treatment for alcoholism; however, there was very little funding available for alcoholism research.[12] By the 1960s, as this chapter will illustrate, concerns had prompted the development of a number of competing organisations, such as the National Council on Alcoholism, which was established in 1962, and the Medical Council of Alcoholism, which was formed in 1967.[13]

The American biostatistician and physician, Elvin Morton Jellinek (1890–1963), published his seminal piece 'Phases of Alcohol Addiction' in 1952 in which he highlighted the notion of 'loss of control' which progressed through a set of stages towards 'rock bottom'.[14] These principles were further developed by the German-born neurologist, Max Glatt (1912–2002), into a 'U shaped' chart depicting a 'slippery slope' with an upward path to recovery.[15] In the 1970s, the British psychiatrist, Griffith Edwards (1928–2012), who became an internationally renowned expert on addiction, coined the term 'alcohol dependence syndrome', which was incorporated in the World Health Organization's *International Classification of Diseases* (ICD) in 1979. Griffith outlined the dependence syndrome in an article published in the *British Medical Journal* in 1976, co-written with American psychiatrist Milton M. Gross.[16] Edward's influence on addiction studies was manifest in a prolific range of publications directed at both academic and popular readerships.[17]

The model of alcoholism eventually adopted by the NHS, and influential during the period under study, was that based on the work of Max Glatt at his therapeutic treatment unit at Warlingham Park, Middlesex during the 1950s.[18] Although there was increasing acceptance of the notion of alcoholism as a 'disease', developments in policy and treatment in Britain were nonetheless fragmented and piecemeal. While some articulated increasing concern about alcohol abuse, there was still widespread denial of the problem. The first branch of Alcoholics Anonymous (AA) was founded in London in 1948 but aroused little interest among those in the medical profession.[19] It is testimony to the disregard of the medical profession that three years later, in 1951, a consultant psychiatrist applied for funds to attend a World Health Organization conference on alcoholism to find that his application was rejected, on the grounds that 'there was no alcoholism in England and Wales'.[20] Glatt, who first came across alcoholics when working as a psychiatrist at Warlingham Park hospital, recalled that when he became interested in alcoholism during the early 1950s, he knew 'not a thing about it' and that 'nothing much was written' about it in Britain.[21] His treatment unit became a model for others that were eventually opened under the NHS and he often received foreign clinicians to his unit who came to learn about his treatment methods. Despite increasing concern about alcoholism in specialist circles, the Ministry of Health continued to deny outright that alcohol was a problem at all in England and Wales.[22]

In the scant statistical evidence that emerged in figures from in-patient units and general practice, men were significantly over-represented. However, prior to the 1970s there was no organised discussion about gender in British debates about alcoholism; it was simply noted to be less common in women. Efforts instead focused upon establishing an accurate national estimate of alcoholics and discussion centred otherwise on how best to treat the condition once diagnosed. The Rowntree Steering Group on Alcoholism, set up in 1956 under the chairmanship of W. B. Morrell from the Rowntree Trust, was particularly concerned with finding a true estimate of numbers affected by alcohol abuse, since numbers varied greatly in existing studies. Jellinek had developed a formula for estimating the percentage of alcoholics in the general population based broadly on the number of deaths from liver cirrhosis in a given year. However, Denis Parr, then a Research Fellow at the Department of Psychiatry, St. George's Hospital in London, put forward a much lower estimate based on numbers presenting in general practice.[23] Glatt was critical of Parr's research, arguing that GPs were not always likely to detect the early stages of alcoholism and he raised concerns that this lower estimate would increase the general apathy about alcohol abuse.[24] The steering group called upon the assistance of social agencies, such as health visitors and probation officers, eventually confirming that much hidden alcoholism existed in the community, thus calling into question Parr's figures.[25]

Other initiatives developed along similar lines. Griffith Edwards, inspired by alcoholism programmes he had seen in America, began discussions during the early 1960s with a group of interested individuals in the Camberwell area of London – a move that developed into the Camberwell Council on Alcoholism (CCA). This group consisted of members drawn from medicine and psychiatry, the clergy, the police, social services and the Chamber of Commerce and it worked to educate doctors and other interested parties. While Glatt's treatment unit tended to treat middle-class drinkers, the CCA was particularly concerned about the plight of 'skid row' alcoholics and habitual drunken offenders.[26] It went on to become nationally influential, in part because of the lack of other strong policy-relevant interest groups in the alcohol arena.[27] Although their objective was 'to gauge the extent of the problem and to investigate personal, social and economic factors concerned in the *causes* of alcoholism', discussion tended to be dominated instead by its 'impact upon the life of the nation', in particular the deleterious social consequences of alcoholism: crime, social disturbance and family breakdown.[28] Alcohol abuse clearly appeared to affect men in much larger numbers than women, but nonetheless, discussions rarely mentioned why this might be. Rare individual accounts from alcoholics themselves demonstrate widespread denial and reluctance to confront the problem. One former alcoholic whose contribution was published in the *Journal of Alcoholism*, for example, recalled that none of his friends, work colleagues or his employer ever took him aside and spoke seriously to him. Instead, he noted that they 'all connived in covering up . . . what now appears to be serious drinking bouts and their attendant hangovers'.[29] This man declared that the situation within which he found himself was simply 'part of the rich pageant of life as [he knew] it', and he concluded that, where alcohol was concerned, he was just 'slightly more blind in a whole kingdom of the partially sighted'.[30]

General medicine

Although researchers eventually acknowledged that much problem drinking remained unreported in the community, the official figures that existed by 1950 suggested that alcohol consumption in Britain was comparatively low.[31] This contributed to the official view from the Ministry of Health that alcohol abuse was 'not a problem'. However, as Thom has shown, a number of other factors framed the discourse on alcohol abuse. Firstly, the power of the temperance movement had waned considerably and thus policy action, when it came, focused on the medical aspects of alcoholism and not on preventative measures. Secondly, the general disarray of mental health services following the introduction of the NHS resulted in a lack of resources for alcohol treatment. Thirdly, and perhaps most importantly, the disease model of alcoholism legitimised medicine's role in treating the condition, viewing it as a 'disease of the unfortunate minority'.[32] As such, debates did not focus in any serious way on the social factors and life stressors that might have contributed to individual drinking habits, nor did they address the strong cultural forces that prevented men from discussing their problems and seeking help. Indeed, the Ministry of Health was explicitly concerned about limiting their enquiries strictly to treatment issues, since prevention would open 'very wide vistas', which were thought to be quite outside the scope of the department'.[33]

Accounts from those working in medicine certainly reflected this approach. Casualty doctors noted that cases of alcoholism usually presented at the 'emergency end of the disease', and, because patients were admitted to general hospitals, not psychiatric wards, as soon as they were 'physically well' they were discharged.[34] The emphasis on the physical nature of the condition was widely evident in accounts from hospital doctors who contributed to a series of seminars on the topic held by the CCA in 1967. One remarked, for example, that alcoholics rarely presented in 'such a mental state' that it would justify compulsory detention under Section 25 of the Mental Health Act.[35] During a subsequent seminar in 1970, the Registrar in charge of Casualty at King's College Hospital similarly described his experience of treating intoxicated patients:

> Should someone present himself as very depressed, we try and find a physical reason to account for this . . . such as an overdose of drugs . . . or some overwhelming disease – I wouldn't spend too long on it. If it's an acute problem, we treat them, but if it's not, then they have to go. Overdose is seen as a psychiatric emergency – alcoholics are not.[36]

The remaining seminar discussion focused on the physical treatments that were available such as stomach irrigation for alcohol poisoning and the use of vitamin injections. 'True' psychiatric cases, one doctor pointed out, were assured a consultation at the Maudsley Hospital; however, he cautioned that the broad remit was 'to find out what is the matter with him, to assess whether he should be chucked out or kept in'.[37] This approach was in many ways at odds with the official approach of the psychiatric profession and the classification of 'alcoholism', which was placed firmly under the heading 'Neurosis, personality disorders and other non-psychotic mental disorders', in the *International Classification of Diseases*.[38] While psychiatrists were more likely to consider that alcohol problems might be related to personality disorders and neurosis, clinicians working within general medicine, often dealing with late-stage alcohol problems as emergencies, highlighted its organic and physical effects.[39] This approach was also in marked contrast to the attitudes of alcohol experts such as Glatt who, although not underestimating the importance of personality, emphasised the 'great influence of social problems on the causation and development of alcoholism'.[40] His position was that alcoholism was both a 'symptom' and a 'disease'; 'family strife may have been caused by the drinking but [was] in itself later a cause for further drinking'.[41] Indeed, one of his methods of treatment involved patients telling their life-stories – a technique he had developed previously when working with neurosis patients.[42] Glatt also worked closely with AA and claimed his methods complemented those employed by the organisation.[43] However, despite his notable influence, the eventual development of alcohol treatment units between the early 1960s and the 1980s was slow and patchy and treatment methods were diverse.[44] Glatt noted that he faced considerable inertia and that 'many doctors and professionals [were] only too keen to avoid involvement with alcoholic patients'.[45] Although some provision was made for women, those who were referred to treatment units were predominantly male, likely to be in their forties and from the higher social classes. 'Skid row' drinkers were less likely to call upon services provided, and consultants were less likely to admit them to in-patient wards. Thom notes that this demographic remained stable until the 1980s.[46]

During the early 1970s, a small group within the CCA put forward a proposal to investigate women alcoholics. Although numbers of women were thought to be very small at a ratio with men of one to four, a review of the literature suggested that there were some specific concerns – among them the fact that within the family unit, women were usually the primary carers of children, and the fact that 'drinking at home' featured much more regularly, making it harder to detect.[47] The nature of this investigation is particularly illuminating. In many ways concerns clearly reflected long-established moralistic overtones about women and alcohol. As others have shown, in the alcohol arena the focus has historically been 'not so much on women as women, but on women as mothers, and on the notion of maternal neglect'.[48] However, the approach employed for this research on women says much about contemporary attitudes towards gender, 'ways of coping' and psychological illness. The investigative framework was notably different to that applied to the seminars, symposia and enquiries into drinking problems in men. To begin with, the group of professionals invited to contribute to discussions included sociologists and marriage guidance counsellors in addition to clinicians and members of the criminal justice system.[49] Subsequently, specific areas for research included: the role of femininity; recent changes in women's social role; the relationship between drinking and marriage; and how conditioning, upbringing and consequent life expectations might influence drinking. In many discussions, the onset of drinking was noted to be triggered by marital breakdown, in contrast to the assumption that alcoholism in men was likely to lead to divorce. Research questionnaires distributed via staff to patients at treatment centres included explicit questions such as: Why did your drinking become a problem? Do you think that being a woman makes a difference to your drinking problem? Was depression a factor in your drinking?[50] Staff working at treatment centres were asked specifically about factors that might be unique to women in patient case histories, referral patterns and treatment methods.

Contributors to the CCA's project observed that women were more likely to be labelled as 'depressive', with the alcoholism treated as a secondary disease, if it was diagnosed at all.[51] Hospital doctors and GPs were more likely to diagnose psychoneurosis to shield a woman from the stigma of alcoholism. Because of this propensity to be diagnosed as 'depressed' and not 'alcoholic', women were subsequently more likely to appear in statistics for psychiatric referral and for treatment with psychotropic drugs. The effects of menstruation, menopause and hysterectomy were explicitly noted to be factors that could influence the onset of drinking, and attention was also paid to possible problems associated with homosexuality, sexual identity and loneliness. These points of reference were in stark contrast to those that emerged in debates about male alcoholics, none of which explored what might be unique about being a 'man' in relation to drinking. Conclusions from this research indeed suggested that women reported drinking when life 'got them down' or when they were 'restless and tense', because it helped them 'forget their worries'.[52] In psychiatric settings, 'marital discord and domestic stress' were specifically observed as 'precipitating factors for hospitalisation in women', whereas alcoholism was less likely to result in a man being referred for psychiatric assessment at all.[53]

These findings were mirrored in a research paper written by a Scottish psychiatrist, A. B. Sclare, who observed that alcohol problems in women could be correlated specifically to environmental factors related to employment or domestic stress.[54] Personal testimonies from men, in contrast, suggest that they were not comfortable with reflective analysis of their feelings or their situation. One recovering male alcoholic for example recalled: 'The question I am often asked is "do you know what caused your drinking?"' to which he added, 'I am not able to isolate any particular cause or causes in myself . . . I am drawn to the conclusion that the most likely hypothesis is that I was conceived on the back of a brewer's dray.'[55] The CCA's enquiry into female alcoholics thus focused not only on dealing with the social consequences of alcohol abuse, but instead included a set of research questions that were much more likely to identify social, cultural and economic factors that prompted problem drinking.

General practice

Inevitably, some patients with alcohol problems presented in primary care. However, GPs were primarily concerned with how to diagnose the problem and deal with sickness certification and focused less upon finding out why their patients might drink in the first place.[56] Many felt that there was so much stigma surrounding alcoholism they were justified in falsifying certificates when a true diagnosis might result in patients losing their job. Glatt conceded that hospital doctors were inclined to do the same thing.[57] Correspondence from the Rowntree Trust Steering Group on Alcohol also suggests that GPs felt 'services on the NHS were so inadequate that many h[ad] decided not to waste their own time or that of their patients by attempting further use of them'.[58] GPs, reflecting on their time in practice, confirmed the general picture that alcoholic patients were usually male and that they would usually present with some kind of somatic disorder that would indicate an alcohol habit. Alternatively, their wives would make a visit to the family doctor to report the problem.[59] Griffith Edward warned GPs that the alcoholic often came into the surgery asking for something for 'bad nerves' or something for 'his stomach', concluding that abnormal drinking may in fact cause, precipitate, imitate or be secondary to every known psychiatric syndrome.[60]

There were important regional differences in the incidence of alcohol abuse, and the characteristics of presentation also varied depending on social class. Although it was eventually determined that Parr's estimate of the numbers of alcoholics nationally was much too low, his study of alcoholism in general practice nonetheless highlighted some distinct regional trends in male drinking. Overall estimates for the south west of England, for example, were relatively low. However, numbers of male alcoholics in the region were particularly high, followed closely by high numbers of male alcoholics in the north of England and the Midlands.[61] Cider drinking among west-country farm labourers resulted in significant alcohol problems that were reflected in Parr's statistics. Personal accounts from GPs who responded to his research questionnaires provided evidence that farm workers regularly drank 'a gallon a day' and this habit would often continue for the duration of their employment. Similar problems were described in the oral histories of retired physicians who had spent their careers in general practice working in Devon and Somerset. One doctor from east Devon, whose practice list consisted largely of farmers and their families, recalled that cider drinking was a 'significant problem', particularly during harvest time. He felt that it was also often related to depression but that it was very difficult to decipher which came first: the depression or the drinking.[62] Professional journals that focused specifically on alcoholism were able to identify a number of other occupations in which individuals might be vulnerable to over-drinking. Concern was directed in particular towards executive workers who drank alcohol socially as part of their role and those with jobs in the hospitality trade where alcohol was widely available. Other types of employment that allowed abuse to go undetected were also noted. Sickness absence among casual labourers, for example, might go undetected where workers could simply resume work when they had recovered from a drinking bout.[63] The incidence of alcohol abuse among fishermen had also been a long-standing concern. A retrospective study of alcoholism among Scottish fishermen between 1966 and 1970 suggested that men working in this trade were 'about six times as likely as other men to die of cirrhosis of the liver and were also more prone to peptic ulceration'.[64] It was once again not clear from reports whether or not fishermen drank due to the unique strains of a life at sea, or whether the job attracted 'unusual men' who already had an increased risk of alcoholism.[65]

For GPs dealing with alcoholism in their community, there was a clear distinction between working-class and executive 'habits'. A common theme among interviews was the working-class culture in which men were paid on a Friday, gave their wives 'housekeeping' money, but then spent the rest of their wages on alcohol over the weekend – a practice described pertinently by one GP as 'brickies on blinders'.[66] This culture may account for high numbers of men affected by alcohol abuse in the Midlands and the north of England where manufacturing industry, building and mining predominated. As another doctor recalled:

> The culture of the working-class man was, he came, he did a heavy job, which was physically demanding, he sweated a lot, lost a lot of

> fluid, and the culture was, he came home, his wife put the meal on the table, and then off he went to the pub, night after night, to put in lots of beer . . . and working men, if you look at the beer consumption, it was absolutely enormous, and it was mostly male. And the pubs were male in those days.[67]

One female GP whose patient list included men who worked for Smithfield and Billingsgate markets in the City of London, recalled that it was difficult to challenge patients about how much they were drinking because 'the norm was very high'. White men in the East End, she recalled, were 'doing it day in, day out'. But in many cases 'they held a job, for a lot of them they managed their life perfectly well, but boy, were they drinking heavily, and were they damaging their health'.[68] Others pointed out that age was a significant factor for men in socially deprived areas; many older men had serious health problems; co-morbidity and alcoholism was 'a big, big thing in east London'.[69] Alcoholism, according to one doctor, was very much associated with depressive illness and other psychiatric conditions, complicated further by the fact that older, alcoholic white men with other health conditions tended also to be non-compliant with their medication.[70]

The general consensus among doctors was that alcohol abuse among professional men was perhaps no less common, but that they 'hid it very well' until the problem deteriorated beyond a certain point.[71] Professionals and semi-professionals were more acutely concerned that their employers did not find out about their alcoholism for fear that they would ultimately lose their jobs. This presented GPs with a dilemma when faced with what diagnosis they should place on the sickness certificate. One doctor remarked:

> They would actually say 'Can you put something else down?' So I, I'd say, 'Well how about stress-related?' And they were happy to accept that. Even though if they hadn't been alcoholic they wouldn't have, they were quite happy to, I used to agree with them . . . 'make it stress-related, but you and I know that it's an alcohol problem'.[72]

David Palmer, when interviewed, agreed that the problem went 'right the way up' the social scale, but that 'the drink [was] different. They drank scotches and gins and things'. Ultimately, he added, whether the men were white- or blue-collar workers, they all drank for 'escapism'.[73] Alcoholism did not respect class, profession or lifestyle, as one other family doctor pointed out: a church-warden patient of his was once found to be behaving strangely, falling asleep in his car and at parish council meetings. They discovered he was stealing the communion wine at about the same time that his wife discovered 'a bottle of whisky in a wellington boot in the garage'. Once again, this doctor felt that the patient's alcoholism had 'probably concealed a degree of depression'.[74]

There was little doubt among GPs reflecting on their time in general practice, that the over-use of alcohol was commonly used among men as a coping mechanism.[75] As was evident in Chapter 2, there was also a general consensus among them that men tended to present with psychosomatic symptoms that were more 'acceptable' and less stigmatising. Sarah Hall, who had a particular interest in the psychological dimension of disease, noted that in her London practice alcohol presented in many ways, but that dyspepsia was one of the most common:

> So, with the dyspepsia, you know, probably, the first thing you thought of is alcohol. And, if you had really ruled that out, you know, then you began to wonder about, whether there was also a psychological element to it. But simply, the person who was always taking Monday and Tuesday off, and so wanting certification. And of course, often they would also come and say they'd got back pain. And, so, some of the back pains were actually problems with alcohol, but they didn't want to admit that, so they just turned it into back pain.[76]

Indeed, employers were warned by alcohol experts to be suspicious of repeated sickness certificates for gastritis, signs of irritability, decreased performance and poor time-keeping.[77] They were also advised to be alert to absences on Monday mornings, particularly 'if a wife phoned in', since this might indicate a weekend of heavy drinking.[78] Such concerns did not go entirely unnoticed by the media, as occasional articles were released in the press highlighting the issue of sickness absence due to alcohol. One headline in 1970 warned that 'Monday is hangover day for British industry', and claimed that 'a quarter of a million men in Britain will be off sick today, when all they have is a bad hangover'.[79] Another news item in the *Daily Express* described the problem as 'a secret illness' and as 'the complaint that nobody wants to talk about'.[80]

Not all GPs were as perceptive as Hall when it came to recognising somatic symptoms caused by alcohol abuse. As Glatt pointed out in 1960, doctors were 'not well-trained to suspect or diagnose the condition in its early phases' and in many cases 'doctors and alcoholics [did] not care a great deal for crossing each other's path'.[81] The personality of individual doctors certainly influenced their patterns of diagnosis. In a lengthy article on this topic that covered numerous research studies, H. J. Walton, a psychiatrist from the University of Edinburgh, found that a substantial proportion of both medical students and experienced GPs reacted unfavourably to patients presenting with psychosomatic disorders without serious organic disease.[82] Although most doctors fully accepted a responsibility towards such patients, those whom Walton described as 'physically-minded' as opposed to 'psychologically-minded' found alcoholic patients to be 'not acceptable' and described them as a 'clinical burden'.[83] An enquiry into GP's opinions about alcoholism also found that although an increasing number of doctors viewed the condition as an illness, 'a disturbing minority still [thought] of it in terms of moral weakness or weakness of willpower, or sin and vice'.[84] This, the author observed, was worth noting precisely because such opinions were likely to be reflected in attitudes towards, and management of alcoholic patients.[85] Concerns about the difficulties associated with understanding alcoholism and alcohol-related behaviour prompted a sociologist from the Addiction Research Unit at the Institute of Psychiatry to remind the medical profession that, although the over-use of alcohol resulted in, on the one hand a 'biochemical and physiological state', on the other hand, the function of 'noticing, recognising, responding to and treating' it should be seen within the context of both personal and societal 'beliefs' about the condition – and wider culturally held values about such issues as personal responsibility and 'appropriate' behaviour. Thus, whatever the medical basis of the condition, much of the decision-making process about diagnosis and treatment depended upon 'explicitly social considerations'.[86] Given doctors' paucity of training in psychological medicine, the lack of postgraduate training for general practice, and the broader stigma and indifference towards alcoholism, it is perhaps not surprising that men who self-medicated for emotional problems were reluctant to seek help from family doctors and were often diagnosed incorrectly when they did so.

Reflections

In an article published in the *British Journal of Addiction* in 1963, Herbert Berger, an American physician, lamented existing approaches towards alcohol abuse.[87] He had deliberately changed the title of his paper from 'The treatment of alcoholism' to 'The prevention of alcoholism', arguing that the word 'treatment' should be 'dropped' from its prominent place in discussions.[88] Berger recommended instead, a 'philosophy of alcoholism' in which 'causative factors' should be central to investigations.[89] His core argument was that alcohol was a 'secondary aetiology' – the prime cause being 'some difficulty' making it 'impossible for the patient to cope with the vicissitudes of his environment'.[90] Berger reminded the medical profession that the need for 'escape' was a normal human attribute and that humans in every culture had practised emotional release from daily frustrations. In this time and place, he noted, 'making the environment more tolerable' included drinking alcohol as medication for the relief of depression and 'as a lubricant to forget one's troubles . . . to blur one's accurate observation of stark reality'. Failing to focus on the environmental causes of alcoholism, he warned, would result simply in 'shifting addictions from one material to another'.[91] In his paper, Berger also criticised AA for its practice of leaving alcoholics to 'hit rock bottom', arguing that in no other speciality of medicine did physicians 'wait until the patient has practically succumbed to a disease before attempting to effect a cure'.[92] Berger thus broadly urged both the medical profession and AA to do more in terms of preventative medicine, concluding that 'no man is an island' and the entire community was needed to attend to the problem.[93]

Berger's comments were expressly relevant to those working in the alcohol arena in Britain. Speaking in 1963 at the annual dinner of the Society for Study of Addiction, Kenneth Robinson MP, acknowledged that there was less than good provision on all fronts in Britain compared with America and some other countries.[94] Commentators noted with regularity that approaches to alcoholism in other countries such as America, Norway and Sweden more readily provided initiatives to help alcoholics that included the use of psychiatrists, psychologists and social workers to explore the social and cultural aspects of the disease.[95] Countries where the temperance movement had previously asserted more influence, despite the divisions this caused, spoke more candidly about alcohol abuse and its problems and were more open to exploring alternative dimensions of the disease. As Selden Bacon, the Director of Alcohol Studies at Rutgers University noted, by the 1960s, the rigid structures of the temperance camp, the anti-temperance camp and the 'avoiders' (who were more opposed to the conflict than to alcohol itself) had begun to lose their power. The resulting interchange of ideas emphasised tested knowledge and an evidence-based approach. Furthermore, as Lord Soper pointed out in the House of Lords debate in 1965, Canada, Australia, New Zealand and Australia received 'a great deal of government assistance' for alcohol research, and in Scandinavian countries, where there was a state monopoly of the manufacture and sale of alcohol, a proportion of the profits were ploughed back into research and education.[96] Consequently, as the previous chapter demonstrated, industrial employers were more likely to provide programmes providing assistance to alcoholic workers. The contrast in Britain was stark: there was widespread denial among industry leaders and within the Ministry of Health, while the state benefited from large revenues from the duty on alcoholic beverages. It is notable that, in Britain during the 1970s, when concern was eventually raised about female alcoholism, research questions were constructed around a more productive framework, less focused on aspects of treatment and diagnosis, and more upon what it might be about the female role that caused women to abuse alcohol. Betsy Thom has argued that the feminist movement of the 1960s was instrumental in this respect, since it had begun to frame women's health issues in political, social and economic terms. It thus provided the ideological motivation for explanations of women's use and misuse of alcohol, emphasising the social and psychological context of drinking.[97] As this book has illustrated, the men's movement in Britain was less influential and there were no prominent initiatives actively questioning the male role and its impact on men's wellbeing.

The problem was exacerbated further by the fact that manufacturers of alcoholic beverages directly targeted men in their advertising campaigns, which promoted drinking as not only a pleasurable pastime, but also increasingly as a way to relieve stress. During the 1950s, these advertisements appeared widely in daily newspapers and also in publications directed exclusively at men, such as *Lilliput* and *Men Only*. Whisky adverts even claimed that alcohol had 'health-giving' properties: 'a White Horse toddy at bedtime', for example was supposed to 'promote warmth and glow of wellbeing' while 'disarming the threat of colds or influenza'.[98] The manufacturers of the fortified wine, Dubonnet, stated that their drink was an effective 'tranquilliser' and that 'at no time does it affect the liver', despite its alcohol by volume (ABV) content of over 14 per cent.[99] During the mid-1960s, alcohol often featured in the advertising matter in the *Journal of the College of General Practitioners*. Guinness in particular was promoted with regularity for consumption both by patients and doctors. One advert featured a cartoon of a man in sports vest and shorts, jogging – while at the same time drinking a pint of Guinness. The caption read: 'Dear Doctor, I have taken Guinness for seven days running and how much better I feel.'[100] Another, aiming directly to entice medical professionals, and picturing a cartoon of an exhausted-looking doctor, suggested that 'When you've been worked off your feet . . . Relax with a Guinness.'[101] Concerns about trends in advertising developed from the 1960s as manufacturers increasingly drew upon sexualised images to promote their products. Lord Soper condemned the alcohol adverts as 'unscrupulous', arguing that they invited young people – if they wanted to be virile – to be constantly taking in alcohol.[102] An article in *The Times* in 1979, urged the alcohol industry to be more responsible, since it had caused trouble confusing 'good' things like holidays and sport with drinking, while being mendacious about the true merits of alcohol.[103] Lemle and Mishkind noted in research published in 1989, that through the second half of the twentieth century social drinking increasingly became a primary cultural symbol of 'manliness'.[104] Heavy drinking symbolised greater masculinity than lighter drinking, and the more a man tolerated his alcohol, the more manly he was deemed.[105]

Accounts from a Mass Observation investigation into public houses and drinking confirm indeed that working-class men were inclined to drink to appear 'tough' and to fit in with their peers. The cultural association between alcohol consumption and masculinity was clearly evident in the words of one respondent who claimed: 'My reason for drinking beer is to appear tough. I heartily detest the stuff, but what would my pals think if I refused? They would call me a cissy.'[106] Another declared that he only went into the pub with his friends 'for the sake of their company'.[107] Many noted the apparent health-giving properties of alcohol, listing its 'good effect on appetite', and its 'laxative and sleep-inducing effects' as reasons for drinking. These reactions, the authors of the study noted, indeed reflected the themes promoted heavily in brewers' advertising.[108] Beer-drinking was also widely associated with increased sexual performance. One pub-drinker declared that 'if [he got] three pints down [him]', he 'was able to have sexual intercourse with the maximum of efficiency and when he woke up in the morning he was able to repeat the process with the utmost satisfaction'.[109] This Mass Observation study was primarily of working-class beer drinkers; however, the publicans who were interviewed observed that spirit drinkers tended to be businessmen, who were 'hard-pressed by work or financial matters, fall[ing] to spirits as a quick consolation to forget matters'.[110] The authors also concluded that a large amount of wine and spirits was being consumed at home by the middle class.[111]

From the accounts of physicians, the growing concerns of those working in the alcohol arena and in industry, it is clear that for men, drinking alcohol was a common means of escapism. In the workplace and during leisure activities, ideas about the degree to which it was seen as appropriate to admit to emotional difficulties discouraged men from seeking help for problems both at work and at home. On a rudimentary level, men appeared unable or unwilling to look introspectively at the cause of their problems. These issues were compounded further by the dominance of the disease theory during the 1950s and 1960s, which assumed the alcoholic to be in the minority, diverting attention away from broader consumption levels and social factors in causation.[112] During the post-war period, GPs and hospital physicians were also poorly trained in psychological medicine and, until the late 1970s, were usually male and therefore affected by the same difficulties when challenged to be reflective or emotionally expressive. Many unwittingly colluded with stereotypical views about femininity and masculinity, providing psychiatric diagnoses for women and somatic diagnoses for men. Quite often, both the male patient and the doctor were satisfied with a somatic diagnosis and looked no further.

4

Psycho-Pharmaceutical Prescriptions and Solutions

Introduction

In a lengthy and well-cited article published in the *Journal of the Royal College of General Practitioners* in 1971, Peter Parish, physician and medical sociologist at University College Swansea, stated that as a result of advances in psychopharmacology and the influences of advertising, 'large sections both of the medical profession and the general public have come to regard psychotropic drugs as a universal panacea for a wide range of social and emotional problems'.[1] The resulting cost to the NHS was considerable. As Parish pointed out, between 1965 and 1970, 47.2 million psychotropic drug prescriptions were dispensed under the National Health Service (NHS), costing a sizeable £21.5 million.[2] The soaring cost of psychotropic drugs prompted much debate in the medical press about their use and efficacy. Interest was particularly focused on prescribing patterns between individual doctors and between practices across the country – and on how doctors gained information about indications for different drugs. Additionally, there were heated debates about the efficacy of different groups of drugs. Although there was much confusion and disagreement on these topics, research articles nonetheless reflected one consistent finding: at least twice as many prescriptions for psychotropic drugs were issued to women than to men. From mid-century, on both sides of the Atlantic, scholars and clinicians have attempted to account for this difference. Some have argued that, from the 1950s there has been an epidemic of psychological illness in women. Others maintain that women are simply more likely to seek medical advice and that doctors have tended to 'code' psychological disorders as female problems.[3] The purpose of this chapter is to consider a range of complex factors that lie beneath prescribing statistics. Analysis of published research on the topic, combined with the recollections of retired doctors, suggests that there are many reasons why women were prescribed drugs more frequently and that official data on prescribing obscures a more complicated picture. Mental 'distress' in men was more common than has been previously acknowledged and was treated in different ways, often with alternative drugs and with self-medication with over-the-counter remedies.

Psychotropic drugs from the 1950s

The post-war period was central to developments in the pharmacological treatment of mental illness and much has been written about the evolution of new treatments from the 1950s. Numerous historians of psychiatry, pharmacology and mental illness have published accounts of their emergence. It is not the remit of this chapter to repeat such histories in detail; however, certain aspects of these developments deserve highlighting. During the period covered by this book, the chemotherapeutic treatment of anxiety disorders, for example, changed significantly with the shift in popularity from old-style hypnotic sedative drugs to the newer tranquillising agents during the 1960s. As has been pointed out already, during the period, depression was also more commonly identified as a condition in its own right, treated specifically with new antidepressants. This chapter will explore debates about the use of these drugs and examine prescribing patterns between doctors.

As is well known, the late 1950s were characterised by cautious optimism surrounding the discovery of the therapeutic effects of the major tranquilliser, chlorpromazine, for the treatment of serious psychosis.[4] David Healy cautions that histories of chlorpromazine have been too narrowly focused on whether or not the drug was responsible for the closure of asylums. He argues that what was equally significant was that by reducing the numbers of patients with serious symptomatic psychosis, less severe symptoms of neurosis and depression duly emerged at the forefront of psychiatric practice.[5] Indeed, chlorpromazine was followed closely by the first compound of a group of drugs that were to become known as the 'minor' tranquillisers for the treatment of anxiety disorders. Meprobamate, sold in the United States under the trademark as Miltown, and in Britain as Equanil, became the best-known drug of its kind until the discovery of chlordiazepoxide (Librium), the first of the benzodiazepine tranquillisers.[6] Diazepam, the second of the benzodiazepines, was introduced in 1963 and its trade name Valium came to be used almost generically to mean 'tranquilliser'.[7] Commentators soon suggested that the calming effects of the benzodiazepines were 'unique' and even 'remarkable', and studies showed that they were much safer in overdose than existing hypnotic sedative preparations.[8] However, concerns were soon raised about the potential for dependence and indeed, by the 1970s, it emerged that large numbers of people were addicted to benzodiazepines.[9]

Increasingly, optimism surrounded the pharmacological treatment of both endogenous and reactive depressions. A group of drugs known as the tricyclics proved promising in the treatment of classic endogenous depression, whereas 'atypical' or reactive depressions appeared to react favourably to monoamine oxidase inhibitors (MAOIs), particularly where symptoms of depression were aggravated by anxiety. In many cases, patients were prescribed both an antidepressant and a benzodiazepine. As Callahan and Berrios have noted, psychotherapeutic, or 'talking' methods of treatment for minor mental illness proved impractical in a primary care setting.[10] As the oral testimonies in this book from physicians suggest, doctors were faced with short consultation times, large lists of patients and minimal ancillary support. The pharmacological treatment of depression and anxiety therefore became entrenched during this period.

It is important to remember that, although the new drugs expanded the pharmacological options available to physicians, the use of prescribed psychoactive substances has a much longer history. Many of the older drugs, such as amphetamines and barbiturate sedatives, continued to be prescribed alongside the newer ones. Some of them were also used in combination preparations alongside other compounds for the treatment of a wide range of psychological and physical complaints ranging from appetite suppressants to treatments for gastric discomfort. By the time of Parish's seminal study of psycho-pharmaceutical prescribing published in 1971, the benzodiazepines, tricyclics and MAOIs were the drugs of choice; however, significant numbers of prescriptions for phenobarbitone and sodium amytal (barbiturates) were still being administered (see Table 4.1).

Between 1965 and 1970, the prescribing of all tranquillising drugs increased from 10.8 million prescriptions to 17.2 million. This rise was largely due to a 110 per cent increase in prescriptions for the minor tranquillisers. During this five-year period, for example, the annual prescribing of Librium increased by 1.15 million and Valium by 4.1 million. Parish noted that such a significant rise could not be accounted for by the concomitant decrease in the use of the older-style sedatives, which had declined only moderately.[11] The period also saw a considerable rise

Table 4.1 Number of prescriptions, psychotropic drugs (England and Wales – in millions)

	1965	1966	1967	1968	1969	1970
Barbiturate hypnotics	17.2	16.8	16.1	15.3	14.2	13.1
Non-barbiturate hypnotics	2.9	3.5	4.8	5.8	6.3	7.1
Tranquillisers	10.8	12.5	14.7	16.0	16.5	17.2
Stimulants/appetite suppressants	5.3	5.2	4.8	3.9	3.6	3.4
Antidepressants	3.5	3.9	4.9	5.3	5.8	6.4
Total	39.7	41.9	45.3	46.3	46.4	47.2

Source: 'The prescribing of psychotropic drugs in general practice', *Journal of the Royal College of General Practitioners*, Supplement 4 (1971), 1. Reproduced with kind permission from the Royal College of General Practitioners.

in the use of non-barbiturate hypnotics, particularly the drugs Mandrax and Mogodon that were prescribed for sedation and insomnia.[12] Antidepressant prescribing increased consistently during the five-year period; however, a pronounced rise in the use of antidepressants did not occur until later in the 1970s and into the 1980s.

From the records of forty-eight GPs examined in Parish's study, 17.1 per cent of prescriptions were for women and 8 per cent were for men.[13] For women, the trend showed a progressive increase in prescriptions up to the age of forty-five. After this age, numbers decreased until the age of seventy when they rose sharply again. Trends in prescribing to men illustrated a more steady, but moderate increase throughout their lifetime.[14] The male to female ratio remained relatively consistent between doctors and between practices (see Table 4.2), but there were inter-practice variations in the overall percentage of patients prescribed psychotropic drugs and large differences in the use of different psychotherapeutic groups.[15] Some physicians preferred to use tranquillising drugs; others opted more commonly for antidepressants. One doctor, for example, used none of the popular psychotropic drugs, and gave most of his patients 'Beplete Syrup' (a vitamin and barbiturate combination). These differences led Parish to caution that reports of overall prescribing were therefore of rather limited value.[16] Stimulants and appetite suppressants were in all cases much more frequently prescribed to women, usually for weight loss, although overall prescribing of amphetamines decreased through the period due to increasing concerns about tolerance and addiction.[17] Parish's study reflected the findings of research undertaken during the previous decade that revealed large variations in prescribing patterns between doctors. A study of prescribing

Table 4.2 Psychotropic drug therapy, sex ratios (17.1% women to 8% of males per population at risk)

Therapeutic sub-group	Number of treatments			Ratio
	Female	Male	Total	Female to male
Barbiturate hypnotics	162	71	233	2.3 to 1
Non-barbiturate hypnotics	173	96	269	1.8 to 1
Tranquillisers	907	437	1,344	2.1 to 1
Stimulants and appetite suppressants	129	19	148	6.8 to 1
Antidepressants	264	110	374	2.4 to 1
Total treatments	1,635	733	2,368	2.21 to 1
Total sample of patients	1,140	528	1,668	2.14 to 1

Source: 'The prescribing of psychotropic drugs in general practice', *Journal of the Royal College of General Practitioners*, Supplement 4 (1971), 20. Reproduced with kind permission from the Royal College of General Practitioners.

patterns in three northern towns, for instance, also illustrated that 'not only the choice of individual remedies but also the proportion of remedies in different therapeutic groups show much difference between individuals, as do the rates per thousand patients on the doctor's lists'.[18] Ultimately, such studies raised many questions about the true extent of psychiatric morbidity but provided few answers. As Parish noted at the end of his discussion, the results of his study had highlighted some interesting problems that required further research. First and foremost of these, he asked, was the question: 'Why are twice as many women as men prescribed psychotropic drugs?'[19]

Behind the data: a complex picture

There are a number of reasons why it was impossible to determine the true extent of psychiatric morbidity in the community, or draw conclusions about the gendered distribution of illness, based on prescribing data. First of all, from the 1960s, doctors were ill-prepared for the sudden increase in therapeutic preparations. Doctors entering practice in the late 1950s and early 1960s had few pharmacological choices available to them. General practitioners recalled that, until the mid-1960s, they primarily used a range of 'tonics' that were dispensed in a variety of colours and available in different strengths. Giles Walden, upon arriving at his first post in 1963, found that the three existing doctors dispensed two types of tonics – one that was dark brown, the other light brown:

'What was in it, I just don't know, but I mean that was their armament really, barbiturates and these tonics with a bit of strychnine in, you know.'[20] Among the medical profession, the term 'tonic' in this period indicated a preparation with muscle-building or 'toning' properties, often containing strychnine; however, the word was used more loosely by the public who perceived tonics to improve health more generally or to remedy some kind of 'deficiency'.[21] Christian Edwards remembered prescribing tablets he described as 'pink, blue and white aspirins', and added that 'the pink worked much better than the blue and not as good as the white, or something'.[22] Richard Stanton, who, after qualifying, fulfilled a number of locum posts, said that he would never forget what he encountered in one doctor's consulting room:

> On this guy's desk-blotter, he had written about twenty drugs around the edge, and that was his whole pharmacy. That was all he ever gave out. I asked one of the partners, 'What's this all about?' He said, 'That's all he ever uses, those twenty drugs.'[23]

A number of doctors pointed out that tonic preparations often acted as a kind of placebo and that in some respects the demand for them was patient-led. Stanton recalled:

> They might actually come in and one of the words that people used was 'Doctor, I think I need a tonic . . .' which of course was put into their minds, because doctors prescribed a tonic. 'Let's go down [to] the doctor and get a tonic, then I'll feel better'. So we responded to that. I mean that, that was the traditional approach.[24]

Giles Walden described a very similar situation:

> All they wanted was their bottle of the usual red stuff, or green stuff [laughing] – or even the blue medicine. 'That's all I want Doc' – you know. And this used to be prescribed and off they went. And to begin with there was little emphasis on trying to find out what it was for or why they needed it. I sort of found myself having to go along with this to begin with . . . but I soon began to question what it was that we were dishing out, and for me, things began to change.[25]

As new drugs for anxiety and depression were developed, the range of treatments became increasingly sophisticated and general practitioners (GPs) were largely required to do their own research into the pharmacological properties of the various groups of drugs. A quick glance at the pharmaceutical reference book, the *British National Formulary* (*BNF*), used widely by GPs, illustrates the marked increase in preparations between the early 1950s and the 1970s. The only drugs listed for psychological disorders and insomnia in the 1952 edition were categorised under the heading, 'Drugs acting on the central nervous system'. These included barbiturates, potassium bromide, amphetamines, analgesics and anaesthetics.[26] Other drugs noted to be of use in stimulating appetite, and as acting in part 'through psychological mechanisms', were listed under the heading 'Bitters and tonics'. Preparations included strychnine and iron, gentian with alkali or acid, and Nux Vomica with alkali. These mixtures have a long history of medicinal use in tonic preparations – strychnine, for example, in non-toxic doses was regarded as a stimulant and often used for respiratory and cardiac conditions.[27] By 1957, the major anti-psychotics, chlorpromazine and reserpine, were added to the list of drugs acting on the central nervous system, and in 1960, a new category of 'sedatives and tranquillisers' appeared. By 1960, there were new warnings about drug dependence and a dedicated section of the reference book entitled, 'Habit-forming drugs' (largely composed of hypnotics, sedatives and analgesics).[28] In 1963, the catalogue of entries expanded extensively to include the new benzodiazepine, Librium; the tricyclic antidepressant, imipramine; a range of MAOI antidepressants; and the minor tranquilliser, meprobamate.[29] Although a new distinct category of 'Antidepressants' appears in 1963, the broad format of the publication remained the same. The new drugs were simply listed in the front section as 'additions', with no detailed discussion about individual preparations. In less than ten years, thus, the pharmacological options available to physicians expanded considerably – yet data on their efficacy was to be hotly debated, and at times disputed, for many years to come. The *BNF* did not change its format significantly until 1974, when the publication split into two separate sections: the first, entitled 'Notes on drugs', provided detailed information and discussion about drugs under specific pharmacological classifications; the second provided a summary of preparations with specifications regarding dosage and contraindications to their use. It is notable that, by the 1974 edition, all reference to the psychological component of tonic preparations disappears altogether as the category of 'Bitters and tonics' disappears, to be replaced with the heading 'Nutrition and blood' – perhaps a discernible marker of the increasing shift towards a reductionist medical model of mental illness.

Given the considerable expansion in available treatments for psychological symptoms, general practitioners were provided with a limited range of methods for keeping abreast of new drugs. Many of them turned to pharmaceutical prescribing reference publications such as the *BNF* and the *Monthly Index of Medical Specialities*, referred to as *MIMS*. Some asked for advice from local hospital consultants in an attempt to gain specialist knowledge, and others conferred with their colleagues in primary care. GPs recalled that, during these years, the *BMJ* and the *Lancet* published very little on psycho-pharmaceuticals that might assist doctors with the day-to-day realities of prescribing.[30] At the centre of debates on sources of therapeutic information was the concern that undergraduate medical training focused primarily on the basic medical sciences and less on pharmacology. During pre-registration training and thereafter, the acquisition of knowledge in this area was primarily the responsibility of the individual doctor.[31] One research article noted specifically that the rapid advances in pharmacology had made a very large number of compounds available for medical treatment, but that there was 'no necessity for a doctor to acquaint himself with any information about these new compounds. If he does attempt to do so, where and how he does this is wholly his own decision'.[32] The study, which included a sample of prescribing over one week by a group of GPs in Liverpool, indicated that when treating serious physical disease, general practitioners were more inclined to rely on their former clinical training. This was predominantly the case for heart disease, for example, with advice from consultant cardiologists where necessary. In contrast, when presented with psychological disorders, peptic ulcer and dyspepsia, doctors were more likely to consult handbooks such as the *BNF* – and take advice from pharmaceutical representatives.[33] The study suggested that British doctors, particularly older doctors, depended on information from drug companies where advances in therapeutics had occurred since their medical training had ceased.[34] Dunnell and Cartwright's study, *Medicine Takers, Prescribers and Hoarders*, published in 1972, reflected these findings, suggesting that one of the most important sources of information about new drugs was the literature produced by drug firms. In this research, 45 per cent of doctors questioned had seen five or more drug-firm representatives in the previous four weeks and only 6 per cent had not seen any.[35]

The growing range of drugs available, the lack of training, the proliferation of advertising and the concurrent increase in prescribing, caused considerable concern and attracted criticism in the medical press. This was summarised opportunely by Derrick Dunlop, Chair of Therapeutics and Clinical Pharmacology at Edinburgh University, who noted: 'Nowadays, when we are Jove-like in the therapeutic thunderbolts we hurl – drugs potent for evil as well as for good – it is of paramount importance for us to be thoroughly conversant with the pharmacological tools of our trade.'[36] Parish, in his comprehensive study of pharmaceutical prescribing, raised specific concerns about the sources of information available to general practitioners, warning that:

> It is difficult to see how the general practitioner can have access to concise and unbiased information and how he has time to sift out objective data, which he needs if he has to make rational therapeutic decisions. Huge sums of money are spent annually to advertise drugs to prescribers, and the prescribing patterns and rates of general practitioners indicate how effective these promotional efforts are.[37]

In May 1965, the Ministry of Health set up a Committee of Enquiry into the Relationship between the Pharmaceutical Industry and the NHS, under the Chairmanship of Lord Sainsbury. In its conclusion, the committee confirmed many of the concerns articulated in the medical press, which stated that some of the sales material produced by pharmaceutical manufacturers failed to measure up to the required standards in informing doctors adequately about new (and existing) preparations.[38] Parish was critical that the claims made by manufacturers placed significant pressure on general practitioners because, with 'such a torrent of information pouring on to him, [he] can cope only by having details of a particular drug and its effects brought clearly to his notice'.[39] Ultimately, Parish maintained that responsible and appropriate prescribing could only be promoted by a system of continuous therapeutic education at undergraduate and postgraduate level.[40]

The influence of pharmaceutical advertising on doctors ultimately contributed to the eclipse of male psychological illness. Manufacturers reinforced and exploited stereotypical gender roles in their marketing material, prompting doctors to prescribe drugs from within a traditional framework that assumed women were more commonly affected by mental disorders. Additionally, drug firms produced combination preparations that were less obviously 'psychotropic' in their action because their primary agent was designed to treat an organic condition, such as peptic ulcer or appetite loss. Many of these drugs were not classed as 'psychotropic', yet they often contained psychoactive compounds – which might either sedate or stimulate.

Studies on psycho-pharmaceutical prescribing during this period were undertaken within the framework of the WHO's classification of psychotropic drugs. The operational definitions were divided into five groups: neuroleptics (major tranquillisers); anxiolytic sedatives (minor tranquillisers); antidepressants (tricyclics and MAOIs); psychostimulants (amphetamines); and psychodysleptics (hallucinogens).[41] A number of other drugs were also being investigated at this time, among them being lithium for use in what was then known as manic-depressive disorder, and methadone for use in the treatment of narcotic addiction. However, preparations for other physical conditions that combined two compounds, one of which was a psychotropic drug, were invariably excluded from the WHO classification framework and subsequently from studies on psycho-pharmaceutical prescribing trends. Parish, for example, stated clearly at the beginning of his study that, 'admixtures' in which the psychotropic drug was not the main constituent were excluded.[42] In broader studies of prescribing trends, combination drugs most usually fell under the classification 'drugs acting on the digestive system' or under the ill-defined category, 'others'.[43] The most commonly prescribed admixtures were those used to treat gastric discomfort from peptic ulcer or indigestion and were, as such, most commonly prescribed to men. They usually contained a compound to reduce stomach acid and a tranquillising agent to reduce anxiety, which, as this book has suggested was strongly associated with peptic ulcer during the period. The manufacturers Roche, for example, widely marketed a drug called Libraxin during the late 1960s and 1970s, which contained the benzodiazepine Librium and clidinium bromide, a compound that reduces stomach cramping and acid production. The company claimed that 'By reducing anxiety and aggression, and by its anticholinergic activity, Libraxin blocks reactions which increase gastric secretions and inflame gastric mucosa.' In fact, claimed Roche: 'Libraxin usefully calms both the stomach and the patient'.[44] The drug, Nactisol, produced by Beecham Laboratories, acted in a similar fashion, containing a compound for ulcer management combined with a barbiturate sedative for cases 'where anxiety complicates ulcer management'.[45] Stelabid, promoted widely during the 1960s by Smith Kline and French, claimed to 'settle the matter' in a 'wide range of gastro-intestinal disorders'. This drug contained an anti-spasmodic with an anti-psychotic compound, and the marketing material claimed that it 'exerts a beneficent calming action which effectively allays the background stress and worry that so often provoke or aggravate such conditions'.[46] Another widely promoted admixture was the drug, Durophet M, which was a sedative/

stimulant combination, used to aid the 'psychological difficulties of dietary restriction' in obesity.[47]

It is difficult to say precisely how widely GPs prescribed these drugs. The position held by editors of the *BNF* on their efficacy was definitively negative, and it is noted in the 1974–6 edition that, compared to other publications from the industry, there were fewer compound preparations discussed in the handbook. Describing them as 'a relic of the whimsical mixtures of our predecessors', the editors were of 'the austere view that such preparations pander to bad practice', and it was recommended instead that, 'each drug should be given in its optimum dosage, which is not possible in a fixed combination'.[48] The same message was reiterated in the subsequent issue (1976–8) under the section on drugs that act on the alimentary system, where the advice was unequivocally that combination drugs should be avoided.[49] This position was supported by a number of doctors during interview where the criticism laid against combination preparations was that if the patient improved following the administering of the drug, it was not possible to tell which compound had produced improvement. Christian Edwards, for example, stated that he was 'brought up on single-drug prescribing' and avoided combinations – 'tempting though it was'. His concern was about side-effects and he put forward an analogy to describe the potential problems: 'It's like riding two bicycles at the same time, you don't know which one to brake on.'[50] Another doctor recalled that the drugs were 'very heavily advertised' but that he had not prescribed them because they 'clashed' with his attitude to medicine, noting that, 'If the patient got better, you had no clue which bit of it was helping.'[51] In contrast, other doctors used them routinely and spoke favourably about the broad concept. Glen Haden maintained that the combination drugs for stomach disorders were 'very effective', and he recalled that he used to prescribe Libraxin in 'vast quantities'.[52] Rupert Espley confirmed that during his early years in practice, the convention of 'putting a little bit of sedative into things' was relatively widespread, and, laughing, he recalled one dispensing surgery where colleagues would 'put a little bit of phenobarbital in the bottle of medicine, according to the amount they felt was needed'. When asked to clarify to which medicines this might apply, Dr Espley replied, 'Oh, in a bottle of medicine for magnesium trisillicate for dyspepsia or something like that.'[53] Undoubtedly, some in the medical community frowned upon the use of combination drugs; nevertheless, the proliferation of adverts for such preparations does suggest that a considerable market existed for those who favoured the approach. As Roger Lea (a West Country GP) observed, the pharmaceutical companies collated large amounts of data on prescribing trends. He eventually refused to meet with drug representatives, because 'they would come in with a headful of data about my prescribing habits, and what I did – you know – how to make me feel good ... I reckoned they were too good at it.'[54]

Since research suggested older GPs were more likely to rely on information from drug companies, it would be reasonable to suggest that these drugs were probably prescribed in significant numbers, and most commonly to men, where anxiety featured as an aspect of some physical disorder. Yet official data on the prescribing of psychotropic drugs did not reflect the use of these preparations and continued to provide compelling evidence that women consumed significantly greater amounts of drugs in all psychotropic categories. In the late 1970s, the Canadian researcher Ruth Cooperstock, who published widely on gender and psychotropic drug use, suggested that the use of these compounds was being underestimated in data; however, little attention was paid to the topic in Britain. Cooperstock claimed that, in Canada, the use of mixed drugs had expanded throughout the 1970s 'to include all varieties of somatic disorders and their emotional sequelae'.[55] Using the drug, Stelabid, as an example, she observed that:

> In 1973, there were as many prescriptions for Stelabid, a mixed psychotropic, as for Stelazine, the pure tranquilizer. Stelabid, however, is termed an antispasmodic drug and is never identified as a psychotropic, consequently deflating the actual proportion consumed.[56]

A year later, in a sociological study of gender-role conflict and benzodiazepine use, Cooperstock maintained that male use of tranquillising agents tended to be related to conflict regarding work performance, 'or more typically, the need to contain somatic symptoms in order to perform an occupational role'. She argued that men in her study were less emotionally expressive than women, 'a consequence of which appeared to be greater emphasis on reports of somatic problems'.[57]

Self-medication

Parish's study of pharmaceutical prescribing patterns revealed that not only had the taking of prescribed medicines increased, but the use of non-prescribed or so-called 'over-the-counter' drugs had also increased dramatically. In 1968, £80 million of non-prescribed medicines were purchased.[58] He pointed out that since only one-third of illness episodes were presented to the general practitioner, it would appear that the practice of self-medication was not influenced by doctors' attitudes and concepts. Dunnell and Cartwright's extensive study of medicine-taking revealed that, of those interviewed, three-quarters of the women and three-fifths of the men had taken some self-prescribed medicine in the past two weeks.[59] The authors emphasised that higher numbers of women taking over-the-counter medicines might be accounted for by the fact that women generally took responsibility for the family shopping and were therefore the ones exposed to persuasive advertising for remedies in shops. They further cautioned that reported behaviour was not necessarily actual behaviour and evidence from the previous chapters in this book suggests that men might well have been reluctant to admit taking remedies for ailments.[60] The figures for non-prescribed medication certainly led Dunnell and Cartwright to conclude that a large 'iceberg' of illness existed in the community at any one time that was not known to the medical profession.[61]

A survey of advertising for home remedies throughout the 1950s and 1960s certainly suggests that there was a sizeable market for medicines and tonics that claimed to relieve stress, and symptoms of indigestion and other digestive disorders. Prior to the 1950s, pharmaceutical companies exploited the wartime market, both in Britain and abroad, expounding the positive effects of tonics to markets in West Africa and Burma, for treatment post-malaria and other tropical illnesses.[62] Adverts were framed within stereotypical gender roles. Sanatogen tonic, for example, was targeted at women for promoting and maintaining beauty. One advert claimed: 'The bloom of youth often leaves a woman early through fevers and the weakening influence of the climate.' Another reminded audiences that: 'A healthy youthful wife is a joy to her husband.' The makers of the tonic also claimed that it would 'banish weakness' and 'restore health' in men.[63] At home, the makers of Rennies indigestion tablets used images of military personnel in their adverts, which appeared regularly in national newspapers. They claimed that 'war-time indigestion' was caused by 'worry, suspense and hurried meals'. 'A couple of Rennies' would help 'stomach pains to stop naturally'.[64] Other adverts drew upon images of suited businessmen and the notion of acid stomach caused by stress at work. One alarming advert released in national newspapers featured a picture of a large burned carpet, accompanied by the text: 'The acid in your stomach would burn a hole in a carpet.' The notion that men should 'stand up' to their indigestion was implicit in all adverts and demonstrated in a promotional piece for Rennies, which depicted a hard-working warden, looking for 'easy instant relief', whose 'job was tough, but his indigestion was tougher'. Another image prompted men not to become 'indigestion martyrs'.[65] War workers, business executives and working class men all appeared in adverts for the same products, but could be distinguished by their dress: military uniform, suits and hard hats or flat cloth caps respectively. Women appeared occasionally in images during the war years, referring to traumatic circumstances such as air raids and appearing in images of factory work, where time pressures and unappetising meals were seen to cause a problem with digestion. However, during the war, the images were predominantly of men.

Post-war, manufacturers of tonics and indigestion remedies employed a range of strategies to engage with the male market. Arguably, the theme of defeating weakness and regaining strength was the most common way in which advertisers resonated with the beliefs and values associated with contemporary masculinity. Socialisation into the male role began early, evident in marketing images that depicted small children, such as the advert for Horlicks shown in Figure 4.1.

In this instance, the manufacturers claim explicitly that 'Little boys are made of GOOD STRONG BONES, good tough muscle, and of loving care'. A mother's loving care therefore required that she provide her sons with the correct nutrition so that they may 'build their bodies into that strength on which health and happiness depend. Setting already the wise habit of a lifetime'.

As numerous authors have noted, advertisements are one of the most important cultural factors reflecting, moulding (and remoulding) everyday life.[66] Although, from this study it is not possible to measure their influence, the motivational psychology behind such adverts is clear from archival collections of draft drawings and copy text filed in advertising agencies' guard books. Figures 4.2 and 4.3, for example, are images in the early stages of design for the product Iron Jelloids, which was a tonic preparation sold widely during the 1950s.

As Figure 4.2 suggests, this product claimed essentially to do two different things. Where a woman is pictured, the adverts suggests that Iron Jelloids might make her look 'lovelier every day', in contrast to the image of a man seen participating in a tug of war, where it is intimated that the product might make men 'feel stronger every day in every way'. For the suited gentleman who featured in the guard book image in Figure 4.3, Iron Jelloids appear to transform the man's sullen, grey complexion, from 'Weakness' to 'A1' condition, the metamorphosis duly represented by a much brighter, healthier and stronger looking appearance.

Figure 4.1 Advertisement for Horlicks, *Radio Times,* 6 December 1957
Source: Reproduced by kind permission of GlaxoSmithKline and the History of Advertising Trust Archive.

Figure 4.2 Iron Jelloids advert design, circa 1950s
Source: Reproduced by kind permission from Reckitt Benckiser and the History of Advertising Trust.

Advertisers increasingly began to draw on well-known figures and television personalities to endorse their products. The makers of Macleans indigestion tablets employed the television host, Gilbert Harding, to advertise their product in 1959. During the 1950s, Harding hosted the BBC Radio show, *I Beg to Differ*, and became infamous for his abrupt,

Figure 4.3 Iron Jelloids advert design, circa 1950s
Source: Reproduced by kind permission of Reckitt Benckiser and the History of Advertising Trust.

outspoken and sometimes rude behaviour. He went on to feature as a regular panellist on the BBC light-entertainment programme, *What's my Line?* Harding's brusque and direct approach was applied skilfully in marketing Macleans Tablets, where he appeared to be expressing his frustration with 'people who just don't bother to think for themselves' and who 'never stop complaining'. For indigestion sufferers, according to Harding, there was simply no excuse for complaining, or for 'suffering' from pain – Macleans Tablets were the obvious answer.

Harding claimed to always carry some in his pocket and suggested that 'anyone with any sense' should do the same (See Figure 4.4).[67]

Although the majority of advertisements directed at men harmonised with the theme of restoring physical strength, vitality and vigour, manufacturers increasingly indicated that men were also vulnerable to psychological stress. Drawing on contemporary scientific studies

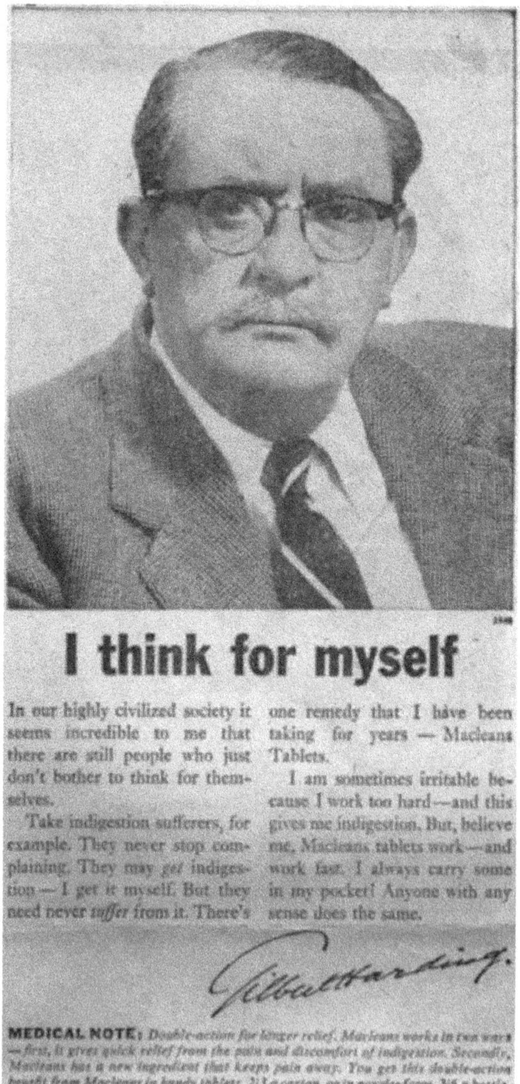

Figure 4.4 Advert for Macleans Tablets, 1959
Source: Reproduced by kind permission from GlaxoSmithKline and the History of Advertising Trust.

of stress, and on broader cultural anxieties about the negative health consequences of modern living, the makers of the tonic, Phosferine, produced numerous adverts depicting men with what they described as 'nervous exhaustion'. The testimonial featured in the advert for Phosferine in Figure 4.5 indeed states explicitly that nerve trouble, for this particular gentleman, caused him to fear train and bus journeys. The cause of 'stress' nonetheless, in this case, was located in the 'gastric nerves', causing loss of appetite and lack of sleep. This was in contrast to the claims increasingly put forward by pharmaceutical companies for prescribed psychotropic drugs, which claimed to act directly on chemicals in the brain and not the nervous system.[68]

Advertisements for over-the-counter preparations also reflected the social changes that took place from the end of the Second World War. Although most women, certainly through the 1950s and into the 1960s, still fulfilled their primary role at home as wives and mothers, men had begun to increase their engagement with family and domestic life. A series of fictional, drama-style advertisements for Horlicks mirrored the developments in gender roles, featuring men in roles as husbands and fathers. The male protagonist in these adverts would invariably be 'grumpy' and exhausted, often upsetting his wife and children. In one advert, published widely in the national press during the mid-1950s, a father is pictured rejecting a hand-made wooden gift from his son, irritated by the noise the boy had created when constructing it. Another scene depicted a policeman whose tiredness had caused him to neglect his son, resulting in delinquent behaviour. Both examples reflect the increasing social and cultural importance of the male role in the home and at the centre of the family. In all cases nonetheless, male protagonists needed prompting by their wives to seek help from the doctor, who invariably confirmed that drinking Horlicks at night might aid sleep and relaxation. Miraculous transformations to mood and manner ensued. The makers of Horlicks also utilised the charms of the well-known actor, novelist and columnist, Godfrey Winn, in a 'problem page' style advert during the late 1950s. Winn was known for his popularity with a female audience and regularly contributed to the BBC Radio show, *Housewives' Choice*. An advert for Horlicks in 1957 featured a letter from a gentleman seeking Winn's advice about insomnia. Not only was the complainant 'miserable' himself, but he confessed that he 'made the whole family the same – especially [his] wife who became a bundle of nerves and had to seek medical aid'. It is likely such letters were entirely fictitious; however, it is interesting that this scenario echoed the accounts put forward by many family doctors who maintained that women often sought medical help for stress and nerves

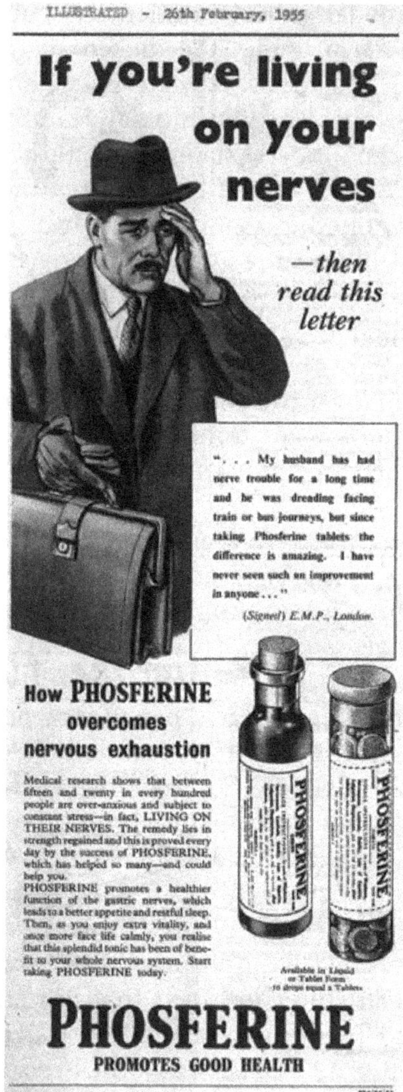

Figure 4.5 Advert for Phosferine, 1955
Source: Reproduced by kind permission from GlaxoSmithKline and the History of Advertising Trust.

caused by living with a family member with psychological problems. At the end of Winn's advice page, he cautioned against 'taking sleeping pills', reassuring readers that his 'Horlicks postbag' was full of similar cases – yet taking Horlicks would undoubtedly ensure that life would become a 'better and happier thing'.[69]

The manufacturers of indigestion remedies either drew an association with poor diet and irregular meals and dyspepsia, or, as was the case with Maclean's Tablets and Rennies, increasingly they claimed a link between worry and indigestion. In Rennies' adverts, the tagline: 'Dyspepsia – sometimes started by worry, invariably stopped by Rennies' appeared often.[70] One promotional advert released by the same company and published in the *Daily Mail* and the *Daily Express* claimed to carry a medical seal of approval and featured a cartoon image of a doctor with a stethoscope around his neck, who had ostensibly 'cured his own stomach trouble after hospital treatment failed'. Worried and overworked, dealing with a large list of patients and struck down with gastric symptoms, the 'doctor' (whose name was omitted) claimed that gastric pain, heartburn and acidity 'disappeared in a matter of seconds after taking a couple of [Rennies]'. Promoting the 'unusual medicinal qualities' of Rennies tablets, the manufacturers claimed that in addition to this doctor, 1,193 other doctors had also written to say they were prescribing the tablets for their patients as the most effective treatment.[71]

Although it is not possible to quantify with any accuracy the extent to which men were purchasing home remedies for minor ailments, the widespread and consistent advertising of such products suggests that a strong and viable market existed. Accounts from doctors certainly suggest that men were more comfortable treating minor ailments themselves than attending the doctor's surgery, and as we have seen, women played a central role in persuading men to seek medical help and in stocking the medicine cabinet as part of the weekly family shop. Over-the-counter remedies certainly afforded men the opportunity to treat conditions themselves and manufacturers often exploited the idea that they were reluctant to seek medical help. An advert for a product called Hemotabs, indicated for use in the treatment of haemorrhoids, provides a typical example. Depicting an image of a male, the makers noted that 'after years of suffering in silence', the product would bring relief.[72]

Reflections

Parish observed in his study during the early 1970s that research on the topic of psycho-pharmaceutical prescribing had been unable to produce 'any firm conclusions'. Results, he pointed out:

> . . . depend upon the size of the sample, the diagnostic classifications, the indices of morbidity, the system of sampling, the methods of recording

> data, and above all, upon the attitudes towards mental illness of the researchers and the general practitioners being investigated.[73]

Until the development of computerised records, not all doctors kept accurate records of prescribing data.[74] Studies were therefore reliant upon those who kept records and were willing to submit them for research. Such doctors were a self-selected group and we know very little about the prescribing habits of those doctors who did not keep accurate records. Reports of mental illness were also only based upon patients who attended their GPs. As Parish pointed out, these too were 'a self-selected group of persons whose attitudes and expectations may differ from those who do not attend and yet suffer from symptoms'.[75] In his report, Parish neatly summarised many of the methodological obstacles faced in previous research:

> In the past, many of these survey findings have not been corrected for age and sex differences, and the period of the surveys has varied from anywhere between one week and five years. It is also obvious that the parameters on which reports of mental disorders in general practice are based need challenging, particularly the present definitions of what is abnormal and what is normal mental health ... When does a 'person' become 'a patient'? Where is the cut-off point in deciding whether a person is 'neurotic'? ... Further, there is little doubt that the estimated extent of 'mental illness' is higher when assessed in the community than when assessed from general practitioners' consulting rooms, and this difference can only be explained by differences in attitude towards mental illness and towards general practitioners.[76]

Research published during the early 1980s began to consider some of these factors in more detail and to reflect on the influence of gender stereotyping upon prescribing. In a longitudinal study of psychotropic drug prescriptions undertaken at the General Practice Research Unit, Institute of Psychiatry in London, doctors were asked to record the complaints presented to them by patients at the initial consultation. The study found that a much greater proportion of women 'described' classical symptoms of depression, whereas a larger proportion of men complained not of depression, but of other physical symptoms – and frequently of sleep disturbance.[77] The study also revealed that more women than men received a tranquilliser for depression (in addition to, or in place of an antidepressant). The researchers were unable to explain why this might be and subsequently urged that this be explored more fully in future research.[78] Commentators began to suggest that psychotropic drugs, and tranquillisers in particular, were being prescribed to remedy symptoms caused by social and not medical problems. As Kevin Koumjian noted in the early 1980s, social problems related to family, work and other spheres of social life were increasingly being defined as medical problems – for which a medical solution could be sought.[79] Sociological, psychological and political interest focused on this topic, in part prompted by claims put forward by the feminist movement that suggested the limited opportunities afforded to women were stifling and oppressive, causing them to experience depression and anxiety.[80] Historians of medicine now debate the extent to which this was in fact the case. However, a point made less frequently was that women were certainly more at ease articulating social problems to their doctor and would seek help and advice in situations where men were more reticent. Much of the research undertaken on both sides of the Atlantic from the late 1970s suggests that women were more comfortable confiding in doctors about strains in family groups, marital difficulties and the pressures of raising children.[81] The increasing medicalisation of daily problems meant that it was therefore almost inevitable that more women would be prescribed psychotropic drugs. Research undertaken by Joanna Murray, again from the General Practice Research Institute, revealed that women on long-term drugs felt that they required medication for a wide range of daily functions, including: travelling, shopping, mixing with people and running their homes.[82] The more intensely commentators focused on women's consumption of psychotropic drugs, the less likely it was that the spotlight might shine on presentations of male distress and the reasons why men were prescribed drugs less frequently.

As the other chapters in this book have shown, there is some evidence that doctors' views about the gendered distribution of mental illness influenced consultations with their patients and subsequent prescribing habits.[83] The view that women were hormonally predisposed to psychiatric symptoms, for example, remained prevalent throughout the 1960s and 1970s – a point that featured in many of my interviews with doctors. Parish too, noted in his study, that disorders of menstruation and the menopause were common physical disorders for which psychotropic drugs were prescribed – in particular the minor tranquillisers, Librium and Valium. According to his research, one in twenty of all patients prescribed such therapy were women with these 'disorders' which included not only puerperal depression and menopausal depression, but also dysmenorrhoea in younger women and other menopausal symptoms which, it was noted, 'appeared to cause much suffering'.[84]

Published sociological research certainly began to suggest that tranquillisers were used increasingly to help individuals tolerate difficult personal circumstances. Many of these individuals were women who were living with partners who might have been displaying psychological symptoms but remained undiagnosed. Researchers pointed to cases, for example, where women were prescribed drugs to help them adapt to conflict in marriage and to intolerable behaviour by alcoholic husbands.[85] Although many women saw no alternative to pharmaceutical treatment, others expressed anger about their physicians' approach and found alternative solutions to their problems.[86] Increasingly, sex role research revealed that male patients, when they did seek medical help, tended to discuss the onset of somatic symptoms – often in relation to work stress. In such cases, psychotropic drugs alleviated incapacitating symptoms, enabling them to continue work. Consistently in research, the most common symptoms related to chest palpitations and gastric symptoms. In rare studies that included combination preparations, the drug Librax emerged as commonly prescribed to men in such situations.[87]

5

Mental Health of Doctors

Introduction

By the 1980s, two particular concerns had begun to catch the attention of those interested in mental health. The first was the realisation that medical professionals (and GPs in particular) appeared to be particularly vulnerable to mental ill health and addiction to drugs and alcohol. The second was a growing concern about the psychological health of those who had emigrated to Britain in the decades following the Second World War. They are explored here because together they are illustrative of many of the broad themes already explored in this book, and serve to advance the core arguments put forward in earlier chapters. Concerns, for example, surrounded the working practice of doctors and the provision of support should they require it. Alcohol consumption among doctors, too, heavily influenced the approaches taken towards patients who presented with possible alcohol addiction. Among ethnic minorities, discussions explored sickness absence and absenteeism, reflecting many of the debates explored in Chapter 2. Among both groups, in different ways, the ability (or otherwise) to recognise psychological illness and the willingness to report it further elucidate our knowledge of male psychological illness. Although their experiences are very different, their stories bring together much of what has been revealed thus far.

Sick doctors

In an influential article that appeared in the *British Journal of Psychiatry* in 1967, M. F. a'Brook and two colleagues, J. D. Hailstone and I. E. J. McLauchlan, undertook a study of physicians receiving in-patient care for psychiatric illness at two hospitals: St Andrew's, Northampton and Atkinson Morley's Hospital, Wimbledon. Given the potentially serious implications of psychiatric illness in medical professionals, the authors expressed their surprise at the dearth of research on the topic. Only two published studies existed on the subject, and these were American. No British research existed, as far as they could discover.[1] The authors found no statistically significant difference in levels of psychiatric disorder between the in-patient group and a control group of doctors – a finding that was to be disputed by further research in later years. The study nonetheless confirmed that there was a serious problem with drug addiction and alcoholism within the medical profession – a finding that had been causing concern for some time. The authors also acknowledged 'the difficulty in differentiating functional somatic symptoms from organic ones in a medically sophisticated patient', and suggested that doctors may well become addicted to alcohol or drugs 'either as a consequence of neurotic symptoms or as a defence against their development'.[2] Some ten years later, Robin Murray, who wrote widely about psychiatric illness in the medical profession, claimed that a'Brook's figures wildly underestimated the gravity and extent of the problem. Murray's investigation into admissions and discharges from Scottish mental hospitals and psychiatric units indicated that doctors were significantly more likely to experience depressive disorders and psychosis as well as drug dependence and alcoholism. Murray was keen to point out that his research had taken into account the size of the population from which the sample had been drawn, making his study more reliable than previous surveys.[3]

Concern about the use of alcohol and drugs among doctors can be traced to the early 1950s. Max Glatt, who featured regularly in debates about alcohol (see Chapter 3), noted that his interest in the problem had been aroused during the early 1950s when studying the contribution made by alcoholism to drunken driving. Many of those who had been admitted to his alcoholic treatment unit at Warlingham Park Hospital were doctors, and over 50 per cent of them had admitted to having been 'in trouble with the law through drunken driving'.[4] Many of those Glatt treated continued to take risks driving whilst under the influence, even after serious accidents. This situation led him to believe that repeated driving in an alcohol-impaired state was 'a common prodromal symptom in alcoholism'.[5] Glatt noted that doctors were greatly over-represented in samples taken from alcoholic populations and supported this contention by providing statistics of liver cirrhosis mortality from the Registrar General which suggested that rates of death were three-and-a half times greater among doctors than among the general population.[6] Drug addiction was also noted to be a significant problem among doctors. a'Brook observed in his study during the late 1960s that barbiturates and amphetamines were the most commonly used drugs.[7] Murray found that the rates for alcoholism and drug dependence were respectively 2.6 and 5.3 higher among doctors than the general population.[8]

On both sides of the Atlantic, suicide had long been considered a concern among members of the medical profession. An editorial in the *British Medical Journal* in 1964 pointed out that high suicide rates among doctors had been recorded since the early decades of the twentieth century. Initial interest in the US had indeed been incited by a cable dispatch from London in 1903 announcing a great increase of suicides among physicians in Great Britain.[9] Between 1949 and 1953, there were sixty-one suicides among male doctors aged between 25 and 64 in England and Wales, and another thirteen among older doctors.[10] The editorial cautioned that these figures were still on the conservative side since reports based on death certification underestimated the true extent of the problem because many cases were not declared as suicide.[11] In a letter to the *BMJ* much later in 1989, a'Brook pointed out that the incidence of suicide in the US had decreased quite significantly by the 1980s due to the development of sick doctor programmes throughout the country. By the 1980s in Britain, in contrast, the incidence of doctors committing suicide was more than three times higher than that for the general population.[12] The overwhelming consensus among researchers was that one of the principal reasons for such high rates was the availability of poisonous drugs. Almost all doctors who killed themselves used drugs and, not only did they have access to them, but also held the required toxicological knowledge.[13] A number of researchers also observed that the medical speciality was an influential feature since a disproportionate number of cases appeared to come from psychiatry.[14] GPs were also thought to be particularly vulnerable to psychiatric disorder and addiction.[15]

Etiological explanations about mental illness, addiction and suicide in doctors were broadly formulated around two opposing camps: one that identified the unique aspects of life working in medicine as the cause; the other proposing that medicine might attract those with personality traits that made them inherently vulnerable to mental illness. A number of commentators suggested that many of the personality traits which characterised a good doctor might predispose him to depression.[16] Others suggested that psychiatry as a speciality may attract more doctors themselves in need of psychiatric help.[17] Murray, for example, while not discounting environmental factors, noted that many alcoholic doctors also had personality disorders.[18] Glatt, in contrast, and in line with his general approach towards alcoholism, stressed the importance of environmental factors, suggesting that the continual excessive emotional and physical demands of medicine might prompt doctors to self-medicate with drugs and alcohol.[19] Some studies suggested that physicians were appreciably more 'anxious' and that this might be directly related to fears of inadequacy in fulfilling the professional role.[20] Others indicated that psychiatric illness in physicians was a vulnerability that existed prior to entry into university and that individuals with an obsessive personality type were attracted to medical school.[21] The age-old dichotomy between environmental and individual causes was, of course, never entirely disentangled, and increasingly, research suggested that both views should be taken into account.[22] In Britain, evidence submitted to the Goodenough Committee in 1944 raised concerns about the failure of medical schools to 'exclude men and women who, though able to pass examinations, ha[d] not the requisite aptitude, character or staying power for a medical career'. The committee agreed that there should be machinery not only to select students from this standpoint but also to weed out students who proved unsatisfactory. However, 'no one was bold enough to state the criteria of rejection, or more specifically, to say whether a propensity to some form of psychological illness should be regarded as a sign of unsuitability'.[23]

One aspect of the problem that attracted broad agreement was the acknowledgement that the shame and stigma surrounding mental illness and addiction affected doctors even more acutely than those outside the medical profession. All research suggested that doctors rarely sought help of their own accord, even when they were concerned, for example, about their own alcohol assumption. Many accounts indicated that medical colleagues would 'turn a blind eye', even if the situation was developing into a crisis.[24] One rare and brutally honest account written by Gareth Lloyd, a physician who had become an alcoholic, is worth repeating in detail since it articulately encapsulates what must have been the situation for many alcoholic doctors. He recalled:

> I began to drink alcohol for symptomatic relief and to drink earlier in the day. No one around me seemed to notice, or if they did so, nothing was said to me. Daily intake of alcohol gradually increased and with this came more symptoms, a worsening overdraft and a loss of interest in my chosen speciality. Each clinic or operating session became an increasing burden to dovetail into a demanding drinking

> pattern . . . by some miracle of effort I maintained good clinical standards and obtained an MRCOG.[25]

Lloyd eventually sought help, but alternated for many years between periods of sobriety and 'falling off the wagon'. He described the situation as 'difficult for a proud man to accept. The frustration of failure, the humiliation of despair, only increased an irrational impulse to find a way to drink safely'. In publishing his own account (and maintaining a long-term interest in alcoholic doctors and their treatment), Lloyd made a plea for greater openness and understanding, concluding that 'surely the time has come to speak more freely of the illness that dare not speak its name'.[26] Glatt echoed Lloyd's sentiments based upon his own experience treating alcoholic doctors:

> As regards alcoholism, the average doctor has not become better educated at medical school about alcoholism than the lay public, and he shares with the layman all the prevalent wrong notions, which maintain the stigma. It therefore does not dawn on the drinking doctor for a long time that he himself could possibly be an alcoholic, 'after all, he is not a psychopath, not a moral weakling, not a skid-row type' . . . He may certainly feel ashamed of his inability to keep himself under better control but he cannot let others know about his 'weakness', and so he may dose himself up with barbiturates or tranquilizers – and may well become dependent on them as well.[27]

As a'Brook noted, when it came to psychiatric symptoms, doctors occupied a privileged position in society, which enabled them to seek advice informally from their colleagues. Some chose to consult a non-psychiatric colleague rather than a psychiatrist and might avoid or refuse referral. Those who did seek psychiatric assistance were often reluctant to admit to it later or to discuss their progress. Indeed, according to a'Brook, 'many doctors with neurotic illnesses never reach[ed] the psychiatrist'.[28] Physicians also often encountered difficulties adopting the patient's role and their psychiatrists frequently '[found] it impossible to adhere to the consistent therapeutic policies that apply to other patients'.[29] The stigma of a psychiatric diagnosis was potentially very damaging to a physician's career, and as a result, some suspected a tendency among psychiatrists to diagnose 'less pathological' conditions in their medical colleagues.[30] Research from in-patient units suggested that physicians often discharged themselves early and discontinued treatment against the advice of their psychiatrists.[31] In one American investigation of the Mayo Clinic in-patient psychiatric services at Rochester Minnesota, a high number of doctors discharged themselves against medical advice, the authors noting explicitly that, 'this may be related to the difficulty the physician has in accepting his illness and his status as a patient'. They added that this situation was subsequently not without strain for hospital staff 'who must cope with their own feelings of insecurity in dealing with the physician as a patient'.[32]

Anthony Allibone, a GP from East Anglia who was chairman of the General Medical Council's Health Committee during the early 1980s, became interested in the health of doctors and explored the subject in a chapter published in the *Medical Annual* in 1983. Drawing on the only available evidence of doctors' views about their health, taken from *The Survey of the Health Care of Doctors* (1977–1979), Allibone noted that 46 per cent of doctors surveyed had at some time delayed seeking medical help when they needed it, and nearly a third said that with hindsight they had delayed longer than was prudent. Many reported that the consequences of not seeking help had had an adverse affect on their husbands or wives.[33] For over half of the respondents, the GP with whom they were registered was a personal friend and for 70 per cent of GPs, their own doctor was a colleague from the same surgery. Perhaps unsurprisingly, self-treatment was common. Although in some circumstances self-treatment was deemed by Allibone to be appropriate (in the case of treatment for a common cold, for example), a number of doctors admitted to treating their own mental illness or alcoholism, something that would be clearly contra-indicated.[34] Allibone opened his chapter with an anonymous contribution from a GP who emphasised the apparent 'conspiracy to reject illness that might reflect on professional competence'. He went on to recall a distressing incident in which a doctor near him had become alcoholic and depressed and eventually shot his wife and children while working in the health centre. The GP was dismayed that the sick doctor 'was somehow unable to communicate his distress to his colleagues'.[35] By the 1980s, such calls for awareness were by no means exceptional and other doctors wrote in to the medical press expressing alarm at the situation. A student midwife, for example, wrote to the correspondence section of the *BMJ* in 1983 complaining that she had recently witnessed one of her colleagues – a doctor – 'break down'. Although, as his friend and colleague, she had often discussed with him the stresses of the job and its consequent effects, the student articulated a great sense of guilt and shame that, even though she had recognised he was depressed, she did nothing as there was no one to whom she felt she could turn: 'Who would listen? Who would care?'[36]

Allibone, in the same correspondence section of the journal, put forward criticism of the framework underpinning the GMC's health committee and the general view that it had been bound 'hand and foot' by an inability to integrate successfully the obligation to 'care' alongside a judicial role.[37] Concerns about the ways in which sick doctors were disciplined had emerged during the Committee of Inquiry into the Regulation of the Medical Committee, under the chairmanship of the British physicist Alexander Walter Merrison, reporting in 1975. The Medical Act of 1978 which followed, although primarily concerned with the broader regulatory aspects of the medical profession and medical education, also separated disciplinary processes from those that dealt with doctors whose performance was impaired by ill health.[38] In practice, however, the health committee that was designed to protect the rights of the doctor was still entirely unsatisfactory. The system failed to cope with the alcoholic doctor and 'was more concerned with his inability to provide a service than with his fitness to practice'.[39] The GMC's submission to the Merrison Committee had revealed that at least half of the doctors appearing before the council on disciplinary charges were suffering from the effects of alcohol misuse, drug abuse or mental illness.[40] However, until the medical committee was set up in 1985, the council could take only disciplinary action against a doctor and was powerless to prevent a doctor from practising unless the issue was one of serious professional misconduct. It often showed a tendency to postpone judgement because of a reluctance to strike a mentally ill doctor off the register. The GMC thus, in part, colluded with the chronic alcoholic doctor in allowing him to continue in practice.[41] It is striking that, over thirty years later, physicians within the NHS still report high rates of psychological distress: depression, substance abuse, alcoholism and suicide, leading commentators more recently to describe a 'disturbing view' of the caring profession and the approach of the GMC as 'one of disinterest, which is temporarily discarded when disaster overtakes'.[42]

Not only was the regulatory framework of the GMC not conducive to exposing and supporting doctors with mental illness and addiction problems, but there was also an uneasy acknowledgement that students at medical school habitually drank heavily as part of an accepted culture before they qualified. Studies began to suggest that a pattern of heavy drinking often began at university and became entrenched during professional life, sometimes leading to a breakdown, on average fifteen to seventeen years into medical practice.[43] Glatt expressed explicit concern about the level of alcohol consumption at university, and, in his work on alcoholic doctors, included an anonymous contribution from one physician who recalled that he was always regarded as the odd man out in medical school because he could not down three pints in a lunch hour.[44] Robin Murray echoed these concerns and cautioned that 'an ability to hold one's liquor is said to be almost mandatory for medical students. The majority of them enjoy trying to measure up to this caricature, but for an unfortunate few, heavy drinking as undergraduates or housemen may be the prelude to later alcoholism.'[45] As Glatt pointed out, alcohol experts had for some time suggested that in nations or groups with high social acceptance of heavy drinking, even average, emotionally stable personalities may expose themselves by habitual heavy social drinking to the risk of becoming (in time) dependent on alcohol. According to Glatt, therefore, it was perhaps not surprising that doctors, who as medical students may often have come to regard occasional heavy drinking as nothing extraordinary, later in life may continue this habit.[46] A further consequence was that a culture of heavy drinking understandably blurred some physicians' appraisal of what was normal or abnormal drinking among their patients. A number of the doctors interviewed for this project confirmed that heavy drinking was an accepted part of medical school. The recollections of David Palmer were typical of many:

> There was a complication in medicine that in fact, medical schools were just awash with alcohol. And these young men drank. They were, in my generation, 85 per cent were male . . . And I have no doubt at all . . . that they were drinking, for bravado, to escape the emotional stress of what was happening to them, and it was a kind of escapism. And they drank ludicrously. And of course what happened was that doctors came out of medical school, my generation anyway, almost thinking that heavy drinking was pretty normal.[47]

Some doctors had colleagues who had succumbed to drink or drug addiction in later life. One GP remembered a friend and fellow physician who became a pethidine addict, in his view due to the stress of the job and the availability of drugs. On alcohol, he remarked, laughing, that the standard joke of the time was: 'What's the definition of an alcoholic? Somebody who drinks more than their doctor.'[48] A study of drug abuse among medical students at Glasgow University in 1971 suggested that, although the problem was small, it was more common in men and that drug use was more likely in those who drank alcohol regularly.

There were inevitably negative consequences for the wives and families of doctors afflicted by mental illness or addiction. Increasingly, commentators from within the medical profession and families themselves began to draw attention to the strain placed on family members. Echoing the findings discussed in Chapter 2 of this book about family presentations of illness, an American study in 1965 showed that it was not uncommon for doctors' wives to present with psychiatric symptoms around the time that their husbands 'broke down'.[49] Many of the participants blamed the cause of their symptoms on relationship difficulties caused by the increasing exclusion from the husband's life as he became more and more involved in his profession.[50] Many of these wives were addicted to drugs such as morphine or morphine-derivatives, prompting the author of the study to conclude that the addiction was related 'dynamically and empirically to the profession of the husbands'.[51] A review article on the subject of psychiatric illness in the medical profession covering research on both sides of the Atlantic reported that marital discord might precipitate or result from psychiatric illness in doctors. Divorce was, perhaps unsurprisingly, twenty times more common among British doctors hospitalised for psychiatric disorders.[52] Echoing the earlier American study, this overview of existing research reported that doctors' wives most usually became ill during their thirties although their illness might well have been present for six or more years. Drug and alcohol abuse were common, as were complaints about sexual relations, thoughts about suicide and somatic disturbances. Although the tone of this article indicated that the expectations and demands of the physician's role were the most likely cause of such problems, some still suggested that the personalities of husband and wife may play a part, particularly where 'a dependent histrionic woman with an intolerable need for affection and nurturing' is attracted to a physician who becomes detached, aloof and a compulsive worker.[53] In contrast, others suggested that wives and families played an important role in helping physicians face up to their problems and were often the ones to apply pressure on them to seek psychiatric help.[54] In Britain, by the 1980s, doctors' wives indeed played an important role in campaigning for less damaging working practices. The wife of a senior GP, Jill Pereira Gray, drew attention to many of the problems facing medical families and the ways in which they were vulnerable to the particular strains associated with the professional medical role. Speaking openly about the topic, she argued, would ensure that the subject of the doctor's family could move, as it rightly should, 'from the shadows to the stage'.[55] Such publicity and pressure lead Allibone to note by 1983 that, as a consequence, there was 'no doubt about changing attitudes which "may profoundly influence doctors'" expectations of medical care for themselves and their families'.[56]

Those who raised concerns about mental illness and addiction in medical professionals put forward three broad recommendations to help sick doctors and prevent them being vulnerable to it in the first place. Firstly, there was overall agreement that more emphasis should be placed at medical school on preventing habitual alcohol consumption and awareness of its dangers. Glatt, for example, argued that doctors should be specifically targeted as a 'high risk' group. Special education at undergraduate level, he suggested, would raise awareness that doctors might be vulnerable to alcoholism on two counts: the temptation of relief drinking and the acceptance of heavy drinking by those around them.[57] Raised awareness would ensure that doctors would not only be less likely to become a casualty themselves, but also '[they] would be in a position to suspect the development of alcoholism early on in [their] patient's drinking career and to arrive at an earlier diagnosis'.[58] Glatt warned that 'the outcome of the still-prevailing laissez-faire attitude to education and the early diagnosis and treatment of alcoholic doctors will be many more avoidable cases of dead doctors and perhaps dead patients'.[59] Others maintained that standards of teaching in psychiatry should be improved at both undergraduate and postgraduate level and suggested that there should be better liaison between psychiatrists and members of other branches of the profession.[60]

Recommendations for special help-groups for doctors, such as the British Doctors' Group, were also put forward. This organisation originated in 1973, when two medical practitioners who were experiencing difficulties with alcohol abuse met up to discuss their difficulties. They discovered that they were able to relate to each other's problems, some of which were unique to life in the medical profession. The group soon took on new members, including female doctors, dentists and doctors addicted to drugs. The meetings were in addition to attendance at AA.[61] Glatt spoke highly of this organisation, describing it as 'one of the most hopeful developments in this field in the country', and maintained that doctors often recovered well within appropriate therapeutic communities.[62] Other schemes eventually developed within specialisms, such as those arranged by the Society of Anaesthetists and the Royal College of Psychiatrists 'to provide rapid, confidential and informal help for the colleague suffering from mental ill health, alcoholism or drug abuse'.[63] The Norfolk Medical Care Scheme was also held as a good example of what was possible. In this scheme, developed by the Norfolk Local Medical Committee, with the support of local members of the Royal College of General Practitioners, a doctor would be identified as a 'link' between the sick doctor and the general practitioner caring for him.[64] In addition to these recommendations, some maintained that medical school admission departments should ensure that well-rounded individuals were selected, 'whose academic achievements complement rather than substitute for a stable personality'.[65]

Finally, when it came to the cause of mental illness in doctors, the ethos of the medical model and the structure of medical training did not entirely escape criticism – particularly in the US. Samuel Corson, professor of psychiatry and biophysics at Ohio State University (who later became known for his work on pet-assisted therapy), wrote an article in 1981 with his wife Elizabeth (who was his laboratory assistant) addressing aspects of social stress in medical education. Applying a biopsychosocial and systems theory approach, the Corsons expressed deep concern that 'physicians have a suicide rate twice that of the population they are trying to keep healthy'. Although fully accepting that psychological stamina was of vital importance to a medical student if they were to become a sound physician, they were critical that so little attention had been focused upon patterns of medical training that may contribute to doctors' morbidity and mortality.[66] The Corsons suggested that it was entirely possible that the highly regimented, stress-inducing methods of medical training contributed to the 'dehumanising' of doctors, driving some of them to addiction and suicide.[67] The authors cited a number of alarming personal accounts from junior doctors who described long hours, sleep deprivation and unreasonable workloads. Added to the mechanistic, dehumanised approach fostered in medical training, the Corsons argued that these factors cumulatively 'mitigate[d] against the ability to learn or to develop attitudes of compassion and caring'.[68] Medical education was thus 'based on dualistic concepts, with the physician being concerned primarily with treating the body as though human beings are inanimate objects, not subject to psychological and emotional influences'.[69] Their conclusions were unequivocal and largely accord with the oral history testimonies of GPs and the broader themes that emerged from Chapter 1 of this book. Firstly, they suggested that the prevailing reductionist medical model had a tendency to 'weed out the most sensitive, creative and humanistic physicians'. Secondly, they argued that, for those who remained in training, the medical model tended to develop a cynical, callous attitude and insensitivity to human needs and suffering. Thirdly, their view was that medical education fostered a competitive atmosphere that might not be fitting or conducive to the caring role. Finally, the authors concluded that the unintended consequences of this model might be the enhanced the risk of iatrogenic errors. They cautioned more broadly that 'the type of physician we train will have the major influence on the kind of health care we will get, including the health of those whose mission it is to provide health care'.[70]

Ethnic presentations of psychological illness

Symptoms of psychological and psychosomatic illness in immigrant communities have long been a source of interest and concern, not only for the medical profession, but also for sociologists, anthropologists, politicians and historians working on the impact of migration. A full analysis is beyond the scope of this book and there is much more important work to be done, particularly with respect to historical work. Nonetheless, where this study touched upon urban communities, the health and welfare obstacles faced by immigrants who had arrived in Britain – and the challenges presented to doctors responsible for helping them – emerged as important themes.

Immigration trends over the twentieth century are well known. Prior to the period under study, the largest migration population in Britain was the Irish. During the period between 1800 and 1914 approximately one million people crossed the Irish Sea to settle in Britain.[71] Although on a smaller scale, the Jews, eastern Europeans, and communities of people from western Europe also journeyed to Britain. Significant numbers of non-Europeans did not arrive until after the Second World War, since when large numbers have migrated from the Caribbean, South Asia, Hong Kong and Africa – while smaller numbers have moved from the Americas.[72] Immigration from the continent has also remained constant, with large numbers of people arriving from Ireland, Poland and Italy – and, in recent years, also from other eastern European states following the accession of new members to the European Union. Post-war, immigrants increasingly settled outside of the traditional communities in London, to the Midlands and other cities.[73]

Not only has immigration changed the demography and economic development of Britain, but also, as numerous commentators have noted, it has radically changed concepts of identity and 'Britishness'.[74] From the 1960s, there was increasing anxiety about the health and well-being of immigrants; however, there were few scientific investigations on the subject due to the fact that 'the study of ethnic differences in patterns of disease . . . often spilled over into political and philosophical areas, stifling objective investigation and rational discussion'.[75] Commentators writing during the 1970s noted that the topic was 'fraught with issues of political, economic and social concern, since understanding and sympathy are not too frequently shown to the migrating individual or group by the receiving society'.[76] With particular reference to mental illness, some have cautioned more recently, that 'to discuss the psychological adjustment of ethnic minorities is to underline yet again the popular conception of them as being primarily a *problem*'.[77] There were a small number of investigations undertaken during the 1930s and 1950s on migration and mental illness; however, post-war, political and cultural sensitivities largely forestalled rational discussion about the ways in which immigrant communities coped with the social and cultural pressures of settling in an unfamiliar environment.[78]

Broader international concerns about how psychiatric illness might present differently in non-western populations had become the focus of study during the mid-1950s in Canada when Eric Wittkower, who later came to work at the Tavistock Clinic in London, established a programme of 'transcultural psychiatry' at McGill University.[79] The movement that developed from the ensuing collaboration between psychiatry and anthropology sought to provide a framework for integrating knowledge in different parts of the world and to provide an institutional core within which international programmes could be harmonised.[80] Transcultural psychiatry, however, soon found itself at odds with the increasingly reductionist biomedical model promoted by psychiatry, which assumed the universality of mental illness. Psychiatry's position opposed the notion put forward by transcultural psychiatry that 'emphasised the importance of understanding disease in the terms of the patient's culture within the framework of cultural relativism'.[81] In Britain, the movement's research focused primarily on immigrants and racism within psychiatry, chiefly the notion that members of ethnic minorities were 'preferentially psychiatrised'.[82] Its stated aims were thus to 'promote the equality of mental health irrespective of race, gender or culture'; and, as recent authors have pointed out, although the term 'culture' was retained, it was primarily the impact of racism that became the focus of the organisation.[83] Indeed, the first book on the subject to be published in Britain, by Bradford psychiatrist Philip Rack, entitled *Race, Culture and Mental Disorder*, was not published until 1982.[84]

Immigration was (and is) of course a complex phenomenon. The decision to emigrate might be deliberate or involuntary – forced by conflict or economic exigency. Movement might be overseas, internationally inland or internally within one country. Researchers noted that immigrant communities experienced pressures that were usually dependent upon two factors: the cultural background of the immigrant and the socioeconomic and cultural characteristics of the community into which they arrive. With the transcultural psychiatry movement in Britain still in its infancy during the 1970s, major environmental change was the defining aspect of migration that inspired interest among the small number of existing researchers. These individuals hoped that the study of mental disorders in a migrant population would offer good opportunities to gain knowledge about the causes of mental illness more generally.[85]

In accord with broader discussions about the causes of mental illness, those who were interested in ethnic presentations and immigrant communities tended to align themselves on one side of the familiar debate about the relative influences of constitution and environment. On the one hand, statistics sometimes supported the 'negative selection' hypothesis that suggests individuals who develop mental illness might be more likely to migrate in the first place. Ødegaard's early study of Norwegian-born immigrants and native-born Americans in Minnesota, for example, found high rates of schizophrenia among Norwegian immigrants and migrants who then returned to Norway. Ødegaard explained this by suggesting a greater tendency for 'pre-schizophrenic individuals to migrate'.[86] A. G. Mezey's 1960 study of psychiatric illness and migration also suggested that personality factors played an important role in bringing about the migration of certain individuals in the first place and, therefore, 'probably underlie[d] the high incidence of schizophrenic disorders in migrants'.[87] Age also emerged as an important factor. Many studies revealed that there was an excess of adolescent and young adult schizophrenia among migrants; however, serious psychotic illness tended to appear more regularly in this age group more generally, regardless of ethnic origin. Sex and class were considered to be additional influencing factors. Among hospital admissions was a preponderance of young males, but the fact that young males seeking work were often the ones to emigrate might again explain this factor.[88] Married persons appeared to have lower hospitalisation rates than single people and rates were much greater for the lower than for the upper and middle classes.[89] Hospitalisation rates for specific ethnic groups tended to be inconclusive, although American studies noted that 'rates for Negroes [w]ere usually much higher than rates for whites'.[90] In general, authors maintained that 'the foreign-born had higher mental hospitalisation rates than native-born regardless of cultural or ethnic origin';[91] however, as this chapter will demonstrate, the way in which individuals presented with illness varied widely between different cultural groups.

The environmental stresses of migration were nonetheless also considered to be important. The way in which an individual had prepared for the change and his or her general state of health prior to migrating were seen as important factors in the development of mental illness.[92] The attitudes of those in the new community and the availability or otherwise of social support networks were also viewed as paramount. In Britain, immigrants from the New Commonwealth and Pakistan tended to settle in inner-city areas such as Tower Hamlets, Lambeth and Islington in London where the housing shortage was already acute. With the exception of those employed in the medical profession, the jobs taken by immigrants were often characterised by insecurity and low wages, and many lived in overcrowded housing with poor amenities.[93] Recent scholarship, drawn from the Community Relations Commission in 1977 and the national census of 1971, has confirmed that many immigrants experienced significant disadvantage in housing, unemployment and family life.[94] In addition to these factors, reports from the 1970s indicate that immigrants endured a range of discriminatory practices in recruitment for jobs and by private landlords.[95]

Most commentators were unable to conclude whether constitutional or environmental factors were responsible for the high rates of mental illness among immigrants and increasingly accepted that there might be a multiplicity of explanations. Existing studies were drawn from hospital in-patient data and dealt only with serious psychotic illness. Very little was known about the less severe affective disorders that remained undiagnosed in the community; however, as we shall see, oral history testimonies from GPs who worked in inner-city communities illuminate some of the problems faced by immigrant communities. Occupational health surveys also indicated distinct patterns of sickness and absenteeism between groups. Early international studies suggested that immigrant workers were absent from work more frequently than indigenous employees, but very little research existed on the subject in Britain.[96] The first significant study at home focused on a large manufacturing company in south-east England. The authors began by explicitly stating that research on mental health and race had hitherto been inhibited by political and cultural sensitivities.[97] The survey found that Asian employees had considerably more sickness absence in all categories. They had more individual spells of sickness and fewer employees in the 'no certified absence' group. On average, Asian workers had twice as many days off work as Caucasians. However, most absences were of short duration, unlike Caucasians and West Indians who were more likely to take longer spells off work.[98] The authors drew a range of inferences from the project and acknowledged that there were a number of non-cultural factors that should be taken into account – first and foremost, much of the documented absenteeism involved younger workers, and this was also a consistent finding among white employees and in other occupational health studies. Immigrant workers nonetheless often endured accommodation problems and were more prone to ill health due to poor living conditions and poverty; however, the authors noted that this would apply to other non-Asian immigrants and could not therefore explain why Asians predominated in figures for sickness absence. A number of culture-specific factors were noted. The English language, for example, was the national language among West Indians, but Asians spoke it less well. Communication problems might reasonably cause integration obstacles, stresses and strains leading to ill health and absenteeism. Drawing on previous studies on pain thresholds, the authors also suggested that cultural sensitivities towards pain and illness provided an alternative explanation for pronounced variation in sickness absence. Pain from muscular strain or arthritis – or pain with a psychological origin – was thought to be experienced differently by groups with different cultural backgrounds and might explain much of the documented sickness absence.[99]

Research on ethnic presentations of psychological illness in general practice was even more limited. Stuart Carne, a London GP working in Hammersmith, commented on the difficulties investigating such a sensitive topic, noting that the very word 'immigrant' was liable to trigger emotive reactions since it was used by some as a term of abuse.[100] Over half of the patients on Carne's list originated outside Britain and he found a range of physical complaints that were more commonly seen in those with non-British nativity. Raised blood pressure was 'a known hazard' in west African patients, while peptic ulceration appeared to be more common in West Indians.[101] Immigrant patients, particularly females, were noted to attend the doctor's surgery more frequently, but required fewer home visits. When compared to British patients, they received less prescribed medication, but were issued sickness certificates more frequently (perhaps in accordance with the findings from occupational health studies).[102] Carne scarcely mentioned psychosomatic presentations of illness, except to say that 'headaches of a non-specific type' were very common in immigrants. However, a hospital physician from Birmingham, Farrukh Hashmi, drew attention to the problems of adaptation endured by immigrants, which invariably caused aches and pains, hypochondriasis and psychosomatic diseases, or 'other signs of anxiety and neurosis'.[103] In a paper on emotions and adaptation published in 1970, Hashmi described many of the cultural presentations that were to become the focus of attention for Arthur Kleinman in his influential work on somatisation some years later. Hashmi observed that, for example, when depressed, Pakistani men often complained of sexual weakness and nocturnal emissions due to the fact that in the East, and in the Pakistani patriarchal society, the father is the dominant figure in the home and a great deal of mystique existed about manhood and sexual potency.[104] In contrast, West Indian men tended to present with physical aches and pains connected to their particular cultural construction of 'manliness', which emphasised the importance of physical strength. Hashmi cautioned that these presentations were usually related to the cultural, social and religious upbringing of the patient and that it was imperative that physicians understood the cultural influences that shaped ethnic presentations of stress and psychological breakdown.[105]

If recognising and treating complex psychological and psychosomatic symptoms in British men within the prevailing western medical model was not problematic enough, GPs working in areas populated with large numbers of immigrants were faced with considerable additional challenges. Carne noted that language difficulties created a communication barrier and that sometimes patients who appeared to be 'speaking the same language use[d] words differently'.[106] Further, he argued that patients tended to come to the doctor with preconceived ideas about what was wrong with them and what was likely to happen at the consultation. For immigrants, previous medical experiences were usually very different to those of English patients who had twenty years of experience of treatment under the NHS.[107] James Robertson, a GP who had spent his whole medical career working in the East End of London, pointed out that 'first generation' Bangladeshi female immigrants spoke poor English and rarely left the home. Often, communication would be through one of the children, typically 'a twelve year old boy, because it was the boy who came out, because you needed a male member of the family to accompany you . . . it had to be your son. So very often it was the sons translating for the mothers'.[108] In areas with high levels of poverty, Robertson explained that comorbidity was a real challenge. Mental illness and serious physical conditions such as lung disease, heart disease and diabetes often existed together and this 'made life very hard' for patients, and difficult for the doctor trying to 'separate out' the dual diagnoses.[109] On his list were large numbers of older men from Somalia, Ireland and Scotland who lived in local hostels. These men, according to Robertson, were often unmarried and socially isolated.

'Major depression' was common among them.[110] Sarah Hall, another GP who worked for many years in the East End of London, recalled that the male Bengali population was also socially isolated, with no support system. Their English was very poor and they had no advocacy interpreters. She noted that 'you wouldn't really know at all what was going on with them'.[111] Mental and physical diseases were often exacerbated by addiction to alcohol and drugs. Heroin addiction became a 'devastating' problem in the East End of London during the 1980s.[112] Compliance with medication regimes also differed between groups. Bangladeshis were in general very compliant with prescriptions and medication, whereas Afro-Caribbean patients were less keen on taking medicines or relying on traditional western medicine.[113]

Psychosomatic presentations were common in both men and women from different ethnic backgrounds; however, Sarah Hall maintained that for women there would 'be a much more rapid shift into a psychiatric domain'.[114] Both GPs with experience treating immigrant communities were of the opinion that patients who somatised were not able to express distress beyond bodily pain. Robertson maintained that if one were to ask any east London GP, they would tell you how difficult it was to manage psychological symptoms in immigrant groups because of what he described as the 'I hurt all over' syndrome.[115] As Hashmi had noted in his paper in 1970, presentations were often culturally specific. Hall suggested, for example, that a psychological diagnosis would be seen as threatening in Bengali culture because it would suggest weakness:

> If the psychological domain meant you were weak, that you might have a family weakness . . . that might be very troublesome when your daughters or sons came to get married, an alliance, you know. So any hint of weakness was really quite difficult.[116]

Hall explained that, while wishing to avoid generalisations about *all* Bengalis, most often, as patients, their favoured discourse was in the physical domain, articulated through some kind of pain – usually gastrointestinal or musculoskeletal. Often a patient would present with a long list of different pains and would be reluctant to accept a psychological diagnosis due to the stigma attached to it. According to Hall, for example, the Bengalis did not have a word for 'depression' in their culture.[117] Often, patients would be uncomfortable with the language and the concepts of western medicine. Eventually, Hall realised that it was mostly counter-productive to apply western concepts and illustrated this with an anecdote about a Bengali man who came to her surgery complaining of waking up paralysed, feeling as though he was being strangled. His concern was that somebody had put 'a jinn' on him,[118] and he had asked the imam to put some incense and amulets around the room. After some discussion, it emerged that the patient had been feeling 'low' and that his wife had left him. Hall attempted to explain that he might be experiencing a condition known in western medicine as a hypnopompic hallucination whereby a person can wake up feeling paralysed. They agreed ultimately that they both had their own 'understanding' about what was happening and the patient ended up needing no further intervention. Hall described this as an 'intercultural encounter' and stressed the importance of what she called 'culture brokers' or health advocates who can help with consultations and understand the patient's culture.[119]

In seeking to help immigrants and those with non-British backgrounds, commentators up until the 1970s had little to offer. Broad recommendations acknowledged that the British needed 'to cultivate tolerance' of immigrant groups and their cultural background.[120] It was generally accepted that housing accommodation should be improved and that local authorities should examine their allocation arrangements. Other recommendations focused on concerns about physical disease and the importance of screening immigrants for infectious diseases on arrival.[121] The notion that patients from non-western backgrounds might present with somatic or physical complaints which were viewed as more acceptable and less stigmatised was not formally articulated until Kleinman's study in 1977, and later developed by Laurence Kirmayer and others. Those from within the transcultural psychiatry movement were indeed later to maintain that: 'Somatisation represents a powerful method of coping with psychological distress. Symptoms are communications of distress, and in many cultures, depression connotes weakness, moral culpability and loss of face.'[122] Although some doctors, like Hall (who continued practising through the 1980s), developed their own skills for navigating complex presentations of disease, during the 1960s and 1970s there was little guidance or research available to aid medical professionals. When the transcultural psychiatry movement developed in Britain, its focus was primarily upon responding to racism within the profession, and not on the 'phenomenological descriptions'[123] – or 'cultural explanations' for disorders. Most doctors applied a western psychiatric framework and 'superimpose[d] those cultural categories'[124] upon their patients. The result was that many symptoms were excluded from a psychological domain and potential psychosocial causes underplayed.

Reflections

The more recent histories of these two groups suggest that many complex factors continue to obfuscate the detection, diagnosis and treatment of psychiatric disorders and addiction in doctors and ethnic minorities. The British Medical Association has provided extensive support services for medical professionals who experience mental illness or addiction and there are additional services available to help those who face a hearing with the GMC. Independent organisations, such as the Sick Doctors' Trust, exist to benefit those with addictions to drugs and alcohol. Nevertheless, the Department of Health's recent document, *Invisible Patients: Report of the Working Group on the Health of Health Professionals* (2010), indicates that a significant problem still exists. This report, which aimed to establish a framework for all healthcare organisations to build healthy workplaces, highlighted a range of ongoing problems related to the well-being of health professionals. It acknowledged that there were still higher rates of depression, anxiety and substance abuse in health professionals than in other groups of workers, noting that the work environment was often inherently more challenging and that workloads were high.[125] One study cited as evidence in the report suggested that 7 per cent of GPs used alcohol frequently 'to cope', and a further NHS Trust survey found that over 60 per cent of junior doctors exceeded the recommended safe alcohol limits. One in ten of these were drinking at hazardous levels.[126] *Invisible Patients* notes that 'suicide rates among doctors are the highest of any health professional group and are more than twice those of the general population'.[127] It is striking how much of the report mirrors the concerns put forward some fifty years ago. Existing research on mental ill health of those working in the medical profession, for instance, was described as 'of limited scope and quality', and despite a 'change in attitudes', stigma was still viewed as a 'powerful deterrent' to seeking help. Informal consulting and self-prescribing were still popular: in the words of one contributor, doctors with mental health problems 'are poorly managed and under managed, and either self-prescribing or getting [their] mate to do it in the corridor'.[128] Presenteeism was also identified as a growing problem in the NHS. The term presenteeism, coined in recent years by economists, denotes the loss of productivity caused by workers who are present at work but unwell.[129] The *Invisible Patients* report explicitly notes that: 'Presenteeism among staff with mental health problems is thought to cost 1.5 times the amount of working time lost through absenteeism,' and cautions that the fear of repercussions increases the likelihood that staff will present at work in poor health.[130] There is nonetheless evidence that some medical and dental schools have begun to formulate educational programmes that foster greater empathy and personal insight, and that in these schools, applicants are selected for personal attributes that are desirable for a caring role.[131]

Among black and minority ethnic (BME) communities, research continues to indicate that different ethnic groups have different rates and experiences of mental health problems. The British charity, Mental Health Foundation, has found that black and minority ethnic groups are more likely to be diagnosed with mental illness and more likely to be admitted to hospital. They are also more at risk of experiencing poor treatment outcomes and are prone to disengage from mainstream mental health services, leading to social exclusion and deterioration in mental health.[132] Numerous other reports suggest that BME communities are poorly served by mental health services and that individuals are reluctant to use existing services because they are not usually culturally sensitive to their needs.[133] Treatment and supportive services are often based upon inaccurate assumptions and stereotypes, such as 'aggressive black men', as policy-makers and service providers fail to understand the cultural and social circumstances of BME communities and their consequent reluctance to seek help.[134] Other surveys suggest that racism is widespread among BME people with mental illness and that many of those affected feel unable to speak out about their mental health. As a consequence, many people experience problems seeking employment, making friends and undertaking basic, everyday activities.[135] Reflecting upon the previous fifty years, it is interesting that research continues to suggest that, although many of those from BME communities with common mental disorders are very likely to have recently seen their GP, they are less likely to have been treated for their psychological problem. A study of mental health care among ethnic minorities in 2008 suggested that: 'Many GPs fail to recognise psychological symptoms in ethnic minorities,' but also that: 'Some minority groups are less likely to present their psychological problems to GPs because they do not consider them to be the most appropriate person to treat them.'[136]

6

Summary

Julian Tudor Hart, a retired GP, widely respected for his contribution to general practice and epidemiological research, recaptured his memories of 'going to the doctor' in a paper published in an edited collection in 2000. Drawing upon a lifetime of experience, he emphasised the importance of the social context of disease. Citing a British study on clinical consultations undertaken in 1975, he reminded readers that this research had indicated '85 per cent of all final diagnoses were reached by simply listening to patients' stories'.[1] Recalling over fifty years of experience of treating patients who presented with ill-defined symptoms with no detectable organic disease, he eloquently articulated much of what has been described throughout this book. Somatic labels, he noted, were often dependent on the current 'fashion'. In his lifetime, hysterical paralysis had become chronic, post-viral fatigue, while ill-defined abdominal pains were consecutively labelled 'grumbling' appendix, spastic colon and irritable bowel syndrome. When it came to psychological illness, Tudor Hart remarked stridently: 'It is hard for later generations to appreciate the hostility of almost all British GPs in the first two thirds of the [twentieth] century to any psychiatric diagnoses other than the gross institutionalised end-stage psychoses they had seen as students.'[2] Drawing on an anecdote from Arthur Watts, who wrote widely about psychological illness in his own general practice, Tudor Hart recounted a story that brutally reflected the realities of psychological illness in primary care. Watts, who described himself at the beginning of his career as having 'a complete blind spot as regards depression', once treated a male patient complaining of constipation. When physical examinations and an X-ray revealed no abnormality, he reassured the patient that there was nothing to worry about and sent him home. Watts recalled: 'He went straight home and put his head in a gas oven. Even when I heard the news, it never dawned on me that I had missed a classic case of depression; indeed, I felt rather indignant that he hadn't believed me.'[3]

Primary care training and practice has undoubtedly been transformed since this time and, since the 1970s, increasing emphasis has been place on the consultation process and the broader context of disease. *The Future General Practitioner*, a key text published in 1972, indeed stated that general practice comprised a set of 'broad goals'; one of these was to see diagnoses composed 'in physical, psychological and social terms'; another was to understand the ways in which 'interpersonal relationships within the family can cause illness or alter its presentation, course and management'. The book also stated that family doctors should be able 'to demonstrate an understanding of the relationship between health and illness on the one hand, and the social characteristics of patients on the other'.[4] The book *Language and Communication in General Practice,* edited by Bernice Tanner and published in 1976, was another important text which aimed to bridge the separation between the didactic information taught in medical school and the communication skills needed in general practice.[5] Currently, one of the central tenets of general practice postgraduate training is a patient-centred approach in which new doctors are encouraged to 'accept the subjective world of patient health beliefs, the family and cultural influences in the different aspects of intervention'.[6] Another outlined area of competence is 'holistic care', in which GPs are required to show their ability 'to understand and respect the values, culture, family structure and beliefs of [their] patients, and understand the ways in which these will affect the experience and management of illness and health'.[7] The current syllabus explicitly states that there is a requirement for new doctors to understand the concept of the bio-psychosocial model as promoted by Engel, and the notion that 'illnesses have both mental and physical components, and that there is a dynamic relationship between them' – a notion they acknowledge has led to criticisms of the purely biomedical model.[8]

Despite these changes, it is a sobering thought that the current rate of suicide in men in Britain is over three times that of women.[9] In 2012, 4,590 men and 1,391 women ended their own lives. Men are three times more likely than women to become alcohol dependent, and 73 per cent of adults who 'go missing' are men. Men are also more than twice as likely to use Class A drugs, and 79 per cent of drug-related deaths occur in men. These wider indicators therefore suggest that there is something very misleading about the commonly perceived notion that women are more likely than men to experience mental disorders.[10] The World Health Organization's paper on gender disparities in mental health states explicitly that gender stereotyping compounds difficulties with the identification and treatment of mental illness. The author notes: 'Female gender predicts being prescribed psychotropic drugs. Even when presenting with identical symptoms, women are more likely to be diagnosed as depressed than men and less likely to be diagnosed as having problems with alcohol.'[11] Gender bias, according to this document, has skewed the research agenda: 'The relationship of women's reproductive functioning to their mental health has also received protracted and intense scrutiny'.[12] The author concludes that reducing gender disparities in mental health 'involves looking beyond mental illness as a disease of the brain' and requires clinicians, researchers and policy-makers to 'socially contextualise the mental disorders affecting individuals and the risk factors associated with them'.[13] Recent research does appear to suggest that modern services might be 'inherently feminised' because of the disproportionately low number of men working in frontline mental health service provision.[14] Most services are also difficult to access outside the nine-to-five timeframe, creating a further obstacle for men who have decided to seek help.[15] We might legitimately ask, therefore, despite developments in services, medical education and in psychopharmacology, how far *have* we come since Arthur Watts and Julian Tudor Hart were practising during the 1950s and 1960s?

In no way does this book seek to blame the medical profession or its practitioners for this situation. On the contrary, it has sought to illustrate the complexities involved and to reveal the role of not only medical services, but also that of employers, wider society and individuals. Dame Carol Black's report on the health of Britain's working-age population makes for equally depressing reading. When the report was published in 2008, the economic costs of sickness absence and worklessness associated with ill-health had reached a cost of over £100 billion per year. Echoing many of the problems identified fifty years ago in Chapter 2 of this book, Black set out a number of key challenges recommended for reform. She argued that the importance of the physical and mental health of working people – in relation to personal, family and social attainment – is still 'insufficiently recognised by our society'.[16] Reflecting the sentiments of GPs discussing the issuing of sickness certification in the 1960s, the report also suggested that GPs still feel ill equipped to offer advice to patients about remaining in or returning to work. Explicitly, the report noted that 'their training has to date not prepared them for this'.[17] Additionally, and perhaps most importantly of all, Black stated that:

> Detachment of occupational health from mainstream healthcare undermines holistic patient care. A weak and declining academic base, combined with the absence of any formal accreditation procedures, a lack of good quality data and a focus solely on those in work, impedes the profession's capacity to analyse and address the full needs of the working age population.[18]

Shortly after the release of Black's report, researchers from the men's health charity, Men's Health Forum, warned that these findings had potentially serious consequences for men who spend more of their lives in the workplace and are much less likely than women to make use of almost all other forms of primary health provision. In their policy briefing paper, the authors noted that the NHS should 'begin to find ways of delivering services to men more effectively than has been the case in the past. Acting in partnership with employers to deliver health improvement services in the workplace offers a real opportunity to do this'.[19]

On an individual level, 'engaging with the emotional lives of men' in the twenty-first century appears to be no less problematic than it was fifty years ago.[20] As recent research has shown, 'gender, for males as for females, helps to shape life experience and behaviour, impacting most strikingly upon help-seeking and engagement with health services'.[21] When men do seek help, much distress is routinely unrecognised because many men 'effectively abandon psychological reflection'.[22] Research suggests that socialisation for the male role leads some men to develop fewer emotional skills, leaving them less able to identify and articulate their feelings. Alexithymia (the inability to express emotions) is increasingly considered to be an aspect of normative masculinity and 'as such poses a major barrier to men seeking therapy'.[23] There is also some evidence to suggest that alexithymia is associated with somatisaion.[24] Frustratingly, many of these observations are not new. Insights presented over thirty years ago by the men's movement in America suggested that 'men have not been socialised to be comfortable either with affective experience or with the processing of their inner experience'.[25] Consequently, 'depression for many men may be a private experience, unshared with others, that men attempt to alleviate or remove by their own efforts without external help'.[26]

The theoretical position presented in *A History of Male Psychological Illness* is that the post-war model of masculinity widely endorsed since the Victorian period has resulted in men being more likely to somatise in distress. The various chapters, thus, in many ways echo the views of Kleinmann, Kirmayer and others. The research also engages with Mechanic's concept of 'illness behaviour' and the notion that 'illness, as well as illness experience, is shaped by sociocultural and social-psychological factors, irrespective of their genetic, physiological or other biological bases'.[27] Indeed, by the 1980s, Mechanic maintained that 'few seriously doubted that the psychosomatic hypothesis was in some sense valid'.[28] It is striking that if one consults Kleinmann's original paper on somatisation, although his focus was on Chinese culture, many of his insights accord with the experiences of male distress in this book. The biomedical model of depression, argued Kleinmann, excludes a wide range of 'depressive phenomena', even in the west. By definition, therefore, physicians will 'find' what is universal, and not that which does not fit its tight boundaries.[29] Although Kleinmann applied this theory to cross-cultural research, it is also consistent with the accounts of male psychological illness put forward in this book. Medical practitioners have indeed 'found' what is universally defined by, and therefore 'seen' within the western biomedical model.[30] Much of what Kleinman observed in the Chinese study is reflected in the western cultural experience of British men from the 1950s: because male mental illness is associated with weakness and therefore stigmatised, for example, the secondary physical complaints are labelled as medical problems, while the psychological issues remain underplayed.[31] Consequently, in the west, 'empirical data on male depression are quite limited; largely because women have been the focus of concern . . . The overriding concern with female depression has obscured the fact that men are not immune to [it]'.[32]

Among psychologists, social scientists and historians, the debate continues unabated. Are women really more prone than men to mental illness? A recent publication by clinical psychologist Daniel Freeman and writer Jason Freeman claimed unequivocally that women are more vulnerable to mental health problems and that this is therefore a major public health issue. The authors set out their argument in a book entitled *The Stressed Sex: Uncovering the Truth about Men, Women and Mental Health* (2013) and in a range of articles in the psychological and national press.[33] Building their thesis from 'large-scale epidemiological surveys', they claim their conclusion is founded upon a representative sample of international populations. In England, for example, Freeman and Freeman use the Adult Psychiatry Morbidity Survey (APMS), a questionnaire sent to approximately 2,550 households randomly selected across a wide geographical and socio-economic spread.[34] However, in basing their data analysis upon surveys that rely on self-reporting, the authors at once increase the likelihood that women will feature more commonly than men in the data. As we have established, men are less likely to recognise, express or report symptoms of dysthymia and other classic psychological symptoms. Crucially, and as this book has demonstrated, any balanced analysis of gender and psychological stress must include somatoform symptoms and atypical presentations of distress. Nearly all of the surveys analysed by Freeman and Freeman deliberately excluded somatoform presentations, sleep disorders and sexual dysfunction – all common ways in which men express anguish and distress. Their article, 'The Stressed Sex?' published in *The Psychologist* in February 2014, prompted a heated response from a group of professional and academic psychologists, who argued that the unwillingness to report psychological symptoms is an 'unassailable methodological problem' when seeking to measure 'sex differences in something as emotive and self-revealing as mental health'.[35] Additionally, the group re-stated the fact that by adhering only to the ICD and DSM criteria, many of the ways in which men manifest psychological distress will be excluded.[36] Indeed, if we continue to adhere to the tightly defined markers determined by the prevailing biological model of mental illness, we will continue to draw similar conclusions from the data. The parallel statistics for male suicide, addiction, homelessness and prison sentencing must surely speak for themselves.

How then might this history of male psychological illness inform current practice and policy? After all, in most cases, historians are not medical professionals and are not usually trained in psychological medicine. These are fields in which we do not work, and do not therefore face the medical contingencies presented daily to those who apply themselves with dedication to their vocation. We should certainly be careful to avoid unmitigated criticism of the biomedical model of medicine. Pathological, biological and physiological developments have, after all, done much on a global scale to alleviate pain and sickness. By drawing on the insights put forward by those such as Engel, neither have I uncritically accepted the notion of a biopsychosocial model, for others have raised valid questions about such an approach – not least that its boundaries and methodology in practice are unclear.[37] It can never be the place of a historian to settle such debates, but we must nevertheless engage with them. The importance of history lies in its ability to contextualise health and sickness. Historical research explores the social and the cultural, as well as the medical and the psychological. We seek to view ideas about male behaviour and psychological illness within the context of their time and to illustrate how it might appear that symptoms emerge in 'new' forms and be understood differently in response to prevailing cultural and medical forces. This book has explored a range of medical, cultural, situational and organisational factors that have influenced men and their experiences of distress since the mid-twentieth century. In that sense, it makes no apology for emphasising the important role of wider sociocultural factors in disease and for endorsing a holistic, interactionist model of mental health.

There is much more yet to be done. The experiences of individual men must now be the logical next stage of enquiry if we are to expand our knowledge of male psychological illness. One challenge might be whether we confront or exploit familiar notions of stoic masculinity in order to persuade men to think about their mental health. A number of recent initiatives to promote mental wellbeing have drawn on the traditional model of masculinity by raising awareness of mental illness at sports venues, for example. Another enterprise that attracted widespread attention was the 'Men's Sheds' movement that originated in Australia and aimed to engage isolated men in communal activity through furniture restoration.[38] In so-doing, they are perhaps reinforcing and promoting the very 'masculine' ideals from which we aim to move away. However, as recent researchers have noted, behaviours and attitudes take a long time to change, and while early intervention might allow young boys to foster healthier ways of expressing emotion, the mind-set of the generations of men who are already adults might be less easy to transform.[39] History does, however, offer the opportunity to expose the ways in which men have coped with distress in the past and to explore many of the social and cultural factors that influence experience. In 1976, Bruce and Barbara Dohrenwend proposed that the debate surrounding which sex was under greater stress, and hence more prone to psychiatric disorder, might be unproductive. Accepting the broad notion that men and women might react differently under psychological stress, they suggested that we would do well to discard unidimensional concepts of psychiatric disorder and 'false questions' about whether women or men were more prone to mental illness. Instead, they recommended we ask instead: 'What is there in the endowments and experiences of men and women that pushes them in these different deviant directions?'[40] Some forty years later, current research still appears to be constrained by the biological paradigm and the somewhat unhelpful notion that one sex might be more vulnerable to mental illness than the other. It is hoped that *A History of Psychological Illness in Men* has begun to add to our knowledge by providing a historical and sociocultural framework upon which social scientists and clinicians might continue to build.

Appendix

Oral history respondents

Name	Entry into general practice	Region	Interviewed
James Robertson	Mid-1970s	East end of London (inner city)	11 September 2012
Sarah Hall	Mid-1970s	East end of London (inner city)	15 October 2012
Christian Edwards	Early 1960s	Hampshire (provincial)	30 July 2012
Graham Hadley	Late 1960s	Midlands (urban/city)	19 October 2009
Jane Russell	Late 1960s	Midlands (urban/city)	19 October 2009
Roger Lea	Late 1960s	Devon (rural)	6 October 2009
Rupert Espley	Late 1950s	Devon (rural)	5 October 2009
Glen Haden	Early 1960s	Somerset (provincial)	20 June 2011
David Palmer	Early 1960s	Devon (provincial)	26 July 2012
Julian Adams	Late 1960s	Somerset (provincial)	20 July 2011
Giles Walden	Early 1960s	Devon (rural)	23 August 2011
Jeffrey Meane	Late 1960s	Somerset (rural)	13 August 2012
John Souton	Mid-1970s	Devon (rural)	16 September 2009
Jeremy Barrington	Late 1950s	Devon (rural)	14 October 2009
Robert Manley	Early 1960s	West Midlands (provincial)	4 January 2012
Richard Stanton	Early 1970s	Devon (provincial)	8 August 2012

Pseudonyms have been used in all cases to protect the anonymity of the GPs and to safeguard the anonymity of people and places mentioned in the interviews. Among the GPs were a number of respondents who fulfilled senior professional and academic posts in addition to the role of practising GP, including a professor of general practice, a former president of the RCGP and a former associate dean of general practice. Several of the respondents came from families with a long and well-respected medical family heritage.

Notes

Introduction

1. *Mad Men*, Lionsgate Television, AMC, 2007.
2. See for example: Lynne Segal, *Slow Motion: Changing Masculinities, Changing Men* (Basingstoke, Palgrave Macmillan, third edition 2007); Susan Faludi, *Stiffed: The Betrayal of Modern Man* (New York, W. Morrow and Co., 1999); James Gilbert, *Men in the Middle: Searching for Masculinity in the 1950s* (Chicago, University of Chicago Press, 2005); Barbara Ehrenreich, *The Hearts of Men: American Dreams and the Flight from Commitment* (New York, Anchor/Doubleday, 1983); Michael Roper, *Masculinity and the British Organization Man since 1945* (Oxford, Oxford University Press, 1984); Frank Mort, *Cultures of Consumption: Masculinities and Social Space in Late Twentieth-Century Britain* (London and New York, Routledge, 1996); and Frank Mort, 'Social and symbolic fathers and sons in post-war Britain', *The Journal of British Studies* (1999), 38 (3), 353–84.
3. It is generally accepted in medical circles that women are more likely than men to be 'diagnosed' with a mental health condition. This is a point discussed recently in Daniel Freeman and Jason Freeman, *The Stressed Sex: Uncovering the Truth about Men, Women and Mental Health* (Oxford, Oxford University Press, 2013).
4. For a discussion of these debates, see Ali Haggett, *Desperate Housewives: Neuroses and the Domestic Environment 1945–1970* (London, Pickering and Chatto, 2012).
5. See 'Gender disparities in mental health', Department of Mental Health and Substance Abuse, World Health Organization (WHO), available at http://www.who.int/mental_health/media/en/242.pdf accessed on 9 August 2013. The WHO notes that there are marked differences in rates of depression between countries, suggesting the importance of macro-social factors and also that mental illness in women in the developing world is intimately related to factors such as poverty, discrimination, socio-economic disadvantage and gender-based violence. See p. 3.
6. For recent discussion, see D. Wilkins, *Untold Problems: A Review of the Essential Issues in the Mental Health of Men and Boys* (Men's Health Forum, 2009), p. 32. For historical data see C. A. H. Watts, *Depressive Disorders in the Community* (Bristol, John Wright and Sons, 1966), p. 119.
7. Wilkins, *Untold Problems*, p. 29.
8. See for example J. G. Bancroft and C. A. H. Watts, 'A survey of patients with chronic illness in a general practice', *Journal of the College of General Practitioners* (1959), 2, 338–45, statistics on 341. This subject is discussed more fully in Chapter 3 of this book.
9. A point made in Wilkins, *Untold Problems*, p. 33.
10. Royal College of General Practitioners' Archive, A CE G 12–1, Psychiatry and the general practitioner working party papers, agendas notes and reports.

11. These ideas are set out fully in Mark Micale, *Hysterical Men: The Hidden History of Male Nervous Illness* (Cambridge MA, Harvard University Press, 2008).
12. See Micale, *Hysterical Men*. See also Elaine Showalter, *The Female Malady: Women, Madness and English Culture 1830–1980* (London, Virago, 1987) and Janet Oppenheim, *Shattered Nerves: Doctors, Patients and Depression in Victorian England* (Oxford, Oxford University Press, 1991).
13. On neurasthenia, see Ruth E. Taylor, 'Death of neurasthenia and its psychological reincarnation', *British Journal of Psychiatry* (2001), 179, 550–7; Edward Shorter, *From Paralysis to Fatigue: A History of Psychosomatic Illness in the Modern Era* (New York, Free Press, 1992).
14. Gastric disorders during the Second World War are explored more thoroughly in Chapter 1 of this book. For war trauma, see Edgar Jones and Simon Wessely, *From Shell Shock to PTSD: Military Psychiatry from 1900 to the Gulf War* (Hove, Psychology Press, 2005); Fiona Reid, *Broken Men: Shell Shock Treatment and Recovery in Britain 1914–1930* (London, Bloomsbury, 2011); Ben Shephard, *A War of Nerves: Soldiers and Psychiatrists, 1914–1994* (London, Pimlico New Edition 2002); and Joanna Bourke, *Dismembering the Male: Men's Bodies, Britain and the Great War* (London, Reaktion, new edition 1999).
15. The theory of performativity is set out in Judith Butler, *Gender Trouble* (Abingdon and New York, Routledge, 1990) and developed further in Judith Butler, *Bodies that Matter* (Abingdon and New York, Routledge, 1993).
16. Philip Hodson, chief spokesperson for the British Association for Counselling and Psychotherapy, Foreword to Wilkins, *Untold Problems*, p. 11.
17. Edward Royle, 'Trends in post-war British social history', in James Obelkevich and Peter Catterall (eds), *Understanding Post-War British Society* (London, Routledge, 1994), pp. 9–18, on p. 12.
18. See Cynthia White, *The Women's Periodical Press in Britain 1946–1976: the Royal Commission on the Press* (London, HMSO, 1977); Cynthia White, *Women's Magazines 1963–1968* (London, Michael Joseph, 1970); and Brian Henry (ed.), *British Television Advertising: the First 30 Years* (London, Century Benham, 1986).
19. Paul Addison, *No Turning Back: The Peacetime Revolutions of Post-War Britain* (Oxford, Oxford University Press, 2010), p. 66.
20. For debates about the extent to which both systems were in fact 'egalitarian', see Michael Sanderson, 'Education and social mobility', in Paul Johnson (ed.), *Twentieth Century Britain: Economic, Social and Cultural Change* (Harlow, Addison Wesley Longman, 1998 edition), pp. 374–91.
21. Royle, 'Trends in post-war British social history', p. 15.
22. James Obelkevich and Peter Catterall, 'Introduction', in James Obelkevich and Peter Catterall (eds), *Understanding Post-War British Society'* (London, Routledge, 1994) pp. 1–8, on p. 1.
23. Chris Harris, 'The family in post-war Britain', in James Obelkevich and Peter Catterall (eds), *Understanding Post-War British Society* (London, Routledge, 1994) pp. 45–57, on p. 50.
24. Harris, 'The family in post-war Britain', p. 49. See Michael Young and Peter Willmott, *Family and Kinship in East London* (London, Routledge and Kegan Paul, 1957) and Elizabeth Bott, *Family and Social Networks* (London, Tavistock, 1957).
25. Raymond Firth, *Two Studies of Kinship* (London, London School of Economics, 1956) and Peter Willmott and Michael Young, *Family and Class in a London*

Suburb (London, Routledge and Kegan Paul, 1960). See also Peter Townsend, *The Family Life of Old People* (London, Routledge and Kegan Paul, 1957).

26. See J. H. Goldthorpe, D. Lockwood, F. Bechhofer and J. Platt, *The Affluent Worker: Industrial Attitudes and Behaviour* (Cambridge, Cambridge University Press, 1968a); J. H. Goldthorpe, D. Lockwood, F. Bechhofer and J. Platt, *The Affluent Worker: Political Attitudes and Behaviour* (Cambridge, Cambridge University Press, 1968b); J. H. Goldthorpe, D. Lockwood, F. Bechhofer and J. Platt, *The Affluent Worker in the Class Structure* (Cambridge, Cambridge University Press, 1969).
27. See Stephen Taylor and Sidney Chave, 'Mental health in Harlow New Town', *Journal of Psychosomatic Research* (1966), 10, 38–44 and E. H. Hare and G. K. Shaw, *Mental Health on a New Housing Estate: A Comparative Study of Health in Two Districts of Croydon* (London, Oxford University Press, 1965).
28. Mike Savage, 'Working-class identities in the 1960s: Revisiting the affluent worker study', *Sociology* (2005), 39 (5), 929–46, on 930.
29. For discussion of the feminist movement between 1945 and the 1970s, see Haggett, *Desperate Housewives*. For a discussion of youth culture, see Addison, *No Turning Back*, p. 98 and Dominic Sandbrook, *White Heat: A History of Britain in the Swinging Sixties* (London, Abacus, 2006), Chapter 6.
30. Addison, *No Turning Back*, p. 200.
31. See for example: Judith Huback, *Wives Who Went to College* (London, William Heinemann, 1957); Alva Myrdal and Viola Klein, *Women's Two Roles: Home and Work* (London, Routledge and Kegan Paul, 1956); and Viola Klein, *Britain's Married Women Workers* (London, Routledge and Kegan Paul, 1965).
32. John Sutherland, *Reading the Decades: Fifty Years of the Nation's Bestselling Books* (London, BBC, 2002), p. 14.
33. Sutherland, *Reading the Decades*, p. 33.
34. For a detailed account of representations of masculinity in British and film, see Andrew Spicer, *Typical Men: The Representation of Masculinity in Popular British Cinema* (London, I B Tauris, 2001). Spicer argues that male stereotypes can be categorised into cultural 'types' – some that arise during a particular historical moment (such as the 'angry young men') and others that are overarching archetypes (such as the 'fool' and the 'rogue' whose cultural histories are extensive). See also Stella Bruzzi, *Bringing up Daddy: Fatherhood and Masculinity in Post-War Hollywood* (London, British Film Institute, 2005).
35. See for example the work of Alistair MacLean whose male characters typify this style.
36. Sutherland, *Reading the Decades*, p. 63. See, as examples, works by Iris Murdoch, Doris Lessing, Penelope Mortimer, Maralyn French and Fay Weldon.
37. For discussion of these authors, see Haggett, *Desperate Housewives*, pp. 19–22.
38. Helen Mayer Hacker, 'The new burdens of masculinity', *Marriage and Family Living* (1957), 19, 227–33, on 227.
39. Ruth Hartley, 'Sex-role pressures in the socialisation of the child', *Psychological Reports* (1959), 5, 457–69.
40. Sidney M. Jourard, 'Some lethal aspects of the male role', in Joseph H. Pleck and Jack Sawyer (eds), *Men and Masculinity* (New Jersey, Prentice Hall, 1974), pp. 21–9, on p. 22.
41. Victor J. Seidler, *The Achilles Heel Reader: Men, Sexual Politics and Socialism* (London, Routledge, 1991), p. ix.

42. Seidler, *The Achilles Heel Reader*, p. xi.
43. For a full analysis of men's liberation groups, see Michael A. Messner, 'The limits of the male sex role: An analysis of the men's liberation and men's rights movements discourse', *Gender and Society* (1998), 12 (3), 255–76. Messner notes that the men's movement broadly split between those who emphasised 'men's rights' and were opposed to feminist claims that patriarchy benefited men at women's expense, and those who aligned themselves with feminists to confront patriarchy.
44. Jourard, 'Some lethal aspects of the male role', p. 23.
45. Anne Rogers and David Pilgrim, *A Sociology of Health and Illness* (Maidenhead, Open University Press, fourth edition, 2010), Chapter 4.
46. John A. Ryle, 'Aetiology: A plea for wider concepts and new study', *Lancet*, 11 July 1942, 29–30. See also John A. Ryle, *Changing Disciplines: Lectures on the History, Method and Motives of Social* Pathology (Oxford, Oxford University Press, 1948).
47. For example, see Stephen Taylor, 'The suburban neurosis', *Lancet*, 26 March 1938, 759–61. For a full account of Taylor's views, see Rhodri Hayward, *The Transformation of the Psyche in British Primary Care 1870–1970* (London, Bloomsbury, 2014).
48. See, for example, the work of Franz Alexander (1891–1964) and Helen Flanders Dunbar (1902–1959).
49. J. L. Halliday, *Psychosocial Medicine: A Study of the Sick Society* (London: William Heinemann, 1948). For a full account of Halliday's theories, and his use of National Insurance claims as 'psychological documents', see Hayward, *The Transformation of the Psyche*, Chapter 3.
50. Mark Jackson, *The Age of Stress, Science and the Search for Stability* (Oxford, Oxford University Press, 2013).
51. Jackson, *The Age of Stress*, p. 177.
52. Dorothy Porter, 'Introduction', to John A. Ryle, *Changing Disciplines* (New Brunswick, NJ, Transaction, 1994 edition), p. xxxi. See also Dorothy Porter, 'The decline of social medicine in Britain in the 1960s', in Dorothy Porter (ed.), *Social Medicine and Medical Sociology in the Twentieth Century* (Amsterdam, Editions Rodopi, 1997), pp. 97–119. Important developments nonetheless include research into the links between smoking and lung cancer by Richard Doll and Austin Bradford Hill, and research into coronary heart disease by J. N. Morris. See J. Pemberton, 'Origins and early history of the Society for Social Medicine in the UK and Ireland', *Journal of Epidemiology and Community Health* (2002), 54, 342–46.
53. Porter, in Ryle, *Changing Disciplines*, p. xxxi.
54. H. J. Walton, 'Effect of the doctor's personality on his style of practice', *Journal of the Royal College of General Practitioners* (1969), 17, 82, supplement 3, 6–17, on 6.
55. Walton, 'Effect of the doctor's personality', 11.
56. Jackson, *The Age of Stress*, pp. 186–7.
57. A problem discussed in C. Gordon, A. R. Emerson and D. S. Pugh, 'Patterns of sickness absence in a railway population', *British Journal of Industrial Medicine* (1959), 16, 230–43. See also Jackson, *The Age of Stress*, p. 200.
58. The lack of attention paid to the influence of social and emotional factors on health at work is examined by R. Jenkins in 'Minor psychiatric morbidity in

employed young men and women and its contribution to sickness absence', *British Journal of Industrial Medicine* (1985), 42, 147–54, on 150. For a polemic debate about the new social theory, see James Le Fanu, *The Rise and Fall of Modern Medicine* (London, Abacus, 2000 edition).

59. This debate, its history and contemporary relevance is discussed in James Colgrove, 'The McKeown thesis: A historical controversy and its enduring influence', *American Journal of Public Health* (2002), 92 (5), 725–9.
60. Colgrove, 'The McKeown thesis', 729.
61. John Ryle, quoted in the editorial 'Social pathology', *Lancet*, 29 March 1947, 413–14, on 413.
62. The origins of the broader cross-cultural movement are discussed further in chapter 5.
63. Arthur Kleinman, 'Depression, somatisation and the "new cross-cultural psychiatry"', *Social Science and Medicine* (1977), 11 (3), 3–10, on 3.
64. Kleinman, 'Depression, somatisation', 3.
65. Arthur Kleinman, *The Illness Narratives: Suffering, Healing and the Human Condition* (New York, Basic Books, 1988), p. xiii.
66. Bio-sketch, Laurence J. Kirmayer, WACP Newsletter, *World Cultural Psychiatry Research Review* (2006), 2 (3), 54–5.
67. Laurence J. Kirmayer, 'Culture, affect and somatisation', *Transcultural Psychiatry* (1984), 21, 159–88, on 160. Kirmayer has been a prominent figure in advancing the notion of transcultural psychiatry in recent years by identifying, for example, the culture-biology interaction, i.e. the ways in which culturally determined behaviour refashions human biology. See Laurence J. Kirmayer, 'Beyond the "new cross-cultural psychiatry": Cultural biology, discursive psychology and the ironies of globalisation', *Transcultural Psychiatry* (2006), 43, 126–44.
68. Kirmayer, 'Culture, affect and somatisation', 161.
69. A point made by Elisabeth Hsu in Elisabeth Hsu, '"Holism" and the medicalisation of emotion: The case of anger in Chinese medicine', in Peregrine Horden and Elisabeth Hsu (eds), *The Body in Balance: Humoral Medicines in Practice* (New York and Oxford, Berghan, 2013), pp. 197–217, on 200.
70. John F. Kihlstrom and Lucy Canter Kihlstrom, 'Somatisation as illness behaviour', *Advances in Mind-Body Medicine* (2001), 17, 240–3, on 243.
71. Kihlstrom and Kihlstrom, 'Somatisation as illness behaviour', 243.
72. George L. Engel, 'The need for a new medical model: A challenge for biomedicine', *Science* (1977), 196, 129–36, on 133.
73. S. Nassir Ghaemi, 'The biopsychosocial model in psychiatry: a critique', *Existenz* (2011), 6 (1), 1–8, on 3.
74. Ghaemi, 'The biopsychosocial model in psychiatry', 4.
75. The basic argument put forward in N. McLaren, 'A critical review of the biopsychosocial model', *Australian and New Zealand Journal of Psychiatry* (1998), 32, 86–92.
76. Suman Fernando, *Mental Health, Race and Culture* (Basingstoke, Palgrave Macmillan, 2010 edition), p. 42. My emphasis.
77. Fernando, *Mental Health*, p. 42.
78. Hacker, 'New burdens of masculinity', p. 227.
79. Hacker, 'New burdens of masculinity', p. 227.
80. John Tosh, *Manliness and Masculinities in Nineteenth-Century Britain* (Harlow, Pearson Longman, 2005), p. 2.

81. Tosh, *Manliness and Masculinities*, p. 3.
82. Joan Scott, 'Gender: A useful category of historical analysis', in Joan Scott (ed.), *Feminism and History* (Oxford, 1996), pp. 152–80. Originally published in *The American Historical Review*, 91 (1986), 1053–75.
83. Joan Scott, *Gender and the Politics of History* (New York, Columbia University, 1999), p. 6.
84. See Stephen Whitehead, 'Masculinity: Shutting out the nasty bits', *Gender, Work and Organization* (2000), 7 (2), 133–7. See also John Tosh, 'What should historians do with masculinity? Reflections on nineteenth-century Britain', *History Workshop Journal* (1994), 38, 179–202.
85. See Maria Lohan, 'Developing a critical men's health debate in academic scholarship', in Brendan Gough and Steve Robertson (eds), *Men, Masculinities and Health: Critical Perspectives* (Basingstoke, Palgrave Macmillan, 2010), pp. 11–29, on p. 12.
86. R. W. Connell and James W. Messerschmidt, 'Hegemonic masculinity: Rethinking the concept', *Gender and Society* (2005), 19, 829–59, on 832.
87. Connell and Messerschmidt, 'Hegemonic masculinity', 833.
88. Margaret Wetherell and Nigel Edley, 'Negotiating hegemonic masculinity: Imaginary positions and psycho-discursive practices', *Feminism and Psychology* (1999), 9 (3), 335–56, on 336.
89. Wetherell and Edley, 'Negotiating hegemonic masculinity', 336.
90. Steve Robertson and Robert Williams, 'The importance of retaining a focus on masculinities in future studies on men and health', in Giles Tremblay and François-Olivier Bernard (eds), *Future Perspectives for Intervention, Policy and Research on Men and Masculinities: An International Forum* (Harriman TN, Men's Studies Press, 2012), pp. 119–33, on pp. 121, 123. See also J. Hearne, 'Is masculinity dead?: A critique of the concept of masculinity/masculinities', in M. Mac an Ghaill (ed.), *Understanding Masculinities* (Buckingham, Open University Press, 1996) and K. Clatterbaugh, *Contemporary Perspectives on Masculinity: Men, Women and Politics in Modern Society* (Oxford, Westview, 2nd edition 1997).
91. Robertson and Williams, 'The importance of retaining a focus on masculinities', p. 125.
92. Micale, *Hysterical Men*, p. 57.
93. John Tosh, *Manliness and Masculinities*, pp. 1–2.
94. Michael Roper, 'Slipping out of view: Subjectivity and emotion in gender history', *History Workshop Journal*, 59 (2005), 57–72, on 62.
95. Karen Harvey and Alexandra Shepard, 'What have historians done with masculinity? Reflections on five centuries of British History, 1500–1950', *Journal of British Studies*, (2005), 44, 274–80, on 277.
96. Roper and Tosh, cited in Roper, 'Slipping out of view', 57.
97. Roper, 'Slipping out of view', 69.
98. For discussion about the use of psychoanalytical theory in history, see Ludmilla Jordanova, *History in Practice* (London, Arnold, 2000), pp. 56, 57.
99. Steve Robertson and Robert Williams, 'Men, public health and health promotion: Towards a critically structural and embodied understanding', in Brendan Gough and Steve Robertson (eds), *Men, Masculinities and Health: Critical Perspectives* (Basingstoke, Palgrave Macmillan, 2009), pp. 48–66, on p. 59.

100. For the history of psychiatric services in Britain, see K. Jones, *A History of the Mental Health Services* (London, Routledge and Kegan Paul, 1972); Andy Bell and Peter Lindley, *Beyond the Water Towers: The Unfinished Revolution in Mental Health Services 1985–2005* (London, The Sainsbury Centre for Mental Health, 2005); and Helen Gilburt and Edward Peck, *Service Transformation: Lessons from Mental Health* (London, The King's Fund, 2014).
101. Indeed, recent research suggests that black and minority communities may be at higher risk of poor mental health and that their experience of mental health services is more likely to be negative; a controversial topic discussed in Wilkins, *Untold Problems*, p. 34.
102. Micale, *Hysterical Men*, pp. 282, 281.
103. Robertson and Williams in 'Men, public health and health promotion', p. 54.
104. A point made recently by Robertson and Williams in 'Men, public health and health promotion', p. 61; and by Micale speaking of earlier times in *Hysterical Men*, p. 281.
105. GPs were recruited from a range of sources, including the alumni department of Birmingham Medical School and from contacts at the Royal College of General Practitioners. Letters were also sent out inviting response from surgeries in the author's locality. An appendix is provided with details of respondents. All interviews are fully anonymised to protect the identity of the respondents, their colleagues and patients.

1 Psychological Illness and General Practice

1. Michael Shepherd, Michael Fisher, Lilli Stein and W. I. N. Kessel, 'Psychiatric morbidity in an urban group practice', *Proceedings of the Royal Society of Medicine* (1959), 52, 269–74, on 265.
2. Greg Wilkinson, 'The General Practice Research Unit at the Institute of Psychiatry', *Psychological Medicine* (1989), 19, 787–90, on 787.
3. David Hannay, 'Undergraduate medical education and general practice', in Irvine Loudon, John Horder and Charles Webster (eds), *General Practice under the National Health Service 1948–1997* (Oxford, Oxford University Press, 1998) pp. 165–81, on p. 167.
4. John Howe, 'Research in general practice: Perspectives and themes', in Irvine Loudon, John Horder and Charles Webster (eds), *General Practice Under the National Health Service 1948–1997* (Oxford, Oxford University Press, 1998), pp. 146–64 on p. 147.
5. Elianne Riska, 'The rise and fall of Type A man', *Social Science and Medicine* (2000), 51, 1665–74, on 1665.
6. Allan V. Horwitz, 'How an age of anxiety became an age of depression', *The Milbank Quarterly* (2010), 88 (1), 112–38, on 120.
7. Horwitz, 'How an age of anxiety', 119.
8. Horwitz, 'How an age of anxiety', 130. See also David Healy, *The Antidepressant Era* (Cambridge, MA, Harvard University Press, 1997) and David Healy, *Let Them Eat Prozac: The Unhealthy Relationship between the Pharmaceutical Industry and Depression* (New York, New York University Press, 2004). See also Christopher Callahan and German E. Berrios, *Reinventing Depression: A History of the*

Treatment of Depression in Primary Care 1940–2004 (Oxford, Oxford University Press, 2005). For an account of anxiety in the preceding period, see Andrea Tone, *The Age of Anxiety: A History of America's Turbulent Affair with Tranquilizers* (New York, Basic Books, 2009).

9. Horwitz, 'How an age of anxiety', 126.
10. See the *International Classification of Diseases and Related Health Problems*, Revision 9 (WHO, 1979), codes 296.2–296.4 and 300–1. Controversy still surrounds the differences between the current DSM V and the ICD-10 (currently under revision). Not only do diagnostic criteria differ between the two, but there is also disagreement about the values and disadvantages of the 'prototype' matching approach favoured by the ICD and the operational or 'defining features', approach favoured by DSM. See Mario Maj, 'Psychiatric diagnosis: Pros and cons of prototypes vs. operational criteria', *World Psychiatry* (2011), 10, 81–2 and Michael First, 'Harmonisation of ICD-11 and DSM – V: Opportunities and challenges', *British Journal of Psychiatry* (2009), 195, 382–90.
11. Mark Jackson, *The Age of Stress: Science and the Search for Stability* (Oxford, Oxford University Press, 2013), p. 141. See also Tone's *Age of Anxiety*. Tone describes the new chapter in what W. H. Auden had declared the 'Age of Anxiety', in which post-war America became 'suffused with atomic anxiety', pp. 93–4. The age of anxiety and the emergence of the concept of 'stress' is also discussed at length in Rhodri Hayward, *The Transformation of the Psyche in British Primary Care 1880–1970* (London, Bloomsbury, 2014), Chapter 3.
12. Jackson, *The Age of Stress*, p. 146.
13. See Jackson, *The Age of Stress*, p. 160. For Alexander and Dunbar, see H. Weiner, 'The concept of psychosomatic medicine', in E. R. Wallace IV and J. Gack (eds), *History of Psychiatry and Medical Psychology* (New York, Springer, 2008), pp. 485–516.
14. Eileen Janes Yeo, 'The social survey in social perspective', in Martin Bulmer, Kevin Bales and Kathryn Kish Sklar (eds), *The Social Survey in Historical Perspective 1880–1940* (Cambridge, Cambridge University Press, 2011), pp. 49–65, on p. 49.
15. Brian Harrison, 'Rowntree, (Benjamin) Seebohm (1871–1954)', *Oxford Dictionary of National Biography*, Oxford University Press, 2004; online edn, January 2008 http://0-www.oxforddnb.com.lib.exeter.ac.uk/view/article/35856, accessed 12 October 2014.
16. Seebohm Rowntree, *Poverty: A Study of Town Life* (London, Macmillan and Co, 1908 edition), pp. vii–viii.
17. W. P. D. Logan and Eileen M. Brooke, *The Survey of Sickness 1943–1952: Studies on Medical and Population Subjects No. 12* (London, HMSO, 1957), p. 11.
18. Logan and Brooke, *The Survey of Sickness*, p. 11.
19. Logan and Brooke, *The Survey of Sickness*, p. 22.
20. Logan and Brooke, *The Survey of Sickness*, pp. 22, 26.
21. Logan and Brooke, *The Survey of Sickness*, p. 26. For comparable studies in the USA, see Callahan and Berrios, *Reinventing Depression*, pp. 30–1.
22. Logan and Brooke, *The Survey of Sickness*, pp. 52, 54.
23. Michael Shepherd, *Psychiatric Illness in General Practice* (Oxford, Oxford University Press, 1981 Second Edition), p. 11.

24. W. P. D. Logan and A. A. Cushion, *General Register Office Studies on Medical and Population Subjects, No. 14, Morbidity Statistics from General Practice, Volume 1* (London, HMSO, 1958), p. 34.
25. Logan and Cushion, *Morbidity Statistics from General Practice, Volume 1*, p. 38.
26. E. R. Bransby, 'The extent of mental illness in England and Wales', *Health Trends* (1974), 6, 56–9, on 57.
27. A. Ryle, 'The neuroses in a general practice population', *Journal of the College of General Practitioners* (1960), 3, 313–28, on 315. See also R. E. Perth, 'Psychosomatic problems in general practice', *Journal of the College of General Practitioners, Research Newsletter* (1957), 4, 295–331. Perth suggested that 40 per cent of the population were at risk.
28. Ryle, 'The extent of mental illness', 313.
29. The shift from asylum-based care to community treatment has been well documented. See, for example, Andrew Scull *Decarceration; Community Treatment and the Deviant – a Radical View* (Cambridge, Polity 1994); Edward Shorter, *A History of Psychiatry: From the Era of the Asylum to the Age of Prozac* (New York, John Wiley, 1997); and also covered in Ali Haggett, *Desperate Housewives: Neuroses and the Domestic Environment 1945–1970* (London, Pickering and Chatto, 2012).
30. Shepherd, *Psychiatric Illness in General Practice*, p. 4.
31. R. E. Kendell, 'The classification of depressions: A review of contemporary confusion', *British Journal of Psychiatry* (1976), 129, 15–28, on 15.
32. Kendell, 'The classification of depressions', 17–18.
33. Shepherd, *Psychiatric Illness in General Practice*, p. 17.
34. Brian Cooper, John Fry and Graham Kalton, 'A longitudinal study of psychiatric morbidity in a general practice population', *British Journal of Preventive and Social Medicine* (1969), 23, 210–17, on 212.
35. Cooper, Fry and Kalton, 'A longitudinal study of psychiatric morbidity', 211.
36. Perth, 'Psychosomatic problems in general practice', 311.
37. Perth, 'Psychosomatic problems in general practice', 307.
38. Keeve Brodman, Albert J. Erdmann and Harold G. Wolff, *Cornell Medical Index: Health Questionnaire* (New York, Cornell University Medical College, 1949), p. 2.
39. Shepherd, *Psychiatric Illness in General Practice*, p. 105.
40. D. P. Goldberg and B. Blackwell, 'Psychiatric illness in general practice: A detailed study using a new method of case identification', *British Medical Journal*, 27 May 1970, 439–43, on 439.
41. For full descriptions of these screening tools, see D. Goldberg, *The Detection of Psychiatric Illness by Questionnaire* (Oxford, Oxford University Press, 1972).
42. Ian McDowell and Claire Newell, *Measuring Health: a Guide to Rating Scales and Questionnaires* (Oxford, Oxford University Press, 1996), p. 178.
43. Dohrenwend, cited in McDowell and Newell, *Measuring Health*, p. 178.
44. McDowell and Newell, *Measuring Health*, pp. 185, 178.
45. Interview with Professor Sir David Goldberg, published in *Psychiatric Bulletin* (2001), 25, 315–20.
46. McDowell and Newell, *Measuring Health*, p. 226.
47. McDowell and Newell, *Measuring Health*, p. 234 and Goldberg and Blackwell, 'Psychiatric illness', 441.
48. McDowell and Newell, *Measuring Health*, p. 234.

49. Shepherd and Clare, *Psychiatric Illness*, p. 26.
50. Shepherd and Clare, *Psychiatric Illness*, pp. 36–7.
51. For case studies, see Shepherd and Clare, *Psychiatric Illness*, p. 50.
52. See for example Aaron Lask, *Asthma: Attitude and Milieu* (London, Tavistock, 1966).
53. C. A. H. Watts, 'The mild endogenous depression', *British Medical Journal*, 5 January 1957, 4–8, on 4.
54. Watts, 'The mild endogenous depression', p. 5.
55. C. A. H. Watts, *Depressive Disorders in the Community* (Bristol, John Wright, 1966), pp. 50–1.
56. Interview with Glen Haden.
57. Interview with Giles Walden.
58. Interview with Richard Stanton.
59. Interview with Richard Stanton.
60. Interview with Robert Manley. Double-strength nerve tonic and other treatments are discussed in Chapter 4 of this book.
61. See for example Cooper, Fry and Kalton, 'A longitudinal study of psychiatric morbidity', 210–17.
62. See John Fry, 'The psychoneurotic in general practice', *Medical World*, June 1954, 657–66, on 661. See also John Fry, 'What happened to our neurotic patients?', *The Practitioner* (1960), 185, 885–9. B FRYC 7–1 Royal College of General Practitioners Archive.
63. John Fry, 'The management of psychosomatic disorders in general practice', *The Practitioner* (1957), 177, 554–63, on 554.
64. BFRY C2-1 John Fry, Research Notes, Peptic Ulcers, C1950–1980, Royal College of General Practitioners Archive.
65. Interview with Graham Hadley.
66. John Fry and David Finer, 'Peptic ulcer in general practice', *British Medical Journal*, 16 July 1955, 169–72, on 173, 169.
67. Fry and Finer, 'Peptic ulcer in general practice', 171.
68. F. Avery Jones, 'Clinical and social problems of peptic ulcer', *British Medical Journal*, 30 March 1957, 719–23, on 722.
69. J. N. Morris and Richard M. Titmuss, 'Epidemiology of peptic ulcer: Vital statistics', *Lancet*, 30 December 1944, 841–45, on 842.
70. Wellcome Witness to Twentieth Century Medicine, *Peptic Ulcer: Rise and Fall* (London, Wellcome, 2000), p. i.
71. Wellcome Witness to Twentieth Century Medicine, *Peptic Ulcer*, p. i.
72. Susan Levenstein, 'Stress and peptic ulcer: Life beyond helicobacter', *BMJ*, 316, 14 February 1998, 538–41, on 538.
73. Levenstein, 'Stress and peptic ulcer', 539.
74. Levenstein, 'Stress and peptic ulcer', 538.
75. For example, Mervyn Susser and Zena Stein put forward a 'cohort theory' of ulcers in which they viewed the rise in numbers as connected to the 'early phase of urbanisation', and the decline as a response to greater social security from the mid-twentieth century. See Mervyn Susser and Zena Stein, 'Civilisation and peptic ulcer', *Lancet*, 20 January 1962, 3–7.
76. See James L. Halliday, 'The rising incidence of psychosomatic illness', *British Medical Journal*, 2 July 1938, 11–14; James L. Halliday, 'Epidemiology and

the psychosomatic affections: A study in social medicine', *Lancet*, 10 August 1946, 185–9; and J. L. Halliday, *Psychosocial Medicine: A Study of the Sick Society* (London, William Heinemann, 1948). For a full account of Halliday's use of national insurance claims as 'psychological documents', see Hayward, *The Transformation of the Psyche*, Chapter 3, 'Social consciences'.

77. Halliday, 'The rising incidence of psychosomatic illness', pp. 13, 14.
78. Rhodri Hayward, 'Enduring emotions: James L. Halliday and the invention of the psychosocial', *Isis* (2009), 100, 827–38, on 835.
79. Halliday, 'Epidemiology and the psychosomatic affections', 187.
80. Halliday, 'Epidemiology and the psychosomatic affections', 187.
81. Halliday, 'Epidemiology and the psychosomatic affections', 187.
82. Halliday, 'Epidemiology and the psychosomatic affections', 188.
83. Halliday, 'Epidemiology and the psychosomatic affections', 189.
84. Halliday, 'Epidemiology and the psychosomatic affections', 189.
85. See Roy Porter, 'Diseases of civilization' in W. F. Bynum and R. Porter (eds), *Companion Encyclopedia of the History of Medicine* (London, Routledge, 1993), pp. 585–600.
86. Halliday, 'Epidemiology and the psychosomatic affections', 189.
87. H. Weiner, 'The concept of psychosomatic medicine', in E. R. Wallace IV and J. Gach (eds), *History of Psychiatry and Medial Pathology* (New York, Springer, 2008), pp. 485–516. See also H. Flanders Dunbar, *Synopsis of Psychosomatic Diagnosis and Treatment* (St Lois, MO: C V Mosby Co., 1948).
88. Weiner, 'The concept of psychosomatic medicine', p. 504. See also F. Alexander, *Psychosomatic Medicine: Its Principles and Applications* (New York, W. W. Norton and Co., 1950).
89. John A. Ryle, 'The natural history of duodenal ulcer', *Lancet*, 13 February 1932, 327–34, on 328.
90. Ryle, 'The natural history of duodenal ulcer', 329.
91. Daniel T. Davies and A. T. Macbeth Wilson, 'Observations on the life-history of the chronic peptic ulcer patient', *Lancet*, 11 December 1937, 1354–60, on 1354.
92. J. N. Morris and Richard Titmuss, 'Epidemiology of peptic ulcer: Vital statistics', *Lancet*, 30 December 1940, 841–45, on 845.
93. Morris and Titmuss, 'Epidemiology of peptic ulcer: Vital statistics', 841 and Ian Miller, 'Stress and abdominal illness in Britain c.1939–1945', *Medical History* (2010), 54, 95–110, on 95.
94. Edgar Jones, '"The gut war": functional somatic disorders in the UK during the Second World War', *History of the Human Sciences* (2012), 25 (5), 30–48, on 34.
95. Jones, '"The gut war"', 35–6.
96. Miller, 'Stress and abdominal illness', 101.
97. Edgar Jones and Simon Wessely, 'Hearts, guts and minds: Somatisation in the military from 1900', *Journal of Psychosomatic Research* (2004), 56, 425–29, on 429.
98. Jones, '"The gut war"', 33.
99. Levenstein, 'Stress and peptic ulcer', 539.
100. See 'Psychological medicine in general practice: A report prepared by a working party of the Council of the College of General Practitioners', *British Medical Journal*, 6 September 1958, 585–90.

101. ACE G12–2, Psychiatry and the General Practitioner Working Party Papers 1956–58, Royal College of General Practitioners Archive.
102. Philip Hopkins, 'Psychiatry in general practice', *Postgraduate Medical Journal*, May 1960, 323–30, on 325.
103. Philip Hopkins, 'The general practitioner and the psychosomatic approach', in Desmond O'Neil (ed.), *Modern Trends in Psychosomatic Medicine* (London, Butterworths, 1955), pp. 4–28, on p. 4.
104. Shepherd and Clare, *Psychiatric Illness in General Practice*, p. 33.
105. David Hannay, 'Undergraduate medical education and general practice', in Irvine Loudon, John Horder and Charles Webster (eds), *General Practice under the National Health Service, 1948–1997* (London, Clarenden Press, 1998), pp. 165–81, on p. 167.
106. Hannay, 'Undergraduate medical education and general practice', p. 168.
107. Hannay, 'Undergraduate medical education and general practice', p. 168.
108. Denis Pereira Gray, 'Postgraduate training and continuing education', in Loudon, Horder and Webster (eds), *General Practice under the National Health Service, 1948–1997*, pp. 182–204, on p. 183.
109. D. W. Hall, 'Vocational training for general practice', *Health Trends* (1973), 5, 80–82, on 80.
110. Pereira Gray, 'Postgraduate training', p. 185. For developments in general practice within the context of the organisation of the NHS, see Geoffrey Rivett, *From Cradle to Grave: Fifty Years of the NHS* (London, King's Fund, 1997), pp. 80–92.
111. Pereira Gray, 'Postgraduate training', p. 188 and Hall, 'Vocational training', 80.
112. Hall, 'Vocational training', 81.
113. Pereira Gray, 'Postgraduate training', p. 192.
114. 'Psychological medicine in general practice: A report prepared by the working party of the Council of the College of General Practitioners', *British Medical Journal*, 6 September 1958, 585–90, on 588.
115. 'Psychological medicine in general practice', 589–90 and 588.
116. Interview with Robert Manley.
117. Interview with David Palmer.
118. A point that emerged in several interviews with doctors who had contact with Sargant – for example, Jeremy Barrington.
119. Interview with Roger Lea.
120. Interview with Richard Stanton.
121. 'Michael Balint', Editorial, *Journal of the Royal College of General Practitioners* (1972), 22, 133–5, on 133.
122. The Tavistock Clinic was founded in London under the leadership of Dr Hugh Crichton-Miller (1877–1959), initially to explore the traumatic effects of First World War shellshock victims. Its vision was extended to provide systematic major psychotherapy on the basis of concepts inspired by psychoanalytic theory, for patients suffering from psychoneuroses and allied disorders. See H. Dicks, *Fifty Years of the Tavistock Clinic* (London, Routledge and Kegan Paul, 1970).
123. Michael Balint, Editorial, 133.
124. Michael Balint, 'The doctor, his patient and the illness', *Lancet*, 2 April 1955, 683–8, on 684.
125. Balint, 'The doctor, his patient and the illness', 684.

126. Michael Balint, 'Psychotherapy and the general practitioner', *British Medical Journal*, 19 January 1957, 156–8, on 157.
127. Michael Balint, Editorial, 133–4.
128. John Horder, 'The first Balint group', *British Journal of General Practice*, December 2001, 1038–9, on 1039.
129. Horder, 'The first Balint group', 1039.
130. Michael Balint, Editorial, 134. This was also the opinion of David Palmer (who became very influential in one regional vocational scheme). See also Marshall Marinker, 'What is wrong and how we know it: Changing concepts of general practice', in Loudon *et al.* (eds), *General Practice*, pp. 65–91, esp., p. 73; and Hayward, *The Transformation of the Psyche*, Chapter 4.
131. *The Future General Practitioner: Learning and Teaching* (Royal College of General Practitioners, 1972). This textbook illustrates a noticeable shift towards the importance of interpersonal relationships, patient-centred care and the consultation process.
132. Interview with Robert Manley. A point confirmed in H. J. Walton, 'Effect of the doctor's personality on his style of practice', *Journal of the Royal College of General Practitioners* (1969), 17 (82, supplement 3), 6–17, on 6.
133. Interview with Glen Haden.
134. Balint, 'The doctor, his patient', 685.
135. Patrick S. Byrne and Barrie E. L. Long, *Doctors Talking to Patients: A Study of the Verbal Behaviour of General Practitioners Consulting in their Surgeries* (London, HMSO, 1976), pp. 8, 9.
136. Byrne and Long, *Doctors Talking to Patients*, p. 191.
137. Walton, 'Effect of the doctor's personality', 8.
138. Walton, 'Effect of the doctor's personality', 11.
139. Walton, 'Effect of the doctor's personality', 12. These findings are echoed in R. R. Bomford, 'The anxious patient and the worried doctor', papers from a joint conference of the College of General Practitioners and the Society of Psychosomatic Research: 'The problems of stress in general practice', *Supplement to the Journal of the College of General Practitioners* (1958), 1 (2), 10–13.
140. Shepherd, *Psychiatric Illness in General Practice*, p. 55.
141. Shepherd, *Psychiatric Illness in General Practice*, p. 33.
142. Shepherd, *Psychiatric Illness in General Practice*, pp. 52, 68.
143. Interview with Christian Edwards.
144. Interview with Richard Stanton.
145. Interview with Giles Walden.
146. Interview with Julian Adams. Gestalt therapy was developed by the Germans, Frederick and Laura Perls, during the 1940s. It focuses particularly on awareness of current circumstances and environment. Gestalt therapy developed in part as a reaction towards psychoanalysis and behaviourism during the mid-twentieth century, which were viewed by some as too deterministic.
147. Interview with Robert Manley.
148. Interview with David Palmer.
149. Interview with David Palmer.
150. Interview with Christian Edwards. Graham Hadley explicitly noted that his wife, who was also a GP and worked with him, ran late with her lists

each day because of the 'worried well' – notably, according to Hadley, with 'bored housewives'.

151. Stephen Taylor, *Good General Practice: A Report of a Survey by Stephen Taylor*, Nufffield Provincial Hospitals Trust (London, Oxford University Press, 1954). See for example pp. 417, 430, 431. Lord Stephen Taylor of Harlow, who was a doctor and former Labour Member of Parliament, became influential in the development of general practice and published regularly about social and political issues that affected health.
152. Watts, *Depressive Disorders*, p. 12.
153. F. J. A. Huygen, *Family Medicine: The Medical Life History of Families* (Nijmegen, The Netherlands, Dekker and Ven de Vegt, 1978), p.11. For a British example of a similar theoretical approach, see Robert Kellner, *Family Ill-Health: An Investigation in General Practice* (London, Tavistock Publications, 1963).
154. Interviews with Roger Lea and John Souton.
155. Hopkins, 'The general practitioner and the psychosomatic approach', p. 11.
156. Marinker, 'Changing concepts of illness', p. 80. A more radical critique of the family was of course also put forward by R. D. Laing and A. Esterson in *Sanity, Madness and the Family* (London, Tavistock, 1964) in which the authors argued that 'the family is the unit of illness: not the individual, but the family', p. 23.
157. Stephen J. Hadfield, 'A field survey of general practice', *British Medical Journal*, 26 September 1953, 684–706, on 685, 686.
158. Hadfield, 'A field survey of general practice', 636.
159. Hadfield, 'A field survey of general practice', 689.
160. Richard Moore, *Leeches to Lasers: Sketches of a Medical Family* (Killala, Ireland, Morrigan, 2002), pp. 218–9.
161. Moore, *Leeches to Lasers*, p. 220.
162. Moore, *Leeches to Lasers*, p. 220.
163. Moore, *Leeches to Lasers*, p. 220.
164. Moore, *Leeches to Lasers*, p. 223.
165. Shepherd, *Psychiatric Illness*, p. 55.
166. David Morrell, 'Introduction and overview' in Loudon *et al.*, *General Practice*, pp. 1–19, on p. 4.
167. David Pilgrim, *Key Concepts in Mental Health* (London, Sage, second edition, 2009), p. 176.
168. For figures and analysis of suicide in England and Wales, see Kyla Thomas and David Gunnell, 'Suicide in England and Wales 1861–2007: A time-trends analysis', *International Journal of Epidemiology* (2010), 39, 1464–75.
169. Emile Durkheim's classic study *Suicide* (London, Routledge, 1955) was cited as a classic epidemiological study.
170. P. Sainsbury, *Suicide in London*, Maudsley Monographs No. 1 (London, Chapman and Hall, 1955).
171. F. A. Whitlock, 'Suicide in England and Wales 1959–63, Part 2: London', *Psychological Medicine* (1973), 3, 411–20, on 411.
172. Norman Kreitman, Vera Carstairs and John Duffy, 'Association of age and social class with suicide among men in Great Britain', *Journal of Epidemiology and Community Health* (1991), 45, 195–202, on 195.

173. Kreitman, Carstairs and Duffy, 'Association of age and social class with suicide', 199. Kreitman was director of the Medical Research Council Unit for Epidemiological Psychiatry in Edinburgh, where, from the 1970s, he undertook research into suicide, female depression and alcohol consumption. He coined the term 'parasuicide', a recognition, not acknowledged at the time, that most episodes of self-harm are not attempts at suicide. See Patricia Casey, Obituary, Norman Kreitman, *Psychiatric Bulletin*, doi: 10.1192/pb.bp.113.043521, accessed 5 March 2015.
174. Kreitman, Carstairs and Duffy, 'Association of age and social class with suicide', 199.
175. F. A. Whitlock, 'Suicide in England and Wales 1959–63, Part 1: the county boroughs', *Psychological Medicine* (1973), 3, 350–65, on 361, 362.
176. Whitlock, 'Suicide in England and Wales 1959–63, Part 1', 362.
177. R. W. Parnell and Ian Skottowe, 'Towards preventing suicide', *Lancet*, 26 January 1957, 206–208.
178. Watts, *Depressive Disorders*, pp. 124, 132.
179. Interview with Jeremy Barrington.
180. Jackson, *The Age of Stress*, p. 186.
181. Jackson, *The Age of Stress*, p. 191. For a full account of these concerns, and research into the social causes of stress and illness see Jackson, *The Age of Stress*, Chapter 5, 'Coping with stress', and Ali Haggett, *Desperate Housewives: Neuroses and the Domestic Environment, 1945–1970* (London, Pickering and Chatto, 2012), pp. 86–95.
182. See for example, Phyillis Chesler, *Women and Madness* (London, Allen Lane, 1974).
183. George W. Brown and Tirril Harris, *Social Origins of Depression: A Study of Psychiatric Disorder in Women* (London, Tavistock, paperback edition, 1979), p. 279.
184. James Y. Nazroo, Angela C. Edwards and George W. Brown, 'Gender differences in the prevalence of depression: Artefact, alternative disorders, biology or roles?, *Sociology of Health and Illness* (1998), 20 (3), 312–30, on 324.
185. See Christopher Tennant and Paul Bebbington, 'The social causation of depression: A critique of the work of Brown and colleagues', *Psychological Medicine* (1978), 8, 565–75.
186. Brown and Tirril, *Social Origins of Depression*, p. 279.
187. See Nazroo, Edwards and Brown, 'Gender differences in the prevalence of depression'.
188. See Walter Gove, 'The relationship between sex roles, marital status and mental illness', *Social Forces* (1972), 51, 34–44. For debate about Gove's work, see Haggett, *Desperate Housewives*, pp. 107–8.
189. Jackson, *The Age of Stress*, p. 194.
190. Bruce P. Dohrenwend and Barbara Snell Dohrenwend, 'Sex differences and psychiatric disorders', *American Journal of Sociology*, (1976), 81, 1447–54, on 1452.
191. Dohrenwend and Dohrenwend, 'Sex differences and psychiatric disorders', 1452.
192. Monica Brisco, 'Sex differences in psychological wellbeing', *Psychological Medicine*, Monograph Supplement, Supplement 1 (1982), 1–46, on 6.

See also Monica E. Brisco, 'Sex differences in perception of illness and expressed life satisfaction, *Psychological Medicine* (1978), 8, 339–45.
193. Brisco, 'Sex differences in psychological wellbeing', 37.
194. Brisco, 'Sex differences in psychological wellbeing', 38.
195. Monica E. Brisco, 'Why do people go to the doctor? Sex differences in the correlates of GP consultation', *Social Science and Medicine* (1987), 25, 5, 507–13, on 511.
196. Brisco, 'Sex differences in psychological wellbeing', 42.
197. Derek L. Phillips and Bernard E. Segal, 'Sexual status and psychiatric symptoms', *American Sociological Review* (1969), 34 (1), 58–72, on 60.
198. Lynda W. Warren, 'Male intolerance of depression: A review with implications for psychotherapy', *Clinical Psychology Review* (1983), 3, 147–56, on 149.
199. Warren, 'Male intolerance of depression', 150.
200. Riska, 'The rise and fall of Type A man', 1666.
201. Barbara Ehrenreich, *The Hearts of Men: American Dreams and the Flight from Commitment* (New York, Anchor Press/Doubleday, 1984), pp. 82–4.

2 Mental Health at Work: Misconceptions and Missed Opportunities

1. Russell Fraser, *The Incidence of Neurosis among Factory Workers*. Medical Research Council (MRC) Industrial Health Research Board, Report No. 90 (London, HMSO, 1947), p. 1.
2. Fraser, *The Incidence of Neurosis among Factory Workers*, p. 4.
3. Fraser, *The Incidence of Neurosis among Factory Workers*, p. 5.
4. Rachel Jenkins, 'Minor psychiatric morbidity in employed young men and women and its contribution to sickness absence', *British Journal of Industrial Medicine* (1985), 42, 147–54, on 149, 150.
5. Vicky Long, *The Rise and Fall of the Healthy Factory: The Politics of Industrial Health in Britain, 1914–60* (Basingstoke, Palgrave Macmillan, 2011), pp. 7–9. Long explores the negotiations between the trade unions, employers, the medical profession and the state.
6. H. A. Waldron, *Occupational Health Practice* (London, Butterworths, 1989 [1973]), p. 9. For a full account of the history of occupational health, see Arthur J. McIvor, *A History of Work in Britain 1880–1950* (Basingstoke, Palgrave, 2001) and Paul Weindling (ed.), *The Social History of Occupational Health* (London, Croom Helm, 1985).
7. Waldron, *Occupational Health Practice*, p. 8.
8. Waldron, *Occupational Health Practice*, p. 10.
9. Waldron, *Occupational Health Practice*, pp. 10–11.
10. Long, *The Rise and Fall*, p. 11.
11. Charles Myers, *Industrial Psychology* (Oxford, Oxford University Press, 1929), p. 9.
12. Sarah Hayes, 'Industrial automation and stress in post-war Britain', in Mark Jackson (ed.), *Stress in Post-War Britain* (London, Pickering and Chatto, 2015), p. 75
13. Hayes, 'Industrial automation', p. 75.

14. Hayes, 'Industrial automation', pp. 75–6. For earlier concerns about industrial fatigue, prompted by the First World War, see M. Greenwood, *A Report on the Cause of Wastage of Labour in Munition Factories* (London, MRC, HMSO, 1918).
15. Hayes, 'Industrial automation', pp. 79, 76. See also T. S. Scott, 'Industrial medicine – An art or a science', *British Journal of Industrial Medicine* (1967), 24, 85–92; and P. A. B. Raffle, 'Automation and repetitive work: Their effect on health', *Lancet,* 6 April 1963, 733–7.
16. World Health Organization, *Mental Health Problems of Automation* (WHO Technical Report Series, 183, 1959), p. 5.
17. WHO, *Mental Health Problems of Automation,* p. 6.
18. WHO, *Mental Health Problems of Automation,* p. 23.
19. Lennart Levi (ed.), 'Preface', *Society, Stress and Disease,* Volume 4, Working Life (Oxford, Oxford University Press, 1981), pp. xi–xii.
20. Hayes, 'Industrial automation', p. 29.
21. For the first detailed study of absenteeism, see Hilde Behrend, 'Voluntary absence from work', *International Labour Review* (1959), 79, 109–40.
22. Behrend, 'Voluntary absence from work', 111.
23. J. K. Chadwick-Jones, Nigel Nicolson and Colin Brown, *Social Psychology of Absenteeism* (New York, Praeger, 1982), p. 130.
24. J. K. Chadwick-Jones, C. A. Brown and N. Nicholson, 'Absence from work: Its meaning, measurement and control', *International Review of Applied Psychology* (1973), 22 (2), 37–54, on 40.
25. P. Froggatt, 'Short-term absence from industry: I Literature, definitions, data and the effect of age and length of service', *British Journal of Industrial Medicine* (1970), 27, 199–210, on 206, 210.
26. Chadwick-Jones, *Social Psychology of Absenteeism,* p. 3.
27. Viviane Isambert-Jamati, 'Absenteeism among women workers in industry', *International Labour Review* (1962), 85, 248–61, on 252.
28. Isambert-Jamati, 'Absenteeism among women', 253.
29. *A Study of Absenteeism among Women* (London, Industrial Research Board, 1943).
30. Isambert-Jamati, 'Absenteeism among women', 255.
31. F. Zweig, *Women's Life and Labour* (London, Victor Gollancz, 1952), p. 111.
32. Zweig, *Women's Life and Labour,* p. 133.
33. See P. Froggatt, 'Short-term absence from industry', 200.
34. Behrend, 'Voluntary absence from work', 126 (my italics).
35. Behrend, 'Voluntary absence from work', 112.
36. Chadwick-Jones, 'Absence from work', 146.
37. Behrend, 'Voluntary absence from work', 112; a finding supported later also by P. Froggatt in 'Short-term absence from industry III', *British Journal of Industrial Medicine* (1970), 27, 297–312, on 307.
38. *Off Sick* (Office for Health Economics, 1971), p. 19.
39. *Off Sick,* p. 5. For example, higher sickness rates were noted among female civil servants. See Debbie Palmer, 'Cultural change, stress and civil servants' occupational health, 1967–1990', in Mark Jackson (ed.), *Stress in Post-War Britain* (London, Pickering and Chatto, 2015).
40. *Off Sick,* pp. 5, 6. A trend noted by all authors, see for example, P. J. Taylor and J. Burridge, 'Trends in death, disablement and sickness absence in the British Post Office since 1891', *British Journal of Industrial Medicine* (1982), 39, 1–10, on 6.

41. *Off Sick*, p. 9.
42. P. J. Taylor, 'Individual variations in sickness absence', *British Journal of Industrial Medicine* (1967), 24, 169–77, on 169.
43. P. J. Taylor, 'Personal factors associated with sickness absence', *British Journal of Industrial Medicine* (1968) 25, 106–18, on 109.
44. David A. Hamburg and Beatrix A. Hamburg, 'Occupational stress, endocrine changes and coping behaviour in the middle years of adult life', in Lennart Levi (ed.), *Society, Stress and Disease*, Volume 4, Working Life (Oxford, Oxford University Press, 1981), pp. 131–43, on p. 138.
45. W. P. D. Logan and Eileen M. Brooke, *The Survey of Sickness 1943–1952, Studies on Medical and Population Studies* (London, HMSO, 1957), p. 51. See also W. P. D. Logan, *Studies on Medical and Population Subjects, No 14: Morbidity Statistics from General Practice Vol II* (London, HMSO, 1960), p. 15.
46. Interview with Jeffrey Meane.
47. Interview with Rupert Espley.
48. Interview with Roger Lea.
49. Interview with Rupert Espley.
50. See Allison Milner *et al.*, 'Suicide by occupation, systematic review and meta-analysis', Review Article, *BJP* (2013), 203, 409–16.
51. Peter Townsend, 'Inequality and the health service', *Lancet* (1974), 303, (7868), 1179–84 on 1179.
52. M. H. Brenner, 'Mortality and the national economy: A review and the experiences of England and Wales', *Lancet* (1979), 2, 568–73, on 568. Debates about the health disadvantages associated with unemployment and financial insecurity proliferated during the 1980s, for, as Brenner noted, there was a time lag effect following loss of employment: suicide was more common within the first year of unemployment, whereas chronic sickness, such as cardiovascular disorders, tended to increase after two or three years of unemployment. See Brenner, 'Mortality and the national economy', 571.
53. *Off Sick*, p. 6.
54. *Off Sick*, p. 8.
55. Logan and Brooke, *Survey of Sickness*, p. 52.
56. J. E. Ager and P. A. B. Raffle, *Patterns of Sickness Absence: Experience of London Transport Workers over Two Decades* (London, London Transport Executive, 1975).
57. See for example, Taylor and Burridge, 'Trends in death, disablement and sickness absence', 8–9.
58. Interview with Sarah Hall.
59. Interview with Glen Haden.
60. *Off Sick*, p. 8.
61. Logan and Brooke, *Survey of Sickness*, p. 53.
62. Logan and Brooke, *Survey of Sickness*, p. 54.
63. Taylor, 'Personal factors associated with sickness absence', 106–18.
64. Taylor, 'Personal factors associated with sickness absence', 111.
65. Taylor, 'Personal factors associated with sickness absence', 114.
66. 21.4% of the 'frequently sick' group had spells of neurosis, in contrast to 12.5% of the controls.
67. Taylor, 'Personal factors associated with sickness absence', 113.
68. Taylor, 'Personal factors associated with sickness absence', 111.

69. Interview with Giles Walden.
70. David Ferguson, 'Some characteristics of repeated sickness absence', *British Journal of Industrial Medicine* (1972), 29, 420–31, on 430.
71. Ferguson, 'Some characteristics of repeated sickness absence', 430.
72. David Ferguson, 'A study of neurosis and occupation', *British Journal of Industrial Medicine* (1973), 30, 187–98, on 187.
73. Ferguson, 'A study of neurosis and occupation', 193.
74. Gunnar Nerall and Ingrid Wahlund, 'Stressors and strain in white collar workers', in Lennart Levi (ed.), *Society, Stress and Disease,* Volume 4, Working Life (Oxford, Oxford University Press, 1981), pp. 120–7.
75. Nerall and Wahlund, 'Stressors and strain in white collar workers', p. 126.
76. Nerall and Wahlund, 'Stressors and strain in white collar workers', p. 126.
77. Michael H. Banks, Chris W. Clegg, Paul R. Jackson, Nigel J. Kemp, Elizabeth M. Stafford and Toby D. Wall, 'The use of the General Health Questionnaire as an indicator of mental health in occupational studies', *Journal of Occupational Psychology* (1980), 53, 187–94, on 188. Godberg's GHQ was published in 1972 – see Chapter 1.
78. Taylor's study of oil refinery workers, for example uses the terms neurosis and nervous breakdown interchangeably.
79. Ferguson, 'Some characteristics', 423.
80. See for example, A. Ryle, 'The neuroses in a general practice population', *Journal of the College of General Practice* (1960), 3, 313–28.
81. See for example, Ferguson, 'A study of neurosis and occupation', 189.
82. R. S. F. Schilling, 'Assessing the health of the industrial worker', *British Journal of Industrial Medicine* (1957), 14, 145–9, on 145.
83. Schilling, 'Assessing the health of the industrial worker', 145.
84. Schilling, 'Assessing the health of the industrial worker', 147.
85. Schilling, 'Assessing the health of the industrial worker', 149, 148.
86. *Off Sick*, p. 17.
87. *Off Sick*, p. 17.
88. Ferguson, 'A study of neurosis and occupation', 189.
89. Interview with Christian Edwards.
90. Interview with David Palmer.
91. Interview with David Palmer.
92. A. M. Adelstein, 'Absence from work attributed to sickness', Conference Report, *British Journal of Industrial Medicine* (1969), 26 (2), 169–70, on 70.
93. Furguson, 'A study of neurosis and occupation', 188.
94. Susan H. Meadows, 'Health examinations of senior staff in industry', *British Journal of Industrial Medicine* (1964), 21, 226–30 on 228.
95. Taylor, 'Personal factors', 117.
96. Mark Jackson, *The Age of Stress: Science and the Search for Stability* (Oxford, Oxford University Press, 2013), p. 146.
97. Recently explored in Palmer, 'Cultural change, stress and civil servants', and cited in Jackson, *The Age of Stress* on p. 201.
98. Jackson, *The Age of Stress*, p. 201.
99. Jackson, *The Age of Stress*, p. 202.
100. Jackson, *The Age of Stress*, p. 201.
101. Jackson, *The Age of Stress*, p. 201.
102. Jackson, *The Age of Stress*, p. 202.

103. Arthur McIvor, *Working Lives: Work in Britain since 1945* (Basingstoke, Palgrave Macmillan, 2013), p. 80.
104. McIvor, *Working Lives*, pp. 80, 81.
105. McIvor, *Working Lives*, p. 106.
106. Eileen Janes Yeo, 'Taking it like a man', *Labour History Review* (2004), 69, 129–33, on 129.
107. McIvor, *Working Lives*, p. 82.
108. McIvor, *Working Lives*, pp. 82, 83.
109. McIvor, *Working Lives*, pp. 84, 89.
110. McIvor, *Working Lives*, p. 163.
111. A point made in McIvor, *Working Lives*, p. 161.
112. David Walker, 'Danger was a thing that ye were brought up wi': Workers' narratives on occupational health and safety in the workplace', *Scottish Labour History* (2011), 46, 54–70, on 57.
113. Walker, 'Danger was a thing', 61.
114. McIvor, *Working Lives*, p. 161.
115. Nick Hayes, 'Did manual workers want industrial welfare? Canteens, latrines and masculinity on British building sites', *Journal of Social History* (2002), 35 (3), 637–58, on 639.
116. Hayes, 'Did manual workers want industrial welfare?', 647.
117. Hayes, 'Did manual workers want industrial welfare?', 651.
118. Walker, 'Danger was a thing', 57.
119. Ronnie Johnston and Arthur McIvor, 'Dangerous work, hard men and broken bodies: Masculinity in the Clydeside heavy industries c. 1930–1970s', *Labour History Review* (2004), 69 (2), 135–51, on 141.
120. McIvor, 'Dangerous work, hard men and broken bodies', 138.
121. McIvor, 'Dangerous work, hard men and broken bodies', 138.
122. Interview with Richard Stanton.
123. Interview with Sarah Hall.
124. Interview with Glen Haden.
125. Interview with Rupert Espley.
126. Pat Ayres, 'Work, culture and gender: The making of masculinities in post-war Liverpool', *Labour History Review* (2004), 69 (2), 154–7, on 156.
127. Michael Roper, *Masculinity and the British Organization Man since 1945* (Oxford, Oxford University Press, 1994), p. 112.
128. Roper, *Masculinity and the British Organization Man*, p. 107.
129. Roper, *Masculinity and the British Organization Man*, pp. 108, 109.
130. Ayres, 'Work, culture and gender', 158.
131. A topic discussed in McIvor, *Working Lives*, on p. 165. For an account that is critical of the unions, see Peter Bartrip, 'Workmen's compensation', in Paul Weindling (ed.), *The Social History of Occupational Health* (London, Croom Helm, 1988), 157–79.
132. McIvor, *Working Lives*, p. 165.
133. See A. McIvor and R. Johnston, *Miners' Lung* (Aldershot, Ashgate, 2007).
134. Joseph Melling, 'The risks of working versus the risks of not working: Trade unions, employers and responses to the risk of occupational illness in British industry, c. 1890–1940s', *ESRC Centre for Analysis of Risk and Regulation Discussion Paper 12*, 14–34, on 16.
135. Melling, 'The risks of working versus the risks of not working', 16.
136. Long, *The Rise and Fall of the Healthy Factory*, p. 111.

137. Long, *The Rise and Fall of the Healthy Factory*, p. 142.
138. Long, *The Rise and Fall of the Healthy Factory*, p. 187.
139. Long, *The Rise and Fall of the Healthy Factory*, p. 188.
140. Long, *The Rise and Fall of the Healthy Factory*, p. 193.
141. Long, *The Rise and Fall of the Healthy Factory*, p. 201.
142. McIvor, *Working Lives*, pp. 176–7.
143. See, for example, Sven Lokander, 'Sick absence in a Swedish company: A sociomedical study', *Acta Medica Scandinavica* (1962), 171.
144. Although this is, of course, disputed by those on the political right who argue that a large public sector stifles growth and innovation.
145. Mary Hilson, *The Nordic Model: Scandinavia since 1945* (London, Reaktion, 2013 edition), p. 93.
146. Hilson, *The Nordic Model*, pp. 101–2.
147. Gerald N. Grob, *Mental Illness and American Society 1875–1940* (New Jersey, Princeton University Press, 1983), p. 150. See also, Jose M. Bertolote, 'The roots of the concept of mental health', *World Psychiatry* (2008), 7, 113–16.
148. Grob, *Mental Illness*, p. 162.
149. Alan A. McLean, 'Occupational mental health: Review of an emerging art', Frank Baker, Peter J. M. McEwan and Alan Sheldon (eds), *Industrial Organizations and Health* (London, Tavistock Publications, 1969), pp. 164–91, on p. 167.
150. McLean, 'Occupational mental health', p. 170.
151. McLean, 'Occupational mental health', p. 173.
152. McLean, 'Occupational mental health', p. 174.
153. W. Donald Ross, *Practical Psychiatry for Industrial Physicians* (Illinois, Charles C Thomas, 1956), p. 22.
154. Ross, *Practical Psychiatry for Industrial Physicians*, pp. 330–4.
155. Ross, *Practical Psychiatry for Industrial Physicians*, p. 210.
156. Ross, *Practical Psychiatry for Industrial Physicians*, p. 368.
157. David Blumenthal, 'Employer-sponsored health insurance in the United States – Origins and implications', *The New England Journal of Medicine*, 6 July 2006, 82–8, on 82.
158. Blumenthal, 'Employer-sponsored health insurance', 83.
159. Blumenthal, 'Employer-sponsored health insurance', 83.
160. Rachel Jenkins, 'Minor psychiatric morbidity in employed young men and women and its contribution to sickness absence', *British Journal of Industrial Medicine* (1985), 42, 147–54, on 150.
161. Measuring scales are discussed fully in Chapter 1 of this book. See D. P. Goldberg and B. Blackwell, 'Psychiatric illness in general practice: A detailed study using a new method of case identification', *British Medical Journal*, 23 May 1970, 439–43. The GHQ was published as a Maudsley Monograph in 1972. Goldberg's background was originally in psychology and his work reflected a wider psychological, biological and social perspective. He also stressed the importance of interview technique.
162. See Banks, Clegg, Jackson, Kemp, Stafford and Wall, 'The use of the General Health Questionnaire'.
163. Jenkins, 'Minor psychiatric morbidity', 149. The only marked sex difference was that the rate of somatic symptoms with psychological origin in women had begun to rise – or were more evident in this style of study – by the 1980s.

164. Jenkins, 'Minor psychiatric morbidity', 152.
165. Jenkins, 'Minor psychiatric morbidity', 152.
166. Jenkins, 'Minor psychiatric morbidity', 153.
167. Banks, Clegg, Jackson, Kemp, Stafford and Wall, 'The use of the General Health Questionnaire', 188.
168. Cary L. Cooper and Judi Marshall, 'Occupational sources of stress: A review of the literature relating to coronary heart disease and mental health', *Journal of Occupational Psychology* (1976), 49, 11–28, on 13.
169. Cooper and Marshall, 'Occupational sources of stress', 14.
170. Cooper and Marshall, 'Occupational sources of stress', 22, 12.
171. Rachel Jenkins, 'Minor psychiatric morbidity and labour turnover', *British Journal of Industrial Medicine* (1985), 42, 534–9.
172. Lennart Levi, 'Quality of the working environment: Protection and promotion of occupational mental health', in Levi (ed.), *Society, Stress and Disease,* Volume 4, Working Life pp. 318–24 on p. 319.
173. R. Jenkins, 'Mental health of people at work', in Waldron (ed.), *Occupational Health Practice* (London, Butterworths, 1989 [1973], pp. 73–99, on p. 97.

3 Men, Alcohol and Coping

1. House of Lords, Fifth Series, 2 December 1965, 270 (1965) columns 1371–1454, on 1410.
2. David Ferguson, 'Some characteristics of repeated sickness absence', *British Journal of Industrial Medicine* (1972), 29, 420–31, on 430.
3. W. K. van Dijk and A. van Dijk-Koffeman, 'A follow-up study of 211 treated male alcoholics', *British Journal of Addiction* (1973), 68, 3–24, on 4.
4. N. Heather and I. Robertson, *Problem Drinking* (Oxford, Oxford University Press, 2004 edition), p. 26. For a discussion of the treatment of 'inebriates' in the nineteenth century see: V. Berridge, 'Punishment or treatment? Inebriety, drink and drugs 1860–2004', *Lancet*, December 2004, 364, 4–5.
5. V. Berridge 'Editorial, the centenary issue', *British Journal of Addiction* (1984), 79, 1–6, on 4.
6. V. Berridge, 'The origins and early years of the society, 1844–1899', *British Journal of Addiction* (1990), 85, 991–1003, on 991, 993. The journal of the society originated in 1903 and was known as the *British Journal of Inebriety* until 1947, changing its title to the *British Journal of Addiction to Alcohol and other Drugs* in 1947 and to the *British Journal of Addiction* in 1980. From 1993 it has been entitled *Addiction.*
7. Berridge, 'The origins and early years of the society', 996.
8. V. Berridge, 'The impact of war 1914–1918', *British Journal of Addiction* (1990), 85, 1017–22, on 1017.
9. See Berridge, 'The impact of war 1914–1918', and also V. Berridge, 'The interwar years: A period of decline', *British Journal of Addiction* (1990), 85, 1023–35.
10. Betsy Thom, *Dealing with Drink, Alcohol and Social Policy, from Treatment to Management* (London, Free Association Books, 1999) p. 15. Thom cautions that although there have been broad shifts in explanatory models, differing

perceptions have continued to co-exist. Current disease theories are still contested. See, for example, S. Peele, 'Addiction as a disease: Policy, epidemiology and treatment consequences of a bad idea', in J. Henningfield, W. Bickel and P. Santora (eds), *Addiction Treatment in the 21st Century: Science and Policy Issues* (Baltimore, Johns Hopkins, 2007), pp. 153–63.

11. V. Berridge, 'The 1940s and 1950s: The rapprochement of psychology and biochemistry', *British Journal of Addiction* (1990), 85, 1037–52, on 1042.
12. Berridge, 'The 1940s and 1950s', 1046.
13. V. Berridge, 'The society from the 1960s to the 1980s', *British Journal of Addiction* (1990), 85, 1053–66, on 1060.
14. E. M. Jellinek, 'Phases of alcohol addiction', *Quarterly Journal of Studies on Alcohol* (1952), 13 (4), 673–84.
15. Heather and Robertson, *Problem Drinking*, p. 58. Glatt became the editor of a new journal, *The Journal of Alcoholism* in 1968.
16. G. Edwards and M. M. Gross, 'Alcohol dependence: Provisional description of a clinical syndrome', *British Medical Journal*, 1 May 1976, 1058–61.
17. G. Watts, 'James Griffith Edwards', Obituary, *Lancet*, 6 October 2012 (338), 1224.
18. Heather and Robertson, *Problem Drinking*, p. 31.
19. Heather and Robertson, *Problem Drinking*, p. 31. For a history of AA, see Ernest Kurtz, *Not God: A History of Alcoholics Anonymous* (Center City MN, Hazleden, 1999 edition), and Alcoholics Anonymous, *Alcoholics Anonymous Comes of Age: A Brief History of AA* (New York, AA World Services Inc., 2012 edition). There is little focus on AA in this book, largely due to the fact that its history is well known, and, aside from an acceptance that many patients might benefit from attending AA in parallel with and after medical treatment, many physicians were sceptical of the organisation. Due to confidentiality issues, research on AA was virtually impossible and many physicians found the organisation difficult to deal with. Max Glatt, in contrast, who promoted a more holistic approach, praised their methods and promoted them. For methodological difficulties surrounding research AA research, see, Paul E. Bebbington, 'The efficacy of alcoholics anonymous: The elusiveness of hard data', *British Journal of Psychiatry* (1976), 128, 572–80.
20. Heather and Robertson, *Problem Drinking*, p. 31.
21. Conversation with Max Glatt, *British Journal of Addiction* (1983), 78, 231–43, on 233.
22. Conversation with Max Glatt, 236.
23. Denis Parr, 'Alcoholism in general practice', miscellaneous papers, personal papers of Sir (William) Allen Daley PP/AWD/H.6/3/2, Wellcome Archives and Manuscripts, also published in *British Journal of Addiction* (1957), 54 (1), 25–39. Sir Allen Daley, medical officer of health, served on numerous committees concerned with preventive medicine and health education, of which the Rowntree Steering Group was one. For the evolution of earlier organisations and societies such as the National Council on Alcoholism, see Thom, *Dealing with Drink*. See also Virginia Berridge, 'The society for the study of addiction 1884–1988', *British Journal of Addiction* (1990), 85, special issue.
24. Max Glatt, 'Remarks on Dr Parr's paper', PP/AWD/H.6/3/3 Wellcome Archives and Manuscripts.

25. G. Prys Williams and M. M. Glatt, 'The incidence of (long-standing) alcoholism in England and Wales', *British Journal of Addiction to Alcohol and Other Drugs* (1966), 61, 257–68. See also W. B. Morrell, 'The Steering Group on Alcoholism of the Rowntree Trust', *British Journal of Addiction to Alcohol and Other Drugs* (1966), 61, 295–9.
26. John Greenaway, *Drink and British Politics since 1830* (Basingstoke, Palgrave Macmillan 2003), p. 164.
27. Thom, *Dealing with Drink*, p. 75.
28. Camberwell Council on Alcoholism (hereafter CCA), Miscellaneous correspondence, SA/CAA/17, 'An Alcohol Information and Discussion Week', *Medical Officer*, 31 December 1965, pp. 353–5, on p. 353, Wellcome Archives and Manuscripts. The Council first met in 1961.
29. M. Bennett, 'Drinking as a career', *Journal of Alcoholism* (1976), 11 (4), 150–2, on 151.
30. Bennett, 'Drinking as a career', 150.
31. Thom, *Dealing with Drink*, p. 20.
32. Thom, *Dealing with Drink*, pp. 22, 25, 34, 39.
33. Thom, *Dealing with Drink*, p. 46.
34. SA/CCA/32 'Information week', transcripts of seminars, 1967, p. 8.
35. SA/CCA/32 'Information week', transcripts of seminars, 1967, p. 13.
36. SA/CCA/44 'CCA seminars on alcoholism' 1970, pp. 5–7.
37. SA/CCA/44 'CCA seminars on alcoholism' 1970, p. 12.
38. *International Classification of Diseases (ICD)*, Revision 8 (1965). It should be noted that the ICD was significantly revised over the period 1950–80; however, alcoholism remained categorised under psychiatric and personality disorders throughout: in revisions 6 and 7 (1948 and 1955 respectively) alcoholism is listed under the heading 'Disorders of character, behaviour and intelligence'; in revisions 8 and 9 (1965 and 1975 respectively) it is listed under 'Personality disorders and other non-psychotic mental disorders'. The term 'alcohol dependence syndrome' replaced 'alcoholism' in revision 9.
39. For a psychiatric appraisal, see G. A. Foulds and Christine Hassall, 'The significance of age of onset of excessive drinking in male alcoholics', *British Journal of Psychiatry* (1969), 115, 1027–32. Although social aspects such as childhood and marriage were considered, the authors of this retrospective study of alcoholics correlated alcoholism and problems in the interpersonal sphere as evidence of personality disorder and neurosis.
40. Conversation with Max Glatt, p. 234.
41. M. M. Glatt, 'A treatment centre for alcoholics in a public mental hospital: Its establishment and working', *British Journal of Addiction* (1955), 52, 55–88, 60, 61.
42. Conversation with Max Glatt, p. 234.
43. Conversation with Max Glatt, p. 234.
44. Thom, *Dealing with Drink*, pp. 41, 63.
45. Conversation with Max Glatt, p. 237.
46. Thom, *Dealing with Drink*, pp. 57–8.
47. SA/CCA/62, CCA 'Women alcoholics: Seminars, student surveys, agencies and work-group meetings', 1973–1975.
48. P. Borsay, 'Binge drinking and moral panics, historical parallels?' *History and Policy* website at http://www.historyandpolicy.org/papers/policy-paper-62.html

[accessed 28 January 2013]. This debate continues today. See R. Herring, V. Berridge and B. Thom, 'Binge-drinking: A confused concept', *Journal of Epidemiology and Community Health* (2008), 62, 476–9. The authors argue that the government and media continue to focus on women drinkers while mortality rates from alcohol are twice as high in men than women.

49. SA/CCA/62 'CCA Women alcoholics', minutes of meeting from the planning group.
50. SA/CCA/62 'CCA Women alcoholics', minutes of meeting from the planning group.
51. SA/CCA/62 CCA 'Women alcoholics', minutes of meeting from the planning group.
52. SA/CCA/62 CCA 'Women alcoholics', minutes of meeting from the planning group.
53. SA/CCA/62 CCA 'Women alcoholics', minutes of meeting from the planning group.
54. A. B. Sclare, 'The female alcoholic', *British Journal of Addiction* (1970), 65, 99–107.
55. SA/CCA/44, CCA '"Cured" by a recovering alcoholic', seminars on alcoholism, paper number 5, Autumn 1970.
56. D. Parr, 'Alcoholism in general practice', C1957, Papers of Sir Allen William Daley PP/AWD/H6/3/2, Wellcome Archives and Manuscripts.
57. SA/CCA/32 CCA 'Information week', p. 501.
58. Correspondence, Rowntree Trust Steering Group on Alcohol 1957–1964, PP/AWD/H6/2.
59. Interview with Rupert Espley.
60. G. Edwards, 'Patients with drinking problems', *British Medical Journal*, 16 November 1968, 435–7, on 436, 437.
61. Denis Parr, 'Alcoholism in general practice', *British Journal of Addiction* (1957) 54, 1, 25–39, on 39.
62. Interview with Rupert Espley.
63. R. M. Murray, 'Alcoholism and employment', *Journal of Alcoholism* (1975), 10 (1), 23–6 on 25.
64. K. J. B. Rix, D. Hunter and P. C. Olley, 'Incidence of treated alcoholism in north-east Scotland, Orkney and Shetland fishermen, 1966–1970', *British Journal of Industrial Medicine* (1982), 39, 11–17, on 11.
65. Rix, Hunter and Olley, 'Incidence of treated alcoholism', 15.
66. Interview with Giles Walden.
67. Interview with David Palmer.
68. Interview with Sarah Hall.
69. Interview with James Robertson.
70. Interview with James Robertson.
71. A point made by Richard Stanton.
72. Interview with Richard Stanton.
73. Interview with David Palmer.
74. Interview with Robert Manley.
75. A recurrent theme in all oral history interviews.
76. Interview with Sarah Hall.
77. Murray, 'Alcoholism and employment', 23–6 on 25.
78. SA/CCA/32 'Information week', p. 9.

79. 'Menace of Monday morning blues', *Daily Express*, 19 January 1970.
80. 'Why 25000 men did not go to work', *Daily Express*, 22 October 1968.
81. M. M. Glatt, 'The key role of the family doctor in the rehabilitation of the alcoholic', *Journal of the College of General Practitioners* (1960), 3, 292–300, on 292.
82. H. J. Walton, 'Effect of the doctor's personality on his style of practice', *Journal of the Royal College of General Practitioners* (1969), 17 (82, supplement 3), 6–17.
83. Walton, 'Effect of the doctor's personality', 14.
84. N. H. Rathod, 'An enquiry into general practitioners' opinions about alcoholism', *British Journal of Addiction* (1967), 62, 103–11, on 109.
85. Rathod, 'An enquiry into general practitioners', 109.
86. David Robinson, 'Alcoholism as a social fact: Notes on the sociologist's viewpoint in relation to a proposed study of referral behaviour', *British Journal of Addiction* (1973), 68, 91–7, on 97, 94.
87. Herbert Berger, 'The prevention of alcoholism', *British Journal of Addiction* (1963), 59, 47–54.
88. Berger, 'The prevention of alcoholism', 47.
89. Berger, 'The prevention of alcoholism', 47, 48.
90. Berger, 'The prevention of alcoholism', 50.
91. Berger, 'The prevention of alcoholism', 49.
92. Berger, 'The prevention of alcoholism', 51.
93. Berger, 'The prevention of alcoholism', 54.
94. Kenneth Robinson, 'Talk at the annual dinner of the society', *British Journal of Addiction* (1963), 60, 6–7, on 6.
95. See for example, W. A. Fransen, 'The social worker's contribution in the care of alcoholics', *British Journal of Addiction* (1964) 60, 65–80, and Thorbjorn Kjolstad, 'Psychotherapy of alcoholics', *British Journal of Addiction* (1965), 61, 35–49.
96. House of Lords, Fifth Series, 2 December 1965, 270 (1965) column 1409.
97. Thom, *Dealing with Drink*, pp. 157–8, 161.
98. Advert for White Horse Whisky, *The Times*, 3 February 1958.
99. Advert for Dubbonet, *The Times*, 15 January 1954. ABV – alcohol by volume.
100. Advert for Guinness, *Journal of the College of General Practitioners* (1965), 9 (3).
101. Advert for Guinness, *Journal of the College of General Practitioners* (1965), 10 (2).
102. House of Lords, Fifth Series, 2 December 1965, 270 (1965), column 1403.
103. *The Times*, 2 January 1979.
104. R. Lemle and M. E. Mishkind, 'Alcohol and masculinity', *Journal of Substance Abuse Treatment*, 6 (1989), 213–22.
105. Lemle and Mishkind, 'Alcohol and masculinity', p. 214.
106. Mass Observation, *The Pub and the People* (London: Faber and Faber [1943], 2009), p. 42.
107. Mass Observation, *The Pub and the People*, p. 43.
108. Mass Observation, *The Pub and the People*, p. 42.
109. Mass Observation, *The Pub and the People*, p. 46.
110. Mass Observation, *The Pub and the People*, p. 49.

111. Mass Observation, *The Pub and the People*, p. 50.
112. Thom notes that a shift away from the disease theory towards a public health model of prevention did not come until the 1980s. Thom, *Dealing with Drink*, p. 130.

4 Pharmacological Solutions

1. P. A. Parish, 'The prescribing of psychotropic drugs in general practice', *Journal of the Royal College of General Practitioners* (1971), 92, Supplement 4, 1–77, on 1. Parish undertook research into – and taught – pharmacology. He stressed the importance of teaching pharmacology to GPs.
2. Parish, 'The prescribing of psychotropic drugs', 1. For an account of the development of prescribing policy and prescription charges, see Darrin Baines, 'The prescription charge and the Hinchcliffe Committee', *Prescriber* (2013), 15 November 2013, 40–2.
3. See Andrea Tone, *The Age of Anxiety: A History of America's Turbulent Affair with Tranquilizers* (New York, Basic Books, 2009), p. 196. For a full discussion of women and psychotropic medication in Britain see Ali Haggett, Desperate Housewives, Neuroses and the Domestic Environment 1945–1970 (London, Pickering and Chatto, 2012).
4. For the history of this discovery, see David Healy, *The Antidepressant Era* (Cambridge Massachusetts, Harvard University Press, 1997), pp. 43–8.
5. David Healy, *The Creation of Psychopharmacology* (Cambridge Massachusetts, Harvard University Press, 2002), p. 4.
6. Mickey C. Smith, *A Social History of the Minor Tranquilizers: A Quest for Small Comfort in the Age of Anxiety* (New York, Pharmaceutical Products Press, 1985), p. 12.
7. Smith, *A Social History of the Minor Tranquilizers*, p. 12.
8. 'Today's Drugs, Benzodiazepines', *British Medical Journal*, 1 April 1967, 36.
9. Malcolm Lader argues that studies in the early 1960s indicated that there was the potential for dependence if benzodiazepines were used in large doses for prolonged periods, but that little notice was taken of negative reports due to the widespread perception of their safety. See M. Lader, 'History of benzodiazepine dependence', *Journal of Substance Abuse* (1991), 8, 53–9.
10. Christopher M. Callaghan and German E. Berrios, *Reinventing Depression: A History of the Treatment of Depression in Primary Care, 1940–2004* (Oxford, Oxford University Press, 2004), p. 38.
11. Parish, 'The prescribing of psychotropic drugs', 6.
12. Parish, 'The prescribing of psychotropic drugs', 3.
13. Parish, 'The Prescribing of psychotropic drugs', 16. The survey included a total patient population of 133,081 registered with forty-eight GPs in the Midlands.
14. Parish, 'The prescribing of psychotropic drugs', 18.
15. Parish, 'The prescribing of psychotropic drugs', 19, 26.
16. Parish, 'The prescribing of psychotropic drugs', 26.
17. Parish, 'The prescribing of psychotropic drugs', 7.
18. John A. H. Lee, Peter A. Draper and Miles Weatherall, 'Medical care: prescribing in three English towns', *Milbank Memorial Fund* (1965), 43, 2, Part 2, 285–90, on 288.

19. Parish, 'The prescribing of psychotropic drugs', 22.
20. Interview with Giles Walden.
21. *British National Formulary* (BNF) (London, British Medical Association, 1952), p. 35.
22. Interview with Christian Edwards.
23. Interview with Richard Stanton.
24. Interview with Robert Manley. See also Richard Moore, *Leeches to Lasers: Sketches of a Medical Family* (Killala, Ireland, Morrigan, 2002). Moore recalled: 'mysterious substances like Syrup of Tolu and Pulv Tragacanth – relics of a bygone age', p. 220.
25. Interview with Giles Walden.
26. *BNF* (1952), p. 44.
27. For a cultural history of strychnine, see John Buckingham, *Bitter Nemesis: The Intimate History of Strychnine* (Boca Raton FL, Taylor and Francis, 2008).
28. *BNF* (London, BMA and The Pharmaceutical Society, 1960), pp. 50, 57.
29. *BNF* (London, BMA and The Pharmaceutical Society, 1963).
30. Interview with Rupert Espley.
31. See C. W. M. Wilson, J. A. Banks, R. E. A. Mapes and Sylvia M. T. Korte, 'Influence of different sources of therapeutic information on prescribing by general practitioners', *British Medical Journal*, 7 September 1963, 599–607.
32. Wilson *et al.*, 'Influence of different sources of therapeutic information', 599.
33. Wilson *et al.*, 'Influence of different sources of therapeutic information', 601.
34. Wilson *et al.*, 'Influence of different sources of therapeutic information', 603. See also C. W. M. Wilson J. A. Banks, R. E. A. Mapes and Sylvia M. T. Korte, 'Pattern of prescribing in general practice', *British Medical Journal*, 7 September 1963, 604–7.
35. Karen Dunnell and Ann Cartwright, *Medicine Takers, Prescribers and Hoarders* (London, Routledge and Kegan Paul, 1972), p. 71.
36. D. M. Dunlop, 'A survey of 17,301 prescriptions on Form E C 10', *British Medical Journal*, 9 February 1952, 292–5, on 295. Dunlop went on to become the first chairman of the Committee on the Safety of Drugs, which was known for many years as the Dunlop Committee. Under his leadership, the Yellow Card Scheme was introduced in 1964, after the thalidomide tragedy highlighted the urgent need for routine monitoring of medicines. See The British Pharmaceutical Society, Hall of Fame: http://www.bps.ac.uk/details/resourcesPage/6215841/Sir_Derrick_Dunlop.html?cat=bps1465bf3219c, accessed 7 January 2015.
37. Parish, 'The prescribing of psychotropic drugs', 62.
38. Parish, 'The prescribing of psychotropic drugs', 63.
39. Parish, 'The prescribing of psychotropic drugs', 69.
40. Parish, 'The prescribing of psychotropic drugs', 70.
41. *Research in Psychopharmacology: Report of a WHO Scientific Group* (Geneva, WHO, 1967), pp. 7–8.
42. Parish, 'The prescribing of psychotropic drugs', 14.
43. See for example, Dunnell and Cartwright, *Medicine Takers*, Chapter 3, and M. Balint, J. Hunt, D. Joyce, M. Marinker and J. Woodcock, *Treatment or Diagnosis: A Study of Repeat Prescribing in General Practice* (London, Tavistock, 1970), Chapter 4.
44. Advert for Libraxin, *British Medical Journal*, 10 January 1970.

45. Advert for Nactisol, *British Medical Journal*, 4 December 1965.
46. Advert for Stelabid, *British Medical Journal*, 4 October 1969.
47. See J. T. Silverstone and B. D. Lascelles, 'A double blind trial of Durophet M in the treatment of obesity in general practice', *Journal of the College of General Practitioners* (1965), 9, 304–10.
48. *BNF* (London, BMA and The Pharmaceutical Society, 1974–6), pp. 5–6.
49. *BNF* (London, BMA and The Pharmaceutical Society, 1976–8), p. 36.
50. Interview with Christian Edwards.
51. Interview with David Palmer.
52. Interview with Glen Haden.
53. Interview with Rupert Espley.
54. Interview with Roger Lea.
55. Ruth Cooperstock, 'Sex differences in psychotropic drug use', *Social Science and Medicine* (1978) 12B, 179–86, on 182.
56. Cooperstock, 'Sex differences in psychotropic drug use', 182.
57. Ruth Cooperstock and Henry L. Lennard, 'Some social meanings of tranquilizer use', *Sociology of Health and Illness* (1979), 1 (3) 332–47, on 335.
58. Parish, 'The prescribing of psychotropic drugs', 66.
59. Dunnell and Cartwright, *Medicine Takers*, p. 21.
60. Dunnell and Cartwright, *Medicine Takers*, pp. 21, 6.
61. Dunnell and Cartwright, *Medicine Takers*, p. 13.
62. Sanatogen guard book 1944, foreign market, History of Advertising Trust.
63. Sanatogen guard book 1944, foreign market, History of Advertising Trust.
64. Advert for Rennies, JWT/GD/007, History of Advertising Trust.
65. Advert for Rennies, JWT/GD/007, History of Advertising Trust.
66. See, for example, Judith Williamson, *Decoding Advertisements: Ideology and Meaning in Advertising* (London, Marion Boyers, 2002 edition), p. 11.
67. Sadly, and perhaps with some irony, Harding died suddenly in 1960, at the age of 53, from a heart attack as he left BBC Broadcasting House.
68. The tricyclic antidepressants, for example, claimed to act on levels of serotonin and norepinephrine – the MAOIs claimed to reduce the breakdown of serotonin. For further information about the 'marketing' of stress, see also, Mark Jackson, *The Age of Stress: Science and the Search for Stability* (Oxford, Oxford University Press, 2013), Chapter 4.
69. Advertisement for Horlicks, February 1957, JWT/GD/101, History of Advertising Trust.
70. Advert for Rennies, 1958, SKB guard book 87, 1957–1958, History of Advertising Trust.
71. Advert for Rennies, 19 May 1938, JWT/GD/007, History of Advertising Trust.
72. Advert for Hemotabs (ND, circa 1950s), SKB guard book (012), History of Advertising Trust.
73. Parish, 'The prescribing of psychotropic drugs', 37.
74. A point made in many of the oral history interviews; however, many doctors preferred the traditional envelope style of storing patients' notes.
75. Parish, 'The prescribing of psychotropic drugs', 38.
76. Parish, 'The prescribing of psychotropic drugs', 38.
77. P. Williams, J. Murray and A. Clare, 'A longitudinal study of psychotropic drug prescription', *Psychological Medicine* (1982), 12, 201–6, on 203, 205.
78. Williams *et al.*, 'A longitudinal study of psychotropic drug prescription', 205.

79. Kevin Koumjian, 'The use of Valium as a form of social control', *Social Science and Medicine* (1981), 245–9, on 245.
80. A topic covered fully in my earlier work, *Desperate Housewives*.
81. See for example, Cooperstock and Lennard, 'Some social meanings of tranquilizer use', 336.
82. Joanna Murray, 'Long-term psychotropic drug-taking and the process of withdrawal', *Psychological Medicine* (1981), 11, 853–8, on 855.
83. Illustrated in a number of the oral history interviews.
84. Parish, 'The prescribing of psychotropic drugs', 41. See also, Watts, *Depressive Disorders in the Community*, pp. 12–15.
85. See examples in Cooperstock and Lennard, 'Some social meanings of tranquilizer use', 338.
86. Cooperstock and Lennard, 'Some social meanings of tranquilizer use', 343.
87. Cooperstock and Lennard, 'Some social meanings of tranquilizer use', 341. Such studies were usually undertaken in the United States.

5 Special Cases: Sick Doctors and Ethnic Presentations of Psychological Illness

1. M. F. a'Brook, J. D. Hailstone and E. J. McLauchlan, 'Psychiatric illness in the medical profession', *British Journal of Psychiatry* (1967), 113, 1013–23, on 1013.
2. a'Brook, Hailstone and McLauchlan, 'Psychiatric illness in the medical profession', 1018.
3. Robin M. Murray, 'Psychiatric illness in male doctors and controls: An analysis of Scottish hospitals in-patient data', *British Journal of Psychiatry* (1977), 131, 1–10, on 3.
4. M. M. Glatt, 'Alcoholism, an occupational hazard for doctors', *Journal of Alcoholism* (1976), 11, 85–91 on 85.
5. Glatt, 'Alcoholism, an occupational hazard for doctors', 85.
6. Glatt, 'Alcoholism, an occupational hazard for doctors', 86.
7. a'Brook, Hailstone and McLauchlan, 'Psychiatric illness in the medical profession', 1017.
8. Murray, 'Psychiatric illness among male doctors', 5.
9. Editorial, 'Suicide among doctors', *British Medical Journal*, 28 March 1964, 789–90, on 789.
10. 'Suicide among doctors', 789.
11. 'Suicide among doctors', 789.
12. M. F. a'Brook, letter to the *British Medical Journal*, 4 March 1989, 603. By the late 1980s, it is notable that, in Britain, the rate of suicide among female doctors had reached an alarming three or four times the rate of the general public – roughly equal to the rate of male doctors.
13. 'Suicide among doctors', 789.
14. R. A. Franklin, 'One hundred doctors at the retreat: A contribution to the subject of mental disorder in the medical profession', *British Journal of Psychiatry* (1977), 131, 11–14, on 12.
15. Franklin, 'One hundred doctors at the retreat', 13.
16. a'Brook, 'Psychiatric illness in the medical profession', 1020.

17. a'Brook, 'Psychiatric illness in the medical profession', 1018.
18. Robin M. Murray, 'Characteristics and prognosis of alcoholic doctors', *British Medical Journal*, 15 December 1976, 1537–59 on 1538.
19. M. M. Glatt, letter to the *British Medical Journal*, 22 September 1979, 732.
20. S. E. D. Short, 'Psychiatric illness in physicians', *Journal of the Canadian Medical Association* (1979), 121, 283–8, on 287.
21. Short, 'Psychiatric illness in physicians', 287.
22. Short, 'Psychiatric illness in physicians', 287.
23. Leading article, 'Doctors' diseases', *British Medical Journal*, 9 December 1967, 467–8, on 467.
24. See for example the account from Robin M. Murray, 'The alcoholic doctor', *British Journal of Hospital Medicine* (1977), 18, 144–9, on 147.
25. Gareth Lloyd, personal paper 'I am an alcoholic', *British Medical Journal*, 18 September 1982, 785–6. (MRCOG – Membership of the Royal College of Obstetricians and Gyneacologists examination.)
26. Lloyd, 'I am an alcoholic', 786.
27. Glatt, 'Alcoholism, an occupational hazard for doctors', 88.
28. a'Brook, 'Psychiatric illness in the medical profession', 1018.
29. Murray, 'The alcoholic doctor', 148.
30. John C. Duffy and Edward M. Litin, 'Psychiatric morbidity of physicians', *Journal of the American Medical Association* (1964), 189, 989–92, on 990.
31. a'Brook, 'Psychiatric illness in the medical profession', 1017.
32. Duffy and Litin, 'Psychiatric morbidity of physicians', 99.
33. A. Allibone, 'The health of doctors', in D. J. Pereira Gray (ed.), *The Medical Annual* (Bristol, Wright, 1983), pp. 141–50 on p. 146.
34. Allibone, 'The health of doctors', 147, 146.
35. Allibone, 'The health of doctors', 141.
36. A. L. Simmonds, letter to the *British Medical Journal,* 10 December 1983, 1796.
37. A. Allibone, letter to the *British Medical Journal*, 10 December, 1983, 1796.
38. Ash Samanta and Jo Samanta, 'Regulation of the medical profession: Fantasy, reality and legality', *Journal of the Royal Society of Medicine* (2004), 97, 211–18, on 211.
39. Notes and news, 'Alcoholism among the medical profession', *Lancet,* 2 December 1978, 1215.
40. Allibone, 'The health of doctors', 142.
41. Notes and News, 'Alcoholism among the medical profession', 1215.
42. B. Marien and F. Mckinna, Editorial, 'The elephant in the room', *Clinical Oncology* (2012), 24, 654–6, on 654.
43. a'Brook *et al.* 'Psychiatric illness in the medical profession', 1013, 1017.
44. Glatt, 'Alcoholism, an occupational hazard for doctors', 87.
45. Murray, 'The alcoholic doctor', 149.
46. Glatt, 'Alcoholism, an occupational hazard for doctors', 87.
47. Interview with David Palmer.
48. Interview with Christian Edwards.
49. J. L. Evans, 'Psychiatric illness in the physician's wife', *American Journal of Psychiatry* (1965), 122, 159–63, cited in a'Brook, 'Psychiatric illness in the medical profession', 1018.
50. Evans, 'Psychiatric illness in the physician's wife', cited in a'Brook, 'Psychiatric illness in the medical profession', 1018.

51. Evans, 'Psychiatric illness in the physician's wife', cited in Leading Article, 'Doctors' diseases', *British Medical Journal*, 9 December 1967, 567–8, on 568.
52. S. E. D. Short, Review Article, 'Psychiatric illness in physicians', *Journal of the Canadian Medical Association* (1979), 121, 238–88, on 284.
53. Short, 'Psychiatric illness in physicians', 284.
54. Duffy, 'Psychiatric morbidity of physicians', 98.
55. Jill Pereira Gray, Editorial, 'The family doctor's family', *Journal of the Royal College of General Practitioners* (1978), 28, 579.
56. Allibone, 'The health of doctors', p. 144.
57. Glatt, 'Alcoholism, an occupational hazard for doctors', 90.
58. Glatt, 'Alcoholism, an occupational hazard for doctors', 90.
59. Glatt, letter to the *British Medical Journal*, 22 September 1979, 732.
60. a'Brook *et al.*, 'Psychiatric illness in the medical profession', 1021.
61. See http://www.bddg.org/10/history-of-bddg/ accessed on 15 January 2015. Nurses and female doctors have increasingly been vulnerable to mental illness, addiction and suicide.
62. Glatt, letter to the *British Medical Journal*, 22 September 1979, 732.
63. Allibone, 'The health of doctors', p. 145.
64. Allibone, 'The health of doctors', p. 149.
65. Short, 'Psychiatric illness in physicians', 287.
66. Samuel A. Corson and Elizabeth O'Leary Corson, 'Working situations and psychophysiological pathology – a systems approach', in Lennart Levi (ed.), *Society, Stress and Disease*, Volume 4, Working Life (Oxford, Oxford University Press, 1981), pp. 226–47, on pp. 236–7.
67. Corson and Corson, 'Working situations', p. 237.
68. Corson and Corson, 'Working situations', p. 237.
69. Corson and Corson, 'Working situations', p. 238.
70. Corson and Corson, 'Working situations', pp. 238–9.
71. Panikos Panayi, *An Immigration History of Britain: Multicultural Racism since 1800* (Harlow, Pearso, 2010), p. 23.
72. Panayi, *An Immigration History of Britain*, p. 24.
73. Panayi, *An Immigration History of Britain*, p. 24.
74. Panayi, *An Immigration History of Britain*, p. 25.
75. C. C. Baker and S. J. Pocock, 'Ethnic differences in certified sickness absence', *British Journal of Industrial Medicine* (1982), 39, 277–82, on 277.
76. Charles Zwingmann and Maria Pfister-Ammende, *Uprooting and After* (New York, Springer Verlag, 1973), pp. 2–3. Studies prior to this were confined to lunatic asylums in the US during the nineteenth century.
77. Roland Littlewood and Maurice Lipsedge, *Aliens and Alienists: Ethnic Minorities and Psychiatry* (New York and Hove, Routledge, 1997 edition), p. xi. Original emphasis.
78. Notable studies include: B. Malzberg, 'Mental disease in New York State according to nativity and parentage', *Mental Hygiene*, 19, 635–60 and Ø. Ødegaard, 'Emigration and insanity: A study of mental disease among the Norwegian-born population of Minnesota', *Acta Psychiatrica et Neurologica*, supplement 4 (Copenhagen, Levin and Munksgard, 1935).
79. Jatinder Bains, 'Race, culture and psychiatry: A history of transcultural psychiatry', *History of Psychiatry* (2005), 16 (2), 139–54, on 139. Theories about the association between the 'civilising process' and insanity have a much longer history dating back to the nineteenth century, leading subsequently

to late nineteenth-century ideas about the 'inferior' intelligence of primitive people within the context of social Darwinism. See Ana Maria G Raimundo Oda *et al.*, 'Some origins of cross-cultural psychiatry', *History of Psychiatry* (2005), 16 (2), 155–69.

80. Bains, 'Race, culture and psychiatry', 141.
81. Bains, 'Race, culture and psychiatry', 145.
82. Simon Dein and Kamaldeep Singh Bhui, 'The crossroads of anthropology and epidemiology: Current research in cultural psychiatry in the UK', *Transcultural Psychiatry* (2013), 50 (6), 769–91, on 771.
83. Dein and Bhui, 'The crossroads of anthropology and epidemiology', 771.
84. Dein and Bhui, 'The crossroads of anthropology and epidemiology', 771.
85. A. G. Mezey, 'Psychiatric aspects of human migrations', *International Journal of Social Psychiatry* (1960), 5, 245–60, on 245.
86. Ødegaard, cited in Mezey, 'Psychiatric aspects of human migration', 248.
87. Mezey, 'Psychiatric aspects of human migrants', 258.
88. Mezey, 'Psychiatric aspects of human migrants', 252.
89. H. B. M. Murphy, 'Migration and the major mental disorders: A reappraisal', in Zwingmann and Pfister-Ammende (eds), *Uprooting and After* (New York, Springer Verlag, 1973) pp. 204–20, on p. 207.
90. Murphy, 'Migration and the major mental disorders', p. 209.
91. Murphy, 'Migration and the major mental disorders', p. 210.
92. Mezey, 'Psychiatric aspects of human migrants', 252.
93. Littlewood and Lipsedge, *Aliens and Alienists*, p. 128.
94. Littlewood and Lipsedge, *Aliens and Alienists*, p. 128.
95. D. J. Smith, *Racial Disadvantage in Britain* (Harmondsworth, Penguin, 1977), cited in Littlewood and Lipsedge, *Aliens and Alienists*, p. 129.
96. Early international studies include: C. P. Collins, 'Sickness absence in the three principal ethnic divisions of Singapore', *British Journal of Industrial Medicine* (1962), 19, 116–22 and WHO, *Health Aspects of Labour Migration: Report on a Working Group Convened by the Regional Office for Europe of the WHO, Algiers, 1973* (Copenhagen, WHO 1974).
97. Baker and Pocock, 'Ethnic differences in certified sickness absence', 277.
98. Baker and Pocock, 'Ethnic differences in certified sickness absence', 279.
99. Baker and Pocock, 'Ethnic differences in certified sickness absence', 281.
100. Stuart Crane, 'Problems of an immigrant population', Section of General Practice, *Proceedings of the Royal Society of Medicine* (1970), 63, 629–31, on 629.
101. Crane, 'Problems of an immigrant population', 630.
102. Crane, 'Problems of an immigrant population', 631.
103. Farrukh Hashmi, 'Immigrants and emotional stress', Section of General Practice, *Proceedings of the Royal Society of Medicine* (1970), 63, 631–2, on 631.
104. Hashmi, 'Immigrants and emotional stress', 632.
105. Hashmi, 'Immigrants and emotional stress', 632.
106. Carne, 'Problems of an immigrant community', 629.
107. Carne, 'Problems of an immigrant community', 629.
108. Interview with James Robertson.
109. Interview with James Robertson.
110. Interview with James Robertson.
111. Interview with Sarah Hall.
112. Interview with James Robertson.
113. A point made in both interviews with Robertson and Hall.

114. Interview with Sarah Hall. James Robertson also noted that somatisation was more common in immigrant groups.
115. Interview with James Robertson.
116. Interview with Sarah Hall.
117. Interview with Sarah Hall.
118. A jinn is a supernatural spirit in Islamic mythology.
119. Interview with Sarah Hall.
120. Carne, 'Problems of an immigrant population', 636.
121. Carne, 'Problems of an immigrant population', 636.
122. Wayne Katon, Arthur Kleinman and Gary Rosen, 'Depression and somatisation: A review', part 1 *The American Journal of Medicine* (1982), 72, 127–35, on 131.
123. A term used by Kleinman in 'Depression, somatization and the "new cross-cultural psychiatry"', 4.
124. Kleinman, 'Depression, somatization and the "new cross-cultural psychiatry"', 4.
125. Department of Health, *Invisible Patients: Report of the Working Group on the Health of Health Professionals* (2010), p. 7.
126. Department of Health, *Invisible Patients*, p. 36.
127. Department of Health, *Invisible Patients*, p. 34. It should be noted that women doctors are now particularly vulnerable to suicide.
128. Department of Health, *Invisible Patients*, pp. 34, 45, 47.
129. See Susan S. Lang, 'Economists coin new word, "presenteeism," to describe worker slowdowns that account for up to 60 percent of employer health costs', *Cornell Chronicle*, 20 April 2004 at http://www.news.cornell.edu/stories/2004/04/new-word-job-health-problem-presenteeism, accessed 9 March 2015.
130. Department of Health, *Invisible Patients*, p. 17.
131. The Peninsula Medical School in south west England was highlighted in this respect. Department of Health, *Invisible Patients*, p. 35.
132. Mental Health Foundation website, 'Black and minority ethnic communities', at http://www.mentalhealth.org.uk/help-information/mental-health-a-z/B/BME-communities/ accessed 13 March 2015.
133. See, for example, Ruby Greene, Richard Pugh and Diane Roberts, *Black and Minority Ethnic Parents with Mental Health Problems and their Children*, Research Briefing (London, Social Care Institute for Excellence, 2008), p. 1.
134. Greene, Pugh and Roberts, *Black and Minority Ethnic Parents*, p. 3.
135. Hamid Rehman and David Owen, *Mental Health Survey of Ethnic Minorities* (Ethnos Research and Consultancy, 2013).
136. Kwame McKenzie, 'Improving mental healthcare for ethnic minorities', *Advances in Psychiatric Treatment* (2008), 14, 285–91, on 287.

Conclusion

1. Julian Tudor Hart, 'Going to the doctor', in R. Cooter and J. Pickstone (eds), *Medicine in the Twentieth Century* (Amsterdam, Harwood Academic Press, 2000), pp. 543–58, on p. 549.
2. Tudor Hart, 'Going to the doctor', p. 553.

3. Arthur Watts, cited in Tudor Hart, 'Going to the doctor', p. 553.
4. Royal College of General Practitioners, *The Future General Practitioner* (London, RCGP, 1972), pp. 4, 6.
5. Bernice Tanner (ed.), *Language and Communication in General Practice* (London, RCGP, 1976).
6. RCGP Curriculum 2010, revised 7 May 2014, p. 5.
7. RCGP Curriculum 2010, p. 19.
8. RCGP Curriculum 2010, pp. 19, 20.
9. Elizabeth Scowcroft, *Suicide Statistics Report 2014, Including Data for 2010–2012* (Samaritans, 2014), p. 8.
10. David Wilkins, *Untold Problems: A Review of the Essential Issues on the Mental Health of Men and Boys* (London, Men's Health Forum, 2011), pp. 15, 6. It is acknowledged that not all people who end their lives are mentally ill; however, there is a much greater risk of suicide among those with mental illness.
11. Jill Astbury, 'Gender disparities in mental health', Mental Health Ministerial Round Tables, 2001, 54th World Health Assembly (Geneva, WHO, Switzerland), p. 2.
12. Astbury, 'Gender disparities in mental health', p. 8
13. Astbury, 'Gender disparities in mental health', p. 17.
14. Linda Morison, Christina Trigeorgis and Mary John, 'Are mental health services inherently feminised?', *The Psychologist* (2014), 27 (6), 414–16 on 414.
15. Morison, Trigeorgis and John, 'Are mental health services inherently feminised?', 415.
16. Dame Carol Black, *Working for a Healthier Tomorrow* (London, TSO, 2008), p. 16.
17. Black, *Working for a Healthier Tomorrow,* p. 16.
18. Black, *Working for a Healthier Tomorrow,* p. 16.
19. Policy briefing paper, *Improving Male Health by Taking Action in the Workplace* (London, Men's Health Forum, 2008), pp. 1–2.
20. Roger Kingerlee, Duncan Precious, Luke Sullivan and John Barry, 'Engaging with the emotional lives of men', *The Psychologist* (2014), 27 (6), 418–20.
21. Kingerlee, Precious, Sullivan and Barry, 'Engaging with the emotional lives of men', 418.
22. Kingerlee, Precious, Sullivan and Barry, 'Engaging with the emotional lives of men', 418.
23. Kingerlee, Precious, Sullivan and Barry, 'Engaging with the emotional lives of men', 421. Alexithymia is a psychiatric term/construct introduced in 1972 by Peter Sifneos. The word, derived from Greek, means inability to express emotion.
24. A. K. Mattila *et al.*, 'Alexithymia and somatisation in general population', *Psychosomatic Medicine* (2008), 70 (6), 716–22.
25. Collectively put forward in a number of papers and articles, cited in Lynda W. Warren, 'Male intolerance of depression: A review with implications for psychotherapy', *Clinical Psychology Review* (1983), 3, 147–56, on 150.
26. Warren, 'Male intolerance of depression', 150.
27. David Mechanic, Editorial, 'The concept of illness behaviour: Culture, situation and personal predisposition', *Psychological Medicine* (1986) 16, 1–7, on 1.
28. Mechanic, 'The concept of illness behaviour', 2.

29. Arthur M. Kleinman, 'Depression, somatisation and the "new cross-cultural psychiatry"', *Social Science and Medicine* (1977), 11, 3–10 on 3–4.
30. A point made by Kleinmann in relation to other cultures in 'Depression, somatisation and the "new cross-cultural psychiatry"', 4.
31. An observation of Chinese culture in Kleinmann, 'Depression, somatisation and the "new cross-cultural psychiatry"', 4.
32. Warren, 'Male intolerance of depression', 148.
33. See Daniel Freemen and Jason Freeman, *The Stressed Sex: Uncovering the Truth about Men, Women and Mental Health* (Oxford, Oxford University Press, 2013) and Daniel Freeman and Jason Freeman, 'The Stressed Sex?', *The Psychologist* (2014), 27 (2), February 2014, 84–7; and James Ball, 'Women 40% more likely to develop mental illness, study finds', *Guardian Online,* 22 May 2013 http://www.theguardian.com/society/2013/may/22/women-men-mental-illness-study, Last accessed 26 January 2015.
34. Freeman and Freeman, *The Stressed Sex*, pp. 29–30.
35. Martin Seager, Linda Morison, David Wilkins, Alison Haggett, Luke Sullivan and John Barry, Letter to the Editor, *The Psychologist*, printed March 2014. Martin Seager, a branch consultant for Samaritans, confirmed that the organisation receives approximately equal numbers of calls from men and women, suggesting that when men are assured anonymity, they might be more willing to report distress.
36. Seager, Morison, Wilkins, Haggett, Sullivan and Barry, Letter to *The Psychologist*, March 2015.
37. See for example, N. McLaren, 'A critical review of the biopsychosocial model', *Australian and New Zealand Journal of Psychiatry* (1998), 32, 86–92 and S. Nassir Ghaemi, 'The biopsychosocial model in psychiatry: A critique', *Existenz* (2011), 6 (1), 1–8.
38. Kingerlee, Precious, Sullivan and Barry, 'Engaging with the emotional lives of men', 418–19.
39. A point made in David Wilkins and Mariam Kemple, *Delivering Male: Effective Practice in Male Mental Health* (London, Men's Health Forum and Mind, 2011).
40. Bruce P. Dohrenwend and Barbara Snell Dohrenwend, 'Sex differences and psychiatric disorders', *American Journal of Sociology*, (1976), 81, 1453.

Bibliography

Archives and manuscripts

Royal College of General Practitioners' Archive

ACE H2–5. Papers of the Postgraduate Education Committee 1954–1964.
ACE H3–2. Undergraduate Education Committee August 1959 to May 1956.
ACE H49–1. Communication and Language in General Practice.

Psychiatry and the General Practitioner Working Party Papers 1956–1958:
A CE G 12–1. Agendas, notes and reports.
A CE 12–2. Reports, essays, opinions, correspondence and drafts of report.

John Fry collection:
B FRY C7–1. Articles on depression and mental illness.
B FRY C7–2. Research notes and publications on depression and mental illness.
B FRY C2–1. Research notes on peptic ulcer.
B FRY C2–2. Clinical notes on peptic ulcer.
B FRY C2–3. Clinical research on peptic ulcer, articles by others.

Wellcome Library, Archives and Manuscripts

PP/AWD/H6/3/1–20. Sir (William) Allen Daley (1887–1969). Miscellaneous papers.

GC/200/G2. Herbert Davis Chalk. Publications.

SA/CCA/15. Camberwell Council on Alcoholism. Correspondence, early meetings.
SA/CCA/17. Camberwell Council on Alcoholism. Miscellaneous correspondence.
SA/CCA/23. Camberwell Council on Alcoholism. Conferences and meetings.
SA/CCA/32. Camberwell Council on Alcoholism. Information week 1967.

History of Advertising Trust Archive

Sanatogen guard book, 1944.
Sanatogen guard book, 1957.
JWT guard book, JWT/GD/007.
JWT guard book, JWT/GD/600.
JWT guard book, JWT/GD/0117.
JWT guard book, JWT/GD/101.
SKB guard book, 'Indigestion remedies' (87), 1957–1958.
SKB guard book, 'Indigestion remedies' (45), 1959.
SKB guard book, (012) (ND, C1950s).
SKB guard book, 'Iron Jelloids' (155), 1950s.
SKB guard book, 'Phospherine' (91), 1952–1967.

Oral history

See appendix

Journal articles and chapters

a'Brook, M. F., J. D. Hailstone and E. J. McLauchlan. 'Psychiatric illness in the medical profession', *British Journal of Psychiatry* (1967), 113, 1013–23.

Adelstein, A. M. 'Absence from work attributed to sickness', conference report, *British Journal of Industrial Medicine* (1969), 26 (2), 169–70.

'Alcoholism among the medical profession', *Lancet,* 2 December 1978, 1215.

Allibone, A. 'The health of doctors', in D. J. Pereira Gray (ed.), *The Medical Annual* (Bristol, Wright, 1983), pp. 141–50.

Avery Jones, F. 'Clinical and social problems of peptic ulcer', *British Medical Journal,* 30 March 1957, 719–23.

Ayres, Pat. 'Work, culture and gender: The making of masculinities in post-war Liverpool', *Labour History Review* (2004), 69 (2), 154–7.

Baines, Darrin. 'The prescription charge and the Hinchcliffe Committee', *Prescriber* (2013), 15 November 2013, 402.

Bains, Jatinder. 'Race, culture and psychiatry: A history of transcultural psychiatry', *History of Psychiatry* (2005), 16 (2), 139–54.

Baker, C. C. and S. J. Pocock. 'Ethnic differences in certified sickness absence', *British Journal of Industrial Medicine* (1982), 39, 277–82.

Balint, Michael. 'The doctor, his patient and the illness', *Lancet,* 2 April 1955, 683–88.

Balint, Michael. 'Psychotherapy and the general practitioner', *British Medical Journal,* 19 January 1957, 156–8.

Bancroft, J. G. and C. A. H. Watts. 'A survey of patients with chronic illness in a general practice', *Journal of the College of General Practitioners* (1959), 2, 338–45.

Banks, Michael H., C. W. Clegg, P. R. Jackson, N. J. Kemp, E. M. Stafford and T. D. Wall. 'The use of the General Health Questionnaire as an indicator of mental health in occupational studies', *Journal of Occupational Psychology* (1980), 53, 187–94.

Bartrip, Peter. 'Workmen's compensation', in Paul Weindling (ed.), *The Social History of Occupational Health* (London, Croom Helm, 1988), pp. 157–79.

Bebbington, Paul E. 'The efficacy of Alcoholics Anonymous: The elusiveness of hard data', *British Journal of Psychiatry* (1976), 128, 572–80.

Behrend, Hilde. 'Voluntary absence from work', *International Labour Review* (1959), 79, 109–40.

Bennett, M. 'Drinking as a career', *Journal of Alcoholism* (1976), 11 (4), 150–52.

Berger, Herbert. 'The prevention of alcoholism', *British Journal of Addiction* (1963), 59, 47–54.

Berridge, V. 'Editorial, the Centenary issue', *British Journal of Addiction* (1984), 79, 1–6.

Berridge, V. 'The impact of war 1914–1918', *British Journal of Addiction* (1990), 85, 1017–22.

Berridge, V. 'The interwar years: A period of decline', *British Journal of Addiction* (1990), 85, 1023–35.

Berridge, V. 'The origins and early years of the Society, 1844–1899', *British Journal of Addiction* (1990), 85, 991–1003.

Berridge, V. 'The 1940s and 1950s: The rapprochement of psychology and biochemistry', *British Journal of Addiction* (1990), 85, 1037–52.

Bertolote, Jose M. 'The roots of the concept of mental health', *World Psychiatry* (2008), 7, 113–16.

Blumenthal, David. 'Employer-sponsored health insurance in the United States – origins and implications', *The New England Journal of Medicine,* 6 July 2006, 82–8.

Bomford, R. R. 'The anxious patient and the worried doctor', Papers from a joint conference of the College of General Practitioners and the Society of Psychosomatic Research: 'The problems of stress in general practice', *Supplement to the Journal of the College of General Practitioners* (1958), 1 (2), 10–13.

Bransby, E. R. 'The extent of mental illness in England and Wales', *Health Trends* (1974), 6, 56–9.

Brisco, Monica E. 'Sex differences in perception of illness and expressed life satisfaction', *Psychological Medicine* (1978), 8, 339–45.

Brisco, Monica E. 'Sex differences in psychological wellbeing', *Psychological Medicine,* Monograph Supplement, Supplement 1 (1982), 1–46.

Brisco, Monica E. 'Why do people go to the doctor? Sex differences in the correlates of GP consultation', *Social Science and Medicine* (1987), 25 (5), 507–13.

Chadwick-Jones, J. K., C. A. Brown and N. Nicholson. 'Absence from work: Its meaning, measurement and control', *International Review of Applied Psychology* (1973), 22 (2), 137–54.

Colgrove, James. 'The McKeown thesis: A historical controversy and its enduring influence', *American Journal of Public Health* (2002), 92 (5), 725–9.

Collins, C. P. 'Sickness absence in the three principal ethnic divisions of Singapore', *British Journal of Industrial Medicine* (1962), 19, 116–22.

Connell, R. W. and James W. Messerschmidt. 'Hegemonic masculinity: Rethinking the concept', *Gender and Society* (2005), 19, 829–59.

Conversation with Max Glatt, *British Journal of Addiction* (1983), 78, 231–43.

Cooper, Cary L. and Judi Marshall, 'Occupational sources of stress: A review of the literature relating to coronary heart disease and mental health', *Journal of Occupational Psychology* (1976), 49, 11–28.

Cooper, Brian, John Fry and Graham Kalton. 'A longitudinal study of psychiatric morbidity in a general practice population', *British Journal of Preventive and Social Medicine* (1969), 23, 210–17.

Cooperstock, Ruth. 'Sex differences in psychotropic drug use', *Social Science and Medicine* (1978) 12B, 179–86.

Cooperstock, Ruth and Henry L. Lennard, 'Some social meanings of tranquilizer use', *Sociology of Health and Illness* (1979), 1 (3), 332–47.

Corson, Samuel A. and Elizabeth O'Leary Corson. 'Working situations and psychophysiological pathology – a systems approach', in Lennart Levi (ed.), *Society, Stress and Disease,* Volume 4, Working Life (Oxford, Oxford University Press, 1981), pp. 226–47.

Crane, Stuart. 'Problems of an immigrant population', Section of General Practice, *Proceedings of the Royal Society of Medicine* (1970), 63, 629–31.

Davies, Daniel T. and A. T. Macbeth Wilson. 'Observations on the life-history of the chronic peptic ulcer patient', *Lancet,* 11 December 1937, 1354–60.

Dein, Simon and Kamaldeep Singh Bhui. 'The crossroads of anthropology and epidemiology: Current research in cultural psychiatry in the UK', *Transcultural Psychiatry* (2013), 50 (6), 769–79.

van Dijk, W. K. and A. van Dijk-Koffeman. 'A follow-up study of 211 treated male alcoholics', *British Journal of Addiction* (1973), 68, 3–24.

'Doctors' diseases', Leading Article, *British Medical Journal*, 9 December 1967, 467–8.

Dohrenwend, Bruce P. and Barbara Snell Dohwenrend. 'Sex differences and psychiatric disorders', *American Journal of Sociology* (1976), 81, 1447–54.

Duffy, John C. and Edward M. Litin. 'Psychiatric morbidity of physicians', *Journal of the American Medical Association* (1964), 189, 989–92.

Dunlop, D. M. 'A survey of 17,301 prescriptions on Form E C 10', *British Medical Journal*, 9 February 1952, 292–5.

Edwards, G. 'Patients with drinking problems', *British Medical Journal*, 16 November 1968, 435–7.

Edwards, G. and M. M. Gross. 'Alcohol dependence: Provisional description of a clinical syndrome', *British Medical Journal,* 1 May 1976, 1058–61.

Engel, George L. 'The need for a new medical model: A challenge for biomedicine', *Science* (1977), 196, 129–36.

Evans, J. L. 'Psychiatric illness in the physician's wife', *American Journal of Psychiatry* (1965), 122, 159–63.

Ferguson, David. 'Some characteristics of repeated sickness absence', *British Journal of Industrial Medicine* (1972), 29, 420–31.

Ferguson, David. 'A study of neurosis and occupation', *British Journal of Industrial Medicine* (1973), 30, 187–98.

First, Michael. 'Harmonisation of ICD-11 and DSM – V: opportunities and challenges', *British Journal of Psychiatry* (2009), 195, 382–90.

Foulds, G. A. and Christine Hassall. 'The significance of age of onset of excessive drinking in male alcoholics', *British Journal of Psychiatry* (1969), 115, 1027–32.

Franklin, R. A. 'One hundred doctors at the retreat: A contribution to the subject of mental disorder in the medical profession', *British Journal of Psychiatry* (1977), 131, 11–14.

Fransen, W. A. 'The social worker's contribution in the care of alcoholics', *British Journal of Addiction* (1964), 60, 65–80.

Freeman, Daniel and Jason Freeman. 'The stressed sex?', *The Psychologist* (2014), 27 (2), February 2014, 84–7.

Froggatt, P. 'Short-term absence from industry: I Literature, definitions, data and the effect of age and length of service', *British Journal of Industrial Medicine* (1970), 27, 199–210.

Froggatt, P. 'Short-term absence from industry: II Temporal variation and inter-association with other recorded factors', *British Journal of Industrial Medicine* (1970), 27, 211–24.

Froggatt, P. 'Short-term absence from industry: III The inference of "proneness" and a search for causes', *British Journal of Industrial Medicine* (1970), 27, 297–312.

Fry, John. 'The psychoneurotic in general practice', *Medical World,* June 1954, 657–66, on 661.

Fry, John. 'The management of psychosomatic disorders in general practice', *The Practitioner* (1957), 177, 554–63.

Fry, John. 'What happened to our neurotic patients?', *The Practitioner*, (1960), 185, 885–9.

Fry, John and David Finer. 'Peptic ulcer in general practice', *British Medical Journal*, 16 July 1955, 169–72.

Ghaemi, S. Nassir. 'The biopsychosocial model in psychiatry: A critique', *Existenz* (2011), 6 (1), 1–8.

Glatt, M. M. 'A treatment centre for alcoholics in a public mental hospital: Its establishment and working', *British Journal of Addiction* (1955), 52, 55–88.

Glatt, M. M. 'The key role of the family doctor in the rehabilitation of the alcoholic', *Journal of the College of General Practitioners* (1960), 3, 292–300.

Glatt, M. M. 'Alcoholism, an occupational hazard for doctors', *Journal of Alcoholism* (1976), 11, 85–91.

Goldberg, D. P. and B. Blackwell, 'Psychiatric illness in general practice: A detailed study using a new method of case identification', *British Medical Journal*, 23 May 1970, 439–43.

Goldberg, D. P. and B. Blackwell. 'Psychiatric illness in general practice: A detailed study using a new method of case identification', *British Medical Journal*, 27 May 1970, 439–43.

Gordon, C., A. R. Emerson and D. S. Pugh, 'Patterns of sickness absence in a railway population', *British Journal of Industrial Medicine* (1959), 16, 230–43.

Gove, Walter. 'The relationship between sex roles, marital status and mental illness', *Social Forces* (1972), 51, 34–44.

Hacker, Helen Mayer. 'The new burdens of masculinity', *Marriage and Family Living* (1957), 19, 227–33.

Hadfield, Stephen J. 'A field survey of general practice', *British Medical Journal*, 26 September 1953, 684–706.

Hall, D. W. 'Vocational training for general practice', *Health Trends* (1973), 5, 80–2.

Halliday, James L. 'The rising incidence of psychosomatic illness', *British Medical Journal*, 2 July 1938, 11–14.

Halliday, James L. 'Epidemiology and the psychosomatic affections: A study in social medicine', *Lancet*, 10 August 1946, 185–9.

Hamburg, David A. and Beatrix A. Hamburg, 'Occupational stress, endocrine changes and coping behaviour in the middle years of adult life', in Lennart Levi (ed.), *Society, Stress and Disease*, Volume 4, Working Life (Oxford, Oxford University Press, 1981), pp.131–43.

Hannay, David. 'Undergraduate medical education and general practice', in Irvine Loudon, John Horder and Charles Webster (eds), *General Practice under the National Health Service 1948–1997* (Oxford, Oxford University Press, 1998) pp. 165–8.

Harris, Chris. 'The family in post-war Britain', in James Obelkevich and Peter Catterall (eds), *Understanding Post-War British Society* (London, Routledge, 1994), pp. 45–57.

Harrison, Brian. 'Rowntree, (Benjamin) Seebohm (1871–1954)', *Oxford Dictionary of National Biography*, Oxford University Press, 2004; online edn, January 2008 http://0-www.oxforddnb.com.lib.exeter.ac.uk/view/article/35856, accessed 12 October 2014.

Hartley, Ruth. 'Sex-role pressures in the socialisation of the child', *Psychological Reports* (1959), 5, 457–69.

Harvey, Karen and Alexandra Shepard. 'What have historians done with masculinity? Reflections on five centuries of British History, 1500–1950', *Journal of British Studies*, 44 (2005), 274–80.

Hashmi, Farrukh. 'Immigrants and emotional stress', Section of General Practice, *Proceedings of the Royal Society of Medicine* (1970), 63, 631–2.

Hayes, Nick. 'Did manual workers want industrial welfare? Canteens, latrines and masculinity on British building sites', *Journal of Social History* (2002), 35 (3), 637–58.

Hayes, Sarah. 'Industrial automation and stress in post-war Britain', in Mark Jackson (ed.), *Stress in Post-War Britain* (London, Pickering and Chatto, 2015).

Hayward, Rhodri. 'Enduring emotions: James L. Halliday and the invention of the psychosocial', *Isis* (2009), 100, 827–38.

Hearne, J. 'Is masculinity dead? A critique of the concept masculinity/masculinities', in M. Mac an Ghaill (ed.), *Understanding Masculinities* (Buckingham, Open University Press, 1996).

Herring, R., V. Berridge and B. Thom. 'Binge-drinking: A confused concept', *Journal of Epidemiology and Community Health* (2008), 62, 476–9.

Hopkins, Philip. 'The general practitioner and the psychosomatic approach', in Desmond O'Neil (ed.), *Modern Trends in Psychosomatic Medicine* (London, Butterworths, 1955), pp. 4–28.

Hopkins, Philip. 'Psychiatry in general practice', *Postgraduate Medical Journal,* May 1960, 323–30.

Horder, John. 'The first Balint group', *British Journal of General Practice,* December 2001, 1038–9.

Horwitz, Allan V. 'How an age of anxiety became an age of depression', *The Milbank Quarterly* (2010), 88 (1), 112–38.

Howe, John. 'Research in general practice: Perspectives and themes', in Irvine Loudon, John Horder and Charles Webster (eds), *General Practice Under the National Health Service 1948–1997* (Oxford, Oxford University Press, 1998), pp. 146–64.

Hsu, Elisabeth. '"Holism" and the medicalisation of emotion: The case of anger in Chinese medicine', in Peregrine Horden and Elisabeth Hsu (eds), *The Body in Balance: Humoral Medicines in Practice* (New York and Oxford, Berghan, 2013), pp. 197–217.

Isambert-Jamati, Viviane. 'Absenteeism among women workers in industry', *International Labour* Review (1962), 85, 248–61.

Jellinek, E. M. 'Phases of alcohol addiction', *Quarterly Journal of Studies on Alcohol* (1952), 13 (4), 673–84.

Jenkins, Rachel. 'Minor psychiatric morbidity in employed young men and women and its contribution to sickness absence', *British Journal of Industrial Medicine* (1985), 42, 147–54.

Jenkins, Rachel. 'Minor psychiatric morbidity and labour turnover', *British Journal of Industrial Medicine* (1985), 42, 534–39

Jenkins, R. 'Mental health of people at work', in H. A. Waldron (ed.), *Occupational Health Practice* (London, Butterworths, 1989 [1973]), pp. 73–99.

Johnston, Ronnie and Arthur McIvor. 'Dangerous work, hard men and broken bodies: Masculinity in the Clydeside heavy industries c. 1930–1970s', *Labour History Review* (2004), 69 (2), 135–5.

Jones, Edgar. '"The gut war": functional somatic disorders in the UK during the Second World War', *History of the Human Sciences* (2012), 25 (5), 30–48.

Jones, Edgar and Simon Wessely. 'Hearts, guts and minds: Somatisation in the military from 1900', *Journal of Psychosomatic Research* (2004), 56, 425–29.

Jourard, Sidney M. 'Some lethal aspects of the male role', in Joseph H. Pleck and Jack Sawyer (eds), *Men and Masculinity* (New Jersey, Prentice Hall, 1974), pp. 21–9.

Katon, Wayne, Arthur Kleinman and Gary Rosen. 'Depression and somatisation: A review', Part 1, *The American Journal of Medicine* (1982), 72, 127–35.

Kendell, R. E. 'The classification of depressions: A review of contemporary confusion', *British Journal of Psychiatry* (1976), 129, 15–28.

Kihlstrom, John F. and Lucy Canter Kihlstrom. 'Somatisation as illness behaviour', *Advances in Mind-Body Medicine* (2001), 17, 240–4.

Kingerlee, Roger, Duncan Precious, Luke Williams and John Barry. 'Engaging with the emotional lives of men', *The Psychologist* (2014), 27 (6), 418–20.

Kirmayer, Laurence J. 'Culture, affect and somatisation', *Transcultural Psychiatry* (1984), 21, 159–88.

Kirmayer, Laurence J. 'Beyond the "new cross-cultural psychiatry": Cultural biology, discursive psychology and the ironies of globalisation', *Transcultural Psychiatry* (2006), 43, 126–44.

Kjolstad, Thorbjorn. 'Psychotherapy of alcoholics', *British Journal of Addiction* (1965), 61, 35–49.

Kleinman, Arthur. 'Depression, somatisation and the "new cross-cultural psychiatry"', *Social Science and Medicine* (1977), 11 (3), 3–10.

Koumjian, Kevin. 'The use of Valium as a form of social control', *Social Science and Medicine* (1981), 245–9.

Lader, M. 'History of benzodiazepine dependence', *Journal of Substance Abuse* (1991), 8, 53–9.

Lee, John A. H., Peter A. Draper and Miles Weatherall. 'Medical care: Prescribing in three English towns', *Milbank Memorial Fund* (1965), 43, 2, Part 2, 285–90.

Lemle, R. and M. E. Mishkind. 'Alcohol and masculinity', *Journal of Substance Abuse Treatment*, 6 (1989), 213–22.

Levenstein, Susan. 'Stress and peptic ulcer: Life beyond helicobacter', *BMJ*, 316, 14 February 1998, 538–41.

Levi, Lennart (ed.). 'Preface', *Society, Stress and Disease*, Volume 4, 'Working Life' (Oxford, Oxford University Press, 1981).

Lloyd, Gareth. 'I am an alcoholic', *British Medical Journal*, 18 September 1982, 785–6.

Lohan, Maria. 'Developing a critical men's health debate in academic scholarship', in Brendan Gough and Steve Robertson (eds), *Men, Masculinities and Health: Critical Perspectives* (Basingstoke, Palgrave Macmillan, 2010), pp. 11–29.

Lokander, Sven. 'Sick absence in a Swedish company: A sociomedical study', *Acta Medica Scandinavica* (1962), Vol. 171, Supplement 377.

Maj, Mario. 'Psychiatric diagnosis: Pros and cons of prototypes vs. operational criteria', *World Psychiatry* (2011), 10, 81–2.

Malzberg, B. 'Mental disease in New York State according to nativity and parentage', *Mental Hygiene*, 19, 635–60.

Marien B. and F. Mckinna, Editorial, 'The elephant in the room', *Clinical Oncology* (2012), 24, 654–6.

Marinker, Marshall. 'What is wrong and how we know it: Changing concepts of general practice', in Irvine Loudon, John Horder and Charles Webster (eds), *General Practice under the National Health Service 1948–1997* (Oxford, Oxford University Press, 1998), pp. 65–91.

Mattila, A. K., E. Kronholm, A. Jula, J. K. Salminen, A. M. Koivisto, R. L. Mielonen and M. Joukamaa. 'Alexithymia and somatisation in general population', *Psychosomatic Medicine* (2008), 70 (6), 716–22.

McKenzie, Kwame. 'Improving mental healthcare for ethnic minorities', *Advances in Psychiatric Treatment* (2008), 14, 285–91.

McLaren, N. 'A critical review of the biopsychosocial model', *Australian and New Zealand Journal of Psychiatry* (1998), 32, 86–92.

McLean, Alan A. 'Occupational mental health: Review of an emerging art', in Frank Baker, Peter J. M. McEwan and Alan Sheldon (eds), *Industrial Organizations and Health* (London, Tavistock Publications, 1969), pp. 164–91.

Meadows, Susan H. 'Health examinations of senior staff in industry', *British Journal of Industrial Medicine* (1964), 21, 226–30.

Mechanic, David. Editorial, 'The concept of illness behaviour: Culture, situation and personal predisposition', *Psychological Medicine* (1986), 16, 1–7.

Melling, Joseph. 'The risks of working versus the risks of not working: Trade unions, employers and responses to the risk of occupational illness in British industry, c. 1890–1940s', *ESRC Centre for Analysis of Risk and Regulation Discussion Paper 12*, 14–34.

Messner, Michael A. 'The limits of the male sex role: An analysis of the men's liberation and men's rights movements discourse', *Gender and Society* (1998), 12 (3), 255–76.

Mezey, A. G. 'Psychiatric aspects of human migrations', *International Journal of Social Psychiatry* (1960), 5, 245–60.

'Michael Balint', Editorial, *Journal of the Royal College of General Practitioners* (1972), 22, 133–5.

Miller, Ian. 'Stress and abdominal illness in Britain c.1939–1945', *Medical History* (2010), 54, 95–110.

Morison, Linda, Christina Trigeorgis and Mary John. 'Are mental health services inherently feminised?', *The Psychologist* (2014), 27 (6), 414–16.

Morrell, David. 'Introduction and overview', in Irvine Loudon, John Horder and Charles Webster (eds), *General Practice under the National Health Service 1948–1997* (Oxford, Oxford University Press, 1998), pp. 1–19.

Morrell, W. B. 'The Steering Group on Alcoholism of the Rowntree Trust', *British Journal of Addiction to Alcohol and Other Drugs* (1966), 61, 295–99.

Morris, J. N. and Richard M. Titmuss. 'Epidemiology of peptic ulcer: Vital statistics', *Lancet*, 30 December 1944, 841–5.

Mort, Frank. 'Social and symbolic fathers and sons in post-war Britain', *The Journal of British Studies* (1999), 38 (3), 353–84.

Murphy, H. B. M. 'Migration and the major mental disorders: A reappraisal', in Charles Zwingmann and Maria Pfister-Ammende (eds), *Uprooting and After* (New York, Springer Verlag, 1973), pp. 204–20.

Murray, Joanna. 'Long-term psychotropic drug-taking and the process of withdrawal', *Psychological Medicine* (1981), 11, 853–8.

Murray, R. M. 'Alcoholism and employment', *Journal of Alcoholism* (1975), 10 (1), 23–6.

Murray, Robin M. 'Characteristics and prognosis of alcoholic doctors', *British Medical Journal*, 15 December 1976, 1537–59.

Murray, Robin M. 'Psychiatric illness in male doctors and controls: An analysis of Scottish hospitals in-patient data', *British Journal of Psychiatry* (1977), 131, 1–10.

Murray, Robin M. 'The alcoholic doctor', *British Journal of Hospital Medicine* (1977), 18, 144–9.

Nazroo, James Y., Angela C. Edwards and George W. Brown. 'Gender differences in the prevalence of depression: Artefact, alternative disorders, biology or roles?', *Sociology of Health and Illness* (1998), 20 (3), 312–30.

Nerall, Gunnar and Ingrid Wahlund. 'Stressors and strain in white collar workers', Lennart Levi (ed.), *Society, Stress and Disease,* Volume 4, Working life (Oxford, Oxford University Press, 1981), pp. 120–7.

Ødegaard, Ø. 'Emigration and insanity: A study of mental disease among the Norwegian-born population of Minnesota', *Acta Psychiatrica et Neurologica,* supplement 4 (Copenhagen, Levin and Munksgard, 1935), 1–206.

Palmer, Debbie. 'Cultural change, stress and civil servants' occupational health, 1967–1990', in Mark Jackson (ed.), *Stress in Post-War Britain* (London, Pickering and Chatto, 2015 forthcoming).

Parish, P. A. 'Prescribing of psychotropic drugs in general practice', *Journal of the Royal College of General Practitioners* (1971), 92, Supplement 4, 1–77.

Parnell R. W. and Ian Skottowe. 'Towards preventing suicide', *Lancet,* 26 January 1957, 206–8.

Parr, Denis. 'Alcoholism in general practice', *British Journal of Addiction* (1957), 54, 1, 25–39.

Peele, S. 'Addiction as a disease: Policy, epidemiology and treatment consequences of a bad idea', in J. Henningfield, W. Bickel and P. Santora (eds), *Addiction Treatment in the 21st Century: Science and Policy Issues* (Baltimore, Johns Hopkins, 2007).

Pemberton J. 'Origins and early history of the Society for Social Medicine in the UK and Ireland', *Journal of Epidemiology and Community Health* (2002), 54, 342–6.

Pereira Gray, Denis. 'Postgraduate training and continuing education', in Irvine Loudon, John Horder and Charles Webster (eds), *General Practice under the National Health Service, 1948–1997* (London, Clarenden Press, 1998), pp. 182–204.

Pereira Gray, Jill. Editorial, 'The family doctor's family', *Journal of the Royal College of General Practitioners* (1978), 28, 579.

Perth, R. E. 'Psychosomatic problems in general practice', *Journal of the College of General Practitioners, Research Newsletter* (1957), 4, 295–31.

Phillips, Derek L. and Bernard E Segal, 'Sexual status and psychiatric symptoms', *American Sociological Review* (1969), 34 (1), 58–72.

Porter, Dorothy. 'Introduction' in John A Ryle, *Changing Disciplines* (New Brunswick, NJ, Transaction, 1994 edition), pp. xi–xxxix.

Porter, Dorothy. 'The decline of social medicine in Britain in the 1960s', in Dorothy Porter (ed.), *Social Medicine and Medical Sociology in the Twentieth-Century* (Amsterdam, Editions Rodopi, 1997), pp. 97–119.

Porter, Roy. 'Diseases of civilization', in W. F. Bynum and R. Porter (eds), *Companion Encyclopedia of the History of Medicine* (London, Routledge, 1993), pp. 585–602.

'Psychological medicine in general practice: a report prepared by a working party of the Council of the College of General Practitioners', *British Medical Journal,* 6 September 1958, 585–90.

Raimundo Oda, Ana Maria G., Claudio Eduardo M. Banzato and Paulo Dalgalarrondo. 'Some origins of cross-cultural psychiatry', *History of Psychiatry* (2005), 16 (2), 155–69.

Rathod, N. H. 'An enquiry into general practitioners' opinions about alcoholism', *British Journal of Addiction* (1967), 62, 103–11.

Riska, Elianne. 'The rise and fall of Type A man', *Social Science and Medicine* (2000), 51, 1665–74.

Rix, K. J. B., D. Hunter and P. C. Olley, 'Incidence of treated alcoholism in north-east Scotland, Orkney and Shetland fishermen, 1966–1970', *British Journal of Industrial Medicine* (1982), 39, 11–17.

Robertson, Steve and Robert Williams, 'Men, public health and health promotion: Towards a critically structural and embodied understanding', in Brendan Gough and Steve Robertson (eds), *Men, Masculinities and Health* (Basingstoke, Palgrave Macmillan 2009), pp. 48–66.

Robertson, Steve and Robert Williams, 'The importance of retaining a focus on masculinities in future studies on men and health', in Gilles Tremblay and François-Olivier Bernard (eds), *Future Perspectives for Intervention, Policy and Research on Men and Masculinities: An International Forum* (Harriman TN, Men's Studies Press, 2012), pp. 119–33.

Robinson, David. 'Alcoholism as a social fact: Notes on the sociologist's viewpoint in relation to a proposed study of referral behaviour', *British Journal of Addiction* (1973), 68, 91–7.

Robinson, Kenneth. 'Talk at the annual dinner of the society', *British Journal of Addiction* (1963), 60, 6–7.

Roper, Michael. 'Slipping out of view: Subjectivity and emotion in gender history', *History Workshop Journal*, 59 (2005), 57–72.

Royle, Edward. 'Trends in post-war British social history', in James Obelkevich and Peter Catterall (eds), *Understanding Post-War British Society* (London, Routledge, 1994).

Ryle, John A. 'The natural history of duodenal ulcer', *Lancet*, 13 February 1932, 327–34.

Ryle, John A. 'Aetiology: A plea for wider concepts and new study', *Lancet*, 11 July 1942, 29–30.

Ryle, A. 'The neuroses in a general practice population', *Journal of the College of General Practice* (1960), 3, 313–28.

Samanta, Ash and Jo Samanta, 'Regulation of the medical profession: Fantasy, reality and legality', *Journal of the Royal Society of Medicine* (2004), 97, 211–18.

Sanderson, Michael. 'Education and social mobility', in Paul Johnson (ed.), *Twentieth Century Britain: Economic, Social and Cultural Change* (Harlow, Addison Wesley Longman, 1998 edition), pp. 374–91.

Savage, Mike. 'Working-class identities in the 1960s: Revisiting the Affluent Worker study', *Sociology* (2005), 39 (5), 929–46.

Schilling, R. S. F. 'Assessing the health of the industrial worker', *British Journal of Industrial Medicine* (1957), 14, 145–9.

Sclare, A. B. 'The female alcoholic', *British Journal of Addiction* (1970), 65, 99–107.

Scott, Joan. 'Gender: A useful category of historical analysis', in Joan Scott (ed.), *Feminism and History* (Oxford, 1996), pp. 152–80.

Scott, T. S. 'Industrial medicine – an art or a science', *British Journal of Industrial Medicine* (1967), 24, 85–92.

Shepherd, Michael, Michael Fisher, Lilli Stein and W. I. N. Kessel. 'Psychiatric morbidity in an urban group practice', *Proceedings of the Royal Society of Medicine* (1959), 52, 269–74.

Short, S. E. D. 'Psychiatric illness in physicians', *Journal of the Canadian Medical Association* (1979), 121, 283–88.

Silverstone, J. T. and B. D. Lascelles. 'A double blind trial of Durophet M in the treatment of obesity in general practice', *Journal of the College of General Practitioners* (1965), 9, 304–10.

'Social pathology', *Lancet*, 29 March 1947, 413–4.

'Suicide among doctors', Editorial, *British Medical Journal*, 28 March 1964, 789–90.

Susser, Mervyn and Zena Stein. 'Civilisation and peptic ulcer', *Lancet*, 20 January 1962, 3–7.

Taylor, P. J. 'Individual variations in sickness absence', *British Journal of Industrial Medicine* (1967), 24, 169–77.

Taylor, P. J. 'Personal factors associated with sickness absence: A study of 194 men with contrasting sickness absence experience in a refinery population', *British Journal of Industrial Medicine* (1968), 25, 106–18.

Taylor, P. J. and J. Burridge. 'Trends in death, disablement and sickness absence in the British Post Office since 1891', *British Journal of Industrial Medicine* (1982), 39, 1–10.

Taylor, Ruth E. 'Death of neurasthenia and its psychological reincarnation', *British Journal of Psychiatry* (2001) 179, 550–57.

Taylor, Stephen. 'The suburban neurosis', *Lancet*, 26 March 1938, 759–61.

Taylor, Stephen and Sidney Chave. 'Mental health in Harlow New Town', Journal *of Psychosomatic Research* (1966), 10, 38–44.

Tennant, Christopher and Paul Bebbington. 'The social causation of depression: A critique of the work of Brown and colleagues', *Psychological Medicine* (1978), 8, 565–75.

Thomas, Kyla and David Gunnell, 'Suicide in England and Wales 1861–2007: A time-trends analysis', *International Journal of Epidemiology* (2010), 39, 1464–75.

Today's Drugs, Benzodiazepines, *British Medical Journal*, 1 April 1967.

Tosh, John. 'What should historians do with masculinity? Reflections on nineteenth-century Britain', *History Workshop Journal* (1994), 38, 179–202.

Tudor Hart, Julian. 'Going to the doctor', in R. Cooter and J. Pickstone (eds), *Medicine in the Twentieth Century* (Amsterdam, Harwood Academic Press, 2000), pp. 543–58.

Walker, David. 'Danger was a thing that ye were brought up wi': workers' narratives on occupational health and safety in the workplace', *Scottish Labour History* (2011), 46, 54–70.

Walton, H. J. 'Effect of the doctor's personality on his style of practice' (1969), *Journal of the Royal College of General Practitioners*, 17, 82, supplement 3, 6–17.

Warren, Lynda W. 'Male intolerance of depression: A review with implications for psychotherapy', *Clinical Psychology Review* (1983), 3, 147–56.

Watts, C. A. H. 'The mild endogenous depression', *British Medical Journal*, 5 January 1957, 4–8.

Watts, G. 'James Griffith Edwards', Obituary, *Lancet*, 6 October 2012 (338), 1224.

Weiner, H. 'The concept of psychosomatic medicine', in E. R. Wallace IV and J. Gack (eds), *History of Psychiatry and Medical Psychology* (New York, Springer, 2008), pp. 485–516.

Wetherell, Margaret and Nigel Edley. 'Negotiating hegemonic masculinity: Imaginary positions and psycho-discursive practices', *Feminism and Psychology* (1999), 9 (3), 335–56.

Whitehead, Stephen. 'Masculinity: Shutting out the nasty bits', *Gender, Work and Organization* (2000), 7 (2), 133–7.

Whitlock, F. A. 'Suicide in England and Wales 1959–63, Part 1: The county boroughs', *Psychological Medicine* (1973), 3, 350–65

Whitlock, F. A. 'Suicide in England and Wales 1959–63, Part 2: London', *Psychological Medicine* (1973), 3, 411–20.

Wilkinson, Greg. 'The General Practice Research Unit at the Institute of Psychiatry', *Psychological Medicine* (1989), 19, 787–90.

Williams, G. Prys and M. M. Glatt. 'The incidence of (long-standing) alcoholism in England and Wales', *British Journal of Addiction to Alcohol and Other Drugs* (1966), 61, 257–68.

Williams, P., J. Murray and A. Clare. 'A longitudinal study of psychotropic drug prescription', *Psychological Medicine* (1982), 12, 201–06.

Wilson, C. W. M., J. A. Banks, R. E. A. Mapes and Sylvia M. T. Korte. 'Influence of different sources of therapeutic information on prescribing by general practitioners', *British Medical Journal*, 7 September 1963, 599–607.

Wilson, C. W. M., J. A. Banks, R. E. A. Mapes and Sylvia M. T. Korte. 'Pattern of prescribing in general practice', *British Medical Journal*, 7 September 1963, 604–7.

Yeo, Eileen Janes. 'Taking it like a man', *Labour History Review* (2004), 69 (2), 129–33.

Yeo, Eileen Janes. 'The social survey in social perspective', in Martin Bulmer, Kevin Bales and Kathryn Kish Sklar (eds), *The Social Survey in Historical Perspective 1880–1940* (Cambridge, Cambridge University Press, 2011), pp. 49–65.

Books

Alcoholics Anonymous. *Alcoholics Anonymous Comes of Age: A Brief History of AA* (New York, AA World Services Inc, 2012 edition).

A Study of Absenteeism among Women (London, Industrial Research Board, 1943).

Addison, Paul. *No Turning Back: the Peacetime Revolutions of Post-War Britain* (Oxford, Oxford University Press, 2010).

Ager, J. E. and P. A. B. Raffle. *Patterns of Sickness Absence: Experience of London Transport Workers over Two Decades* (London, London Transport Executive, 1975).

Astbury, Jill. 'Gender disparities in mental health', Mental Health Ministerial Round Tables, 2001, 54th World Health Assembly (Geneva, WHO, Switzerland).

Balint, Michael, John Hunt, Dick Joyce and Marshall Markinker. *Treatment or Diagnosis: A Study of Repeat Prescribing in General Practice* (London, Tavistock, 1970).

Black, Dame Carol. *Working for a Healthier Tomorrow* (London, TSO, 2008).

Bott, Elizabeth. *Family and Social Networks* (London, Tavistock, 1957).

Bourke, Joanna. *Dismembering the Male: Men's Bodies, Britain and the Great War* (London, Reaktion, New Edition 1999).

British National Formulary (London, British Medical Association, 1952).

British National Formulary (London, BMA and The Pharmaceutical Society, 1960).

British National Formulary (London, BMA and The Pharmaceutical Society, 1963).

British National Formulary (London, BMA and The Pharmaceutical Society, 1974–1976).

British National Formulary (London, BMA and The Pharmaceutical Society, 1976–1978).

Brodman, Keeve, Albert J. Erdmann and Harold G. Wolff. *Cornell Medical Index: Health Questionnaire* (New York, Cornell University Medical College, 1949).

Brown, George W. and Tirril Harris. *Social Origins of Depression: A Study of Psychiatric Disorder in Women* (London, Tavistock, paperback edition, 1979).

Bruzzi, Stella. *Bringing up Daddy: Fatherhood and Masculinity in Post-War Hollywood* (London, British Film Institute, 2005).

Buckingham, John. *Bitter Nemesis, The Intimate History of Strychnine* (Boca Raton FL, Taylor and Francis, 2008).

Butler, Judith. *Gender Trouble* (Abingdon and New York, Routledge, 1990).

Butler, Judith. *Bodies that Matter* (Abingdon and New York, Routledge, 1993).

Byrne, Patrick S. and Barrie E. L. Long. *Doctors Talking to Patients: A Study of the Verbal Behaviour of General Practitioners Consulting in their Surgeries* (London, HMSO, 1976).

Callahan, Christopher and German E. Berrios. *Reinventing Depression: A History of the Treatment of Depression in Primary Care 1940–2004* (Oxford, Oxford University Press 2005).

Chadwick-Jones, J. K., Nigel Nicolson and Colin Brown. *Social Psychology of Absenteeism* (New York, Praeger, 1982).

Chesler, Phyllis. *Women and Madness* (London, Allen Lane, 1974).

Clatterbaugh, K. *Contemporary Perspectives on Masculinity: Men, Women and Politics in Modern Society* (Oxford, Westview, second edition 1997).

Department of Health. *Invisible Patients: Report of the Working Group on the Health of Health Professionals* (2010).

Dunnell, Karen and Ann Cartwright. *Medicine Takers, Prescribers and Hoarders* (London, Routledge and Kegan Paul, 1972).

Durkheim, Emile. *Suicide* (London, Routledge, 1955).

Ehrenreich, Barbara. *The Hearts of Men: American Dreams and the Flight from Commitment* (New York, Anchor/Doubleday, 1983).

Faludi, Susan. *Stiffed: The Betrayal of Modern Man* (New York, W Morrow and Co., 1999).

Fernando, Suman. *Mental Health, Race and Culture* (Basingstoke, Palgrave Macmillan, 2010 edition).

Firth, Raymond. *Two Studies of Kinship* (London, London School of Economics, 1956).

Flanders Dunbar, H. *Synopsis of Psychosomatic Diagnosis and Treatment* (St Lois, MO: C V Mosby Co., 1948).

Fraser, Russell. *The Incidence of Neurosis Among Factory Workers*: MRC Industrial Health Research Board, Report No. 90 (London, HMSO, 1947).

Freeman, Daniel and Jason Freeman. *The Stressed Sex: Uncovering the Truth about Men, Women and Mental Health* (Oxford, Oxford University Press, 2013).

Gilbert, James. *Men in the Middle: Searching for Masculinity in the 1950s* (Chicago, University of Chicago Press, 2005).

Goldberg, D. *The Detection of Psychiatric Illness by Questionnaire* (Oxford, Oxford University Press, 1972).

Goldthorpe, J. H., D. Lockwood, F. Bechhofer and J. Platt. *The Affluent Worker: Industrial Attitudes and Behaviour* (Cambridge, Cambridge University Press, 1968a).

Goldthorpe, J. H., D. Lockwood, F. Bechhofer and J. Platt. *The Affluent Worker: Political Attitudes and Behaviour* (Cambridge, Cambridge University Press, 1968b).

Goldthorpe, J. H., D. Lockwood, F. Bechhofer and J. Platt. *The Affluent Worker in the Class Structure* (Cambridge, Cambridge University Press, 1969).

Greene, Ruby, Richard Pugh and Diane Roberts. *Black and Minority Ethnic Parents with Mental Health Problems and their Children*, Research Briefing (London, Social Care Institute for Excellence, 2008).

Greenaway, John. *Drink and British Politics since 1830* (Basingstoke, Palgrave Macmillan 2003).

Greenwood, M. *A Report on the Cause of Wastage of Labour in Munition Factories* (London, MRC, HMSO, 1918).

Grob, Gerald N. *Mental Illness and American Society 1875–1940* (New Jersey, Princeton University Press, 1983).

Haggett, Ali. *Desperate Housewives Neuroses and the Domestic Environment 1945–1970* (London, Pickering and Chatto, 2012).

Halliday, J. L. *Psychosocial Medicine: A Study of the Sick Society* (London: William Heinemann, 1948).

Hare, E. H. and G. K. Shaw. *Mental Health on a New Housing Estate: A Comparative Study of Health in Two Districts of Croydon* (London, Oxford University Press, 1965).

Hayward, Rhodri. *The Transformation of the Psyche in British Primary Care 1870–1970* (London, Bloomsbury, 2014).

Healy, David. *The Antidepressant Era* (Cambridge Massachusetts, Harvard University Press, 1997).

Healy, David. *Let Them Eat Prozac: The Unhealthy Relationship between the Pharmaceutical Industry and Depression* (New York, New York University Press, 2004).

Heather, N. and I. Robertson, *Problem Drinking* (Oxford, Oxford University Press, 2004 edition).

Henry Brian (ed.) *British Television Advertising: The First 30 Years* (London, Century Benham, 1986).

Hilson, Mary. *The Nordic Model: Scandinavia since 1945* (London, Reaktion, 2013 edition).

Huback, Judith. *Wives Who Went to College* (London, William Heinemann, 1957).

Huygen, F. J. A. *Family Medicine: The Medical Life History of Families* (Nijmegen, The Netherlands, Dekker and Ven de Vegt, 1978).

Improving Male Health by Taking Action in the Workplace, Policy briefing paper (London, Men's Health Forum, 2008).

International Classification of Diseases (*ICD*), Revision 8 (WHO, 1965).

International Classification of Diseases and Related Health Problems, Revision 9 (WHO, 1979).

Jackson, Mark. *The Age of Stress: Science and the Search for Stability* (Oxford, Oxford University Press, 2013).

Jones, Edgar and Simon Wessely. *From Shell Shock to PTSD: Military Psychiatry from 1900 to the Gulf War* (Hove, Psychology Press, 2005).

Jordanova, Ludmilla. *History in Practice* (London, Arnold, 2000).

Kellner, Robert. *Family Ill-Health: An Investigation in General Practice* (London, Tavistock Publications, 1963).

Klein, Viola. *Britain's Married Women Workers* (London, Routledge and Kegan Paul, 1965).

Kleinman, Arthur. *The Illness Narratives: Suffering, Healing and the Human Condition* (New York, Basic Books, 1988).

Kurtz, Ernest. *Not God: A History of Alcoholics Anonymous* (Centre City MN, Hazleden, 1999 edition).

Lask, Aaron. *Asthma: Attitude and Milieu* (London, Tavistock, 1966).

Le Fanu, James. *The Rise and Fall of Modern Medicine* (London, Abacus, 2000 edition).

Littlewood, Roland and Maurice Lipsedge. *Aliens and Alienists: Ethnic Minorities and Psychiatry* (New York and Hove, Routledge, 1997 edition).

Logan, W. P. D. and A. A. Cushion. *General Register Office Studies on Medical and Population Subjects, No. 14, Morbidity Statistics from General Practice, Volume 1* (London, HMSO, 1958).

Logan, W. P. D. and Eileen M. Brooke. *The Survey of Sickness 1943–1952, Studies on Medical and Population Studies* (London, HMSO, 1957).

Long, Vicky. *The Rise and Fall of the Healthy Factory: The Politics of Industrial Health in Britain, 1914–60* (Basingstoke, Palgrave Macmillan, 2011).

Loudon, Irvine, John Horder and Charles Webster (eds). *General Practice under the National Health Service 1948–1997* (Oxford, Oxford University Press, 1998).

Mass Observation. *The Pub and the People* (London: Faber and Faber [1943], 2009).

McDowell, Ian and Claire Newell. *Measuring Health: A Guide to Rating Scales and Questionnaires* (Oxford, Oxford University Press, 1996).

McIvor, Arthur J. *A History of Work in Britain 1880–1950* (Basingstoke, Palgrave, 2001).

McIvor, Arthur. *Working Lives: Work in Britain since 1945* (Basingstoke, Palgrave Macmillan 2013).

Micale, Mark. *Hysterical Men: The Hidden History of Male Nervous Illness* (Cambridge MA, Harvard University Press, 2008).

Moore, Richard. *Leeches to Lasers: Sketches of a Medical Family* (Killala, Ireland, Morrigan, 2002).

Mort, Frank. *Cultures of Consumption: Masculinities and Social Space in Late Twentieth-Century Britain* (London and New York, Routledge, 1996).

Myers, Charles. *Industrial Psychology* (Oxford, Oxford University Press, 1929).

Myrdal, Alva and Viola Klein. *Women's Two Roles: Home and Work* (London, Routledge and Kegan Paul, 1956).

Off Sick (Office for Health Economics, 1971).

Oppenheim, Janet. *Shattered Nerves: Doctors, Patients and Depression in Victorian England* (Oxford, Oxford University Press, 1991).

Panayi, Panikos. *An Immigration History of Britain: Multicultural Racism since 1800* (Harlow, Pearso, 2010).

Pilgrim, David. *Key Concepts in Mental Health* (London, Sage, second edition 2009).

Rehman, Hamid and David Owen. *Mental Health Survey of Ethnic Minorities* (Ethnos Research and Consultancy, 2013).

Reid, Fiona. *Broken Men: Shell Shock Treatment and Recovery in Britain 1914–1930* (London, Bloomsbury, 2011).

Research in Psychopharmacology: Report of a WHO Scientific Group (Geneva, WHO, 1967).

Rivett, Geoffrey. *From Cradle to Grave: Fifty Years of the NHS* (London, King's Fund, 1997).
Rogers, Anne and David Pilgrim. *A Sociology of Health and Illness* (Maidenhead, Open University Press, fourth edition, 2010).
Roper, Michael. *Masculinity and the British Organization Man since 1945* (Oxford, Oxford University Press, 1994).
Ross, Donald W. *Practical Psychiatry for Industrial Physicians* (Illinois, Charles C Thomas, 1956).
Rowntree, Seebohm. *Poverty: A Study of Town Life* (London, Macmillan and Co, 1908 edition).
Royal College of General Practitioners. *The Future General Practitioner* (London, RCGP, 1972).
Ryle, John A. *Changing Disciplines: Lectures on the History, Method and Motives of Social Pathology* (Oxford, Oxford University Press, 1948).
Sainsbury, P. *Suicide in London*, Maudsley Monographs No. 1 (London, Chapman and Hall, 1955).
Sandbrook, Dominic. *White Heat: A History of Britain in the Swinging Sixties* (London, Abacus, 2006).
Scott, Joan. *Gender and the Politics of History* (New York, Columbia University, 1999).
Scowcroft, Elizabeth. *Suicide Statistics Report 2014, Including Data for 2010–2012* (Samaritans, 2014).
Scull, Andrew. *Decarceration; Community Treatment and the Deviant – A Radical View* (Cambridge, Polity 1994).
Segal, Lynne. *Slow Motion: Changing Masculinities, Changing Men* (Basingstoke, Palgrave Macmillan, third edition 2007).
Seidler, Victor J. *The Achilles Heel Reader: Men, Sexual Politics and Socialism* (London, Routledge, 1991).
Shephard, Ben. A *War of Nerves: Soldiers and Psychiatrists, 1914–1994* (London, Pimlico New Edition 2002).
Shepherd, Michael. *Psychiatric Illness in General Practice* (London, Oxford University Press, 1966).
Shorter, Edward. *From Paralysis to Fatigue: A History of Psychosomatic Illness in the Modern Era* (New York, Free Press, 1992).
Shorter, Edward. *A History of Psychiatry: From the Era of the Asylum to the Age of Prozac* (New York, John Wiley, 1997).
Showalter, Elaine. *The Female Malady: Women, Madness and English Culture 1830–1980* (London, Virago, 1987).
Smith, Mickey C. *A Social History of the Minor Tranquilizers: A Quest for Small Comfort in the Age of Anxiety* (New York, Pharmaceutical Products Press, 1985).
Spicer, Andrew. *Typical Men: The Representation of Masculinity in Popular British Cinema* (London, I B Tauris, 2001).
Sutherland, John. *Reading the Decades: Fifty Years of the Nation's Bestselling Books* (London, BBC, 2002).
Tanner, Bernice (ed.). *Language and Communication in General Practice* (London, RCGP, 1976).
The Future General Practitioner: Learning and Teaching (Royal College of General Practitioners, 1972).
Taylor, Stephen. *Good General Practice: A Report of a Survey by Stephen Taylor*, Nufffield Provincial Hospitals Trust (London, Oxford University Press, 1954).

Thom, Betsy. *Dealing with Drink, Alcohol and Social Policy, from Treatment to Management* (London, Free Association Books, 1999).

Tone, Andrea. *The Age of Anxiety: A History of America's Turbulent Affair with Tranquilizers* (New York, Basic Books, 2009).

Tosh, John. *Manliness and Masculinities in Nineteenth-Century Britain* (Harlow, Pearson Longman, 2005).

Townsend, Peter. *The Family Life of Old People* (London, Routledge and Kegan Paul, 1957).

Waldron, H. A. *Occupational Health Practice* (London, Butterworths, 1989 [1973]).

Watts, C. A. H. *Depressive Disorders in the Community* (Bristol, John Wright and Sons, 1966).

Weindling, Paul (ed.). *The Social History of Occupational Health* (London, Croom Helm, 1985).

Wilkins, David. *Untold Problems: A Review of the Essential Issues on the Mental Health of Men and Boys* (London, Men's Health Forum, 2010).

Wilkins, David and Mariam Kemple. *Delivering Male: Effective Practice in Male Mental Health* (London, Men's Health Forum and Mind, 2011).

Wellcome Witness to Twentieth Century Medicine, *Peptic Ulcer: Rise and Fall* (London, Wellcome, 2000).

White, Cynthia. *Women's Magazines 1963–1968* (London, Michael Joseph, 1970).

White, Cynthia. *The Women's Periodical Press in Britain 1946–1976: The Royal Commission on the Press* (London, HMSO, 1977).

Williamson, Judith. *Decoding Advertisements: Ideology and Meaning in Advertising* (London, Marion Boyers, 2002 edition).

Willmott, Peter and Michael Young. *Family and Class in a London Suburb* (London, Routledge and Kegan Paul, 1960).

World Health Organization, *Mental Health Problems of Automation* (WHO Technical Report Series, 183, 1959).

World Health Organisation, *Health Aspects of Labour Migration: Report on a Working Group Convened by the Regional Office for Europe of the WHO, Algiers, 1973* (Copenhagen, WHO 1974).

Young, Michael and Peter Willmott. *Family and Kinship in East London* (London, Routledge and Kegan Paul, 1957).

Zweig, F. *Women's Life and Labour* (London, Victor Gollancz, 1952).

Zwingmann, Charles and Maria Pfister-Ammende. *Uprooting and After* (New York, Springer Verlag, 1973).

Permissions

All chapters in this book were first published in AHMPDB, by Springer by Ali Haggett; hereby published with permission under the Creative Commons Attribution License or equivalent. Every chapter published in this book has been scrutinized by our experts. Their significance has been extensively debated. The topics covered herein carry significant information for a comprehensive understanding. They may even be implemented as practical applications or may be referred to as a beginning point for further studies.

We would like to thank the editorial team for lending their expertise to make the book truly unique. They have played a crucial role in the development of this book. Without their invaluable contributions this book wouldn't have been possible. They have made vital efforts to compile up to date information on the varied aspects of this subject to make this book a valuable addition to the collection of many professionals and students.

This book was conceptualized with the vision of imparting up-to-date and integrated information in this field. To ensure the same, a matchless editorial board was set up. Every individual on the board went through rigorous rounds of assessment to prove their worth. After which they invested a large part of their time researching and compiling the most relevant data for our readers.

The editorial board has been involved in producing this book since its inception. They have spent rigorous hours researching and exploring the diverse topics which have resulted in the successful publishing of this book. They have passed on their knowledge of decades through this book. To expedite this challenging task, the publisher supported the team at every step. A small team of assistant editors was also appointed to further simplify the editing procedure and attain best results for the readers.

Apart from the editorial board, the designing team has also invested a significant amount of their time in understanding the subject and creating the most relevant covers. They scrutinized every image to scout for the most suitable representation of the subject and create an appropriate cover for the book.

The publishing team has been an ardent support to the editorial, designing and production team. Their endless efforts to recruit the best for this project, has resulted in the accomplishment of this book. They are a veteran in the field of academics and their pool of knowledge is as vast as their experience in printing. Their expertise and guidance has proved useful at every step.

Their uncompromising quality standards have made this book an exceptional effort. Their encouragement from time to time has been an inspiration for everyone.

The publisher and the editorial board hope that this book will prove to be a valuable piece of knowledge for students, practitioners and scholars across the globe.

Index

T

W

Printed in the USA
CPSIA information can be obtained
at www.ICGtesting.com
LVHW010814221023
761596LV00005B/494